Farnborough
to Sydney

CHI
AHMEDABAD
NAGPUR
CHITTAGONG
CALCUTTA
YANGON
MYEIK
KUALA LUMPUR
SINGAPORE
PALEMPANG
JAKARTA
SEMARANG
SURABAYA
TIMOR
TRUSCOTT
ELLIOTT
ALICE SPRINGS
AYERS ROCK
OODNADATTA
IVANHOE
SYDNEY

N
E
S

BIRD

For my mother, Pat Curtis.

BIRD

TRACEY
CURTIS-TAYLOR

with Douglas Wight

MIRROR BOOKS

MIRROR BOOKS

1

Written with Douglas Wight

Published in Great Britain and Ireland in 2023 by
Mirror Books, a Reach PLC business.

www.mirrorbooks.co.uk
@TheMirrorBooks

Print ISBN 9781915306173
eBook ISBN 9781915306180

Cover design by Rick Cooke
Typesetting by Christine Costello
Edited by Harri Aston

Printed and bound in Great Britain by
CPI Group (UK) Ltd, Croydon, CR0 4YY

CONTENTS

Prologue

SUDDENLY, it was like we were staring down at the surface of another planet. At the foot of towering, striated crimson and chalk white cliffs lay a vast body of ink black water, its glassy surface broken intermittently by steep pillars of rock stretching up towards us.

Roaring above such a staggering landscape at just a few hundred feet in my Boeing Stearman biplane, with co-pilot and engineer Ewald Gritsch in the front cockpit, my heart soared. The day's first flight, an early morning scenic trip along the rim of the Grand Canyon with Simon Fanthorpe, our cameraman, had felt very special but compared to what we witnessed now from my open cockpit vantage point, that was merely the warm-up.

Tracking east from the Grand Canyon to the Vermilion Cliffs, a steep and winding escarpment of rock glowing red in the morning sun, had brought us to Lake Powell, a reservoir on the Colorado River, and this other worldly sensation.

I was grateful for the GoPros attached to the wing and that Simon was flying alongside us in a Cessna 185 flown by local pilot Patrick 'Pat' McGarry. The air-to-air filming was hopefully going to capture something of the immensity and grandeur of what we were flying through for our documentary film about my expeditions across five continents following the pioneers of the air.

Leaving the canyon behind us, as we continued east through the cloudless sky I gripped the joystick, trembling in anticipation of what we were about to witness. A few miles further on there it was...

Stretching out before us was a vast desert tableland, interspersed with instantly recognisable red sandstone buttes as far as the eye could see. We had arrived in Monument Valley, a landscape so iconic and sacred to the Navajos and other Native American tribes it felt in truth as if we were flying through the land of the gods.

Roaring through at just a few hundred feet above ground, past these glowing rock faces, I laughed with the sheer, intoxicating joy of it all. It was as if the earth below us had wound back to its prehistoric beginning, admitting us into another dimension of geological time and space. From the air – and at such a low level – you see and feel something of the dynamic metamorphic forces that created such a landscape. Flying it was so savagely beautiful and profound, I was in a state of entrancement, hardly conscious of the Stearman, or even my own body.

Was this how those pioneering US transcontinental Air Mail pilots had felt, back in the 1920s when the dream of flight was so new and this rugged vista had yet to provide the backdrop for the American West in so many movies?

We were 10 days and nearly 2,000 miles into the flight emulating those pilots, tracing the old air mail route from the historic Boeing Field in Seattle down the Pacific seaboard, stopping at various points to refuel. On this last section we had departed Los Angeles, heading northeast into the Mojave Desert on the 3,000-mile trajectory that would take us from west coast to east coast and eventually to New York.

Since embarking on this epic journey in the Stearman, I had wondered what it would have been like for those pilots to see such shining vistas for the first time – coastlines, mountains, desert and prairies – each day a new dawn, but always with the pressure to keep flying in all weathers to get the mail delivered on time. It must have been awe-inspiring.

Our plan today was to stop at the small Monument Valley Airport for lunch and even that was dramatic, as beyond the landing strip a huge vertical rock face of several hundred feet erupted straight out of the ground. A missed landing would render a go-round a hazardous undertaking in any aircraft. The short strip wouldn't have been a problem for modern planes, but it was very narrow and, coming in on close approach with a tail-dragger like the Stearman, there was no forward visibility and after touching down I couldn't see the runway ahead of me. I came in blind and kept it straight with my feet on the rudder, using my peripheral vision to maintain the direction. In the thin air at this high altitude, the ground roll felt fast, but the Stearman soon drew to a halt with the pronounced upslope and some firm braking.

I hadn't realised beforehand that where we landed was the location for several westerns and a scattering of tourists had gathered to take pictures with an Indian chief on a horse in the foreground. In another time lapse it was as though we had stumbled into the 19th century and even the Stearman represented an impossible modernity. Nearby was an old stagecoach, gaily painted yellow and red and positioned on a terrace with the famous landscape as a backdrop. Next to it was a flagpole with the Stars and Stripes blazing against the vivid blue sky and below it was a hand-written sign bearing the legend 'God Bless America'. Standing there, in that moment of time and space, I felt in some way we shared this benediction.

'It's like the evolution of mail delivery encapsulated right here,' I said, surveying this scene. 'First there was the pony express, then the stagecoach and then the ground-breaking air mail pilots in biplanes. And now, here we are again.'

We got airborne half an hour later, taking off downhill towards the open terrain. It was late afternoon when we decided to make a refuelling stop at Winslow before embarking on our final flight of the day to Phoenix. Once again there was a surprise in store, as only when we landed did I realise the airport's full name was Winslow-Lindbergh, after the pioneering aviator, who was also one of the most famous US Air Mail pilots. Charles Lindbergh helped develop the route after his historic solo Atlantic crossing in the *Spirit of St Louis*. The airport's sole hanger was an air mail relic from the heady days of the late 1920s so held enormous historical significance for me. We delayed our take-off and spent the next hour filming in and around the hangar, one of the most original from the period, and it was stirring to imagine the tall, spare figure of Lindbergh with his sheath of maps on this very spot.

I could scarcely believe the day I was having and I knew then that I would remember every second of it. Still on a high from the spectacular scenery I'd witnessed, I waxed on about how special it had all been.

'Listen,' Pat said, 'if you liked that, you'll love what's not far from here.'

'What's that?' I asked, my curiosity stoked.

'Around 15 miles to the west of here is a big crater. It's nearly a mile wide, a perfect circle. It was supposedly blown out by a meteor strike.'

'You are kidding me?' I had read about this meteor strike which had occurred during the Pleistocene age, nearly two million years ago. There was a time when geologists speculated that this was the meteor that caused the extinction of the dinosaurs and I was thrilled to discover it was so close. It seemed another marvellous coincidence and the thought of flying over it in this radiant sunset would be the perfect finale to this most memorable of days. I climbed in, still in a beatific mood and eager for one last awe-inspiring sight.

At 5.10pm we were ready for take-off. The conditions could not have been better. The late sun cast a golden luminosity over the desert and as we took off towards the west with a light crosswind from the north. The only consideration was the altitude. Winslow lies at 4,941 feet above sea level and the warm temperature meant it would be the usual thin air or 'high-density altitude' for the take-off with an aspirated piston engine.

PROLOGUE

For any aviator, take-off is one of the most critical points – the time when you don't want anything to go wrong – and whenever you fly the possibility that something could is always there at the back of your mind. In the early days of aviation, crashing was an occupational hazard and a relatively common event. Charles Lindbergh famously jumped out of four aeroplanes – not, it should be said, the *Spirit of St Louis* – when he was an air mail pilot and, of course, two of the most famous female pioneers, Amelia Earhart and Amy Johnson, were killed in flying accidents. It's always there.

However, the Stearman had never let me down and had coped fantastically well in the intense heat of the Sahara and Australian deserts, and the high-density altitudes in Africa during my 10,000-mile journey from Cape Town to Goodwood in 2013. Earlier today, in fact, I had flown in higher density altitudes taking off from both Grand Canyon Airport and Monument Valley, so I had no particular concern about taking off from Winslow.

We took off after the Cessna departed using the western runway. I reduced the richness of the fuel mixture as part of my engine checks to compensate for the high altitude. It was a long ground roll for the take-off, which was normal in such circumstances and we rose over the runway threshold heading straight towards the sun. We climbed normally but just seconds later the engine lost power.

Suddenly, we lost 300 revs, enough to arrest the climb given that the engine power was already reduced by the high-density altitude. With barely 70ft of height, the Stearman was going down.

I quickly checked forward on the joystick to prevent the aircraft from stalling. My first thought was fuel, and I slammed the mixture control to full rich, but nothing happened. There was no time to do anything else.

'Bloody hell, we're going in,' I yelled to Ewald over the intercom.

That was all too obvious. We were losing height. Fast.

To the right of us was a railway line and the town of Winslow and straight ahead, some 200 yards away, were power lines. To avoid these, I made a shallow left turn through 30° towards the open desert.

The Stearman hit the ground with such force it ripped the joystick from my hand. We hurtled forwards several yards and were then suddenly propelled into a full 360° cartwheel. The right-hand undercarriage leg had hit one of the rugged sage bush root mounds which populated the desert and sent us into the violent somersault. I gripped on with all my strength as we whirled around, earth and sky spinning madly as the Stearman shattered itself against the ground with a deafening roar. It finally came to a shuddering halt. I closed my eyes, trying to take in that moment of arrest. As a cloud of red dust settled around us, the plane was right way up, bellied on its fuselage, a heaving mass of broken wood and ripped wires. The only sounds were creaking, like a ship at dock, the almost imperceptible sigh of energy dissipating into silence... and dripping.

Shit, I thought, for a second time. Fuel. Could the whole thing go up?

I unclipped my harness and climbed out in what was almost a parody of normality. Ewald was already out, brushing himself off and surveying the damage.

'Are you okay?' I said, breathlessly.

'Yes,' he nodded. 'You?'

'Fine.'

It was true. Amazingly, neither of us was injured. While all hell had raged around us the big double wings had absorbed the energy of the crash and we'd been completely protected in the middle of the centrifuge. I looked up and waved frantically to the film crew, now circling overhead in the Cessna, to show them we were okay.

The dripping I'd heard was fuel trickling steadily out of the top tanks. The rest of the contaminated fuel, which had clogged the engine carburettor after take-off and caused the partial power loss, was now dripping from the previously pristine white wings, staining them an oily blue.

Despite the spillage, there didn't seem to be an immediate risk of the plane igniting. Maybe if I had been on the ball, I would have turned everything off when we started to plummet – the fuel, the mixture, the ignition, but I didn't. I was just concentrating on flying the aeroplane and by then it had been out of control. The main thing is I didn't stall. That would have killed us with a vertical plunge to earth.

As I took off my goggles and helmet my initial feeling was not one of relief at cheating death, however, but utter, heart-stopping dismay at the state of my beloved Stearman. Slowly surveying the appalling damage, I drew a deep, choking breath which was more of a sob. The aeroplane, which had carried us safely across continents, halfway around the world and back, was all but destroyed.

The silver blades of the propeller were bent backwards over the engine from the impact with the ground and those beautiful wings were broken and shattered. The fabric skin was torn away and the wooden spars and delicate ribs protruded at sundry odd angles like splintered bones. Thirty feet away lay the undercarriage leg, the dismembered limb which had been ripped off by that wretched sage bush.

The Stearman lay there twitching like a mortally wounded animal.

In the dying embers of that day, the carcass, framed by a blood-red sunset, was lifted out of the desert and taken back to the old 1920s air mail hangar in Winslow. It was unbearable for me to watch this harrowing spectacle. I knelt in the sand, rocking slightly, with my back to these excavations and stared out over the flat, empty landscape, now grown dim in the twilight.

Life had suddenly lost all elevation. This was the end. The end of the Stearman, the end of everything I had worked for the last seven years, the end of the dream.

As if that wasn't bad enough I could sense the vultures circling, and I could picture the headlines already: 'Bird in a Biplane brought crashing down to earth.'

For some, this was all their Christmases come at once. A chance to go in for the kill. Where would I find the strength to keep fighting them off?

But worse than that, there was something else.

As I reached down and felt the dust of that dry earth run through my fingers, I knew I had been here before, in a tight pit of despair as another dream died.

It all came flooding back.

Memories long since buried – of the last time I held something rare and beautiful in my hand, before it was wrenched from my grasp forever.

The Call of the Wild

FOR as long as I can remember I have been gripped by a sense of adventure.

My earliest memory was standing on the deck of an ocean liner bound for Canada. It was 1964 and I might have only been a two-year-old toddler but I can still recall the pitching deck and the wind on my face as our family embarked on a grand sea voyage halfway around the world.

My parents, Timothy and Patricia Curtis, had decided to emigrate to escape the drudgery and deprivations of post-war Britain. They both came from Manchester, the sprawling industrial city in the north-west of England. My father was born in 1935 and my mother the following year. Mum was old enough to remember scrambling into the air raid shelters during the German bombing raids and waiting in terror for the bombs to hit. She could mimic the peculiar whining sound of the bombers as they approached by simultaneously humming and rotating her lower jaw in a kind of grotesque mastication. It made the hair on the back of my neck stand up just to hear the sullen menace of it. And she told us about the extermination of millions of Jews in the gas chambers, an almost inconceivable horror and my first apprehension of death.

My father's family were more fortunate. Evacuated to the Lake District during the war, Dad, and his three older sisters, had an idyllic, *Swallows and Amazons* style existence near Tarn Hows, ranging over the Coniston fells, playing in the woods and swimming in the lakes and smaller tarns. It was here he became captivated by Jack London's books, most notably *The Call of the Wild*, which directly inspired the decision to emigrate to Canada 20 years later. The sudden death of his mother in 1963 provided the small bequest which paid for our passage the following year.

On board that ocean liner, our family then consisted of my older sister Julie and my twin sister Debbie and me. Our younger brother Russell would arrive four years later.

Dad was a journalist by trade and, arriving in Canada without a job, found employment with the publishing house, Maclean-Hunter, which produced specialist magazines about heavy construction and engineering projects. Dad's new job was in Toronto but soon he moved to their Winnipeg office, and finally got posted to Vancouver, where he became field editor for the whole of the west coast. While Dad went on ahead to prepare the ground, Mum followed with us three girls on a Canadian Pacific train. From this luxurious vantage point, we watched the prairies rolling past in an unbroken horizontal line, and the breath-taking verticality of the Rocky Mountains. Like so many pioneers in their wagon trains before us, we were on another epic journey westwards to an unknown but hopeful future.

We finally settled 70 miles inland along the Fraser Valley in a remote mountain settlement called McConnell Creek. Although Dad endured a 140-mile round trip commute each day, our move to that idyllic backwater heralded a golden age for our family. It was a marvellous beginning.

Our house was a modest bungalow clad in weatherboard, set back from the road, with an adjoining open carport and the unlikely formality of a semi-circular drive enclosing a front lawn. We had many animals – cats with kittens, countless generations of rabbits and one beleaguered guinea pig which didn't survive long. Some of our neighbours kept horses, which Debs and I loved and longed to ride. One night, my sisters and I slept out on the veranda under the stars and as we woke we could scarcely believe our eyes – there, on the lawn, shimmering in the morning mist was a horse. Our excitement could hardly have been greater had it been a unicorn but it was a stunted little pony of indeterminate breeding. It had strayed onto our property in search of fresh grass and looked decidedly grumpy as we looped a dressing gown belt around its neck and tried to saddle it with a pillow. The idyl barely lasted an hour before its owner came to retrieve it.

One of our many and varied games was pretending to be birds. My sisters and I were given kites one year by visiting relatives but neither had the skill nor patience to coax them into the air. Instead, we ran with them on a short string, flapping and straining wildly above our heads, making a cacophony of 'cawing' sounds, pretending to be crows. We were 'kite runners' in the literal sense but in our imagination we were flying high.

In addition to this endless entertainment out of doors, I very early realised that I was born with one significant advantage in life – my ever-present soul mate. When Debs and I were born in 1962, delivered at home in Stamford, Lincolnshire, by a midwife who was only mildly less surprised than my mother to find two babies on her hands instead of one, I was the first to arrive and Debs, two pounds lighter, made her dramatic appearance 10 minutes later. We are fraternal twins, hatched from two separate eggs fertilised at the same time. We have never resembled each other. I am dark, as my father was, and Debs is fair and blue-eyed like my mother. I have always been taller and the physical dissimilarity marked even greater differences in personality and temperament. Debs has always been the more self-assured personality, very gregarious and possessed of an innate worldly wisdom. She would relate to people in a way which I couldn't or didn't want to. Julie, our older sister by two years, was also blonde with blue eyes and a strong character with an occasionally fearful temper. I was less volatile than either of my sisters and, as the middle sibling, often kept a fractious peace between them.

Julie, Debs and I were a very close little trio in those early years, our identities almost indistinguishable from each other. We called ourselves the Three Mrs Greens. I can't remember why but it still amuses us to call each other that to this day. We operated as a pack, completely absorbed in our own world, and hardly bothered with anybody else.

When Mum fell pregnant, Dad took us girls to an air show at Abbotsford and it was there we had a very brief encounter with a different kind of bird. I was particularly captivated by a display of skywriting, a phenomenon produced by a noisy little aeroplane roaring up and down, forming letters with its exhaust smoke and, as a final flourish, the pilot traced the outline of a perfect white heart in the sky. The lettering hovered against the blue and then gradually dissipated into the air.

That seemed to presage the beginning of the end of everything else as well.

Although the arrival of my brother Russell – the much longed for son – completed our family, change was in the air.

After eight and a half years in Canada, my father decided we would return to England. Ostensibly, this was to re-join the wider family and to give us the benefit of a real English education, but in truth the situation was rather more complicated. There was some kind of crisis but I didn't know this until many years after the event. It seems that my father lost his job after he turned down a promotion which would have involved us moving to Calgary in Alberta. Strangely, he chose not to discuss the job offer with my mother before rejecting it out of hand. When he attempted to reverse the situation at her insistence it was already too late. He found another job but something had been irretrievably lost. After a few months of freelance writing, he threw in the towel.

I was 10 years old by the time we arrived back in England and moved to a small farming town called Appleby-in-Westmorland in the north-western county of Cumbria. It was here, without any previous experience of the catering industry, that my father decided that we would open a pizza restaurant.

That was in 1972, well before pizza became a fast food and supermarket staple, and we were only the second such restaurant to open in the whole country. Where we lived was a very conservative community and no doubt many of the resident Cumbrians regarded this foreign incursion into their town with a degree of suspicion. Theirs was a trencherman's meat and potatoes culture and the locals had never heard of pizza, let alone eaten it. They regarded us as outsiders or 'offcomers', the Cumbrian expression for people who came from somewhere else.

Leading off the town's medieval square was a narrow side street called High Wiend. There, in rented two-storey premises, with adjoining buildings on each side, was the location for our pizza restaurant. It was called The Potlatch after the word indigenous peoples of the Pacific Northwest Coast of Canada used for a feast.

Dad spent several months renovating downstairs, converting the two rooms into the seating area and installing a long, narrow kitchen with the requisite pizza oven. We lived in the tiny, cramped flat upstairs. My two sisters and I shared a bedroom which overlooked the street and our little brother occupied a small room adjacent, with a wardrobe balanced on a triangle shelf at the end of his truncated bed. Mum and Dad slept in the sitting room on a box divan that Dad had built which turned into a bed. There was one small bathroom with a tub and no shower and a narrow aisle of a kitchen with a single shelf table which ran the length of it. This is where we kids sat in a row on stools to eat our breakfast as if at an American diner.

We all worked in the restaurant at various stages and it was a great family effort. My mother was front of shop and served the customers while Dad rolled pizzas in the back, frequently ducking out the rear door for a quick cigarette. I never cared for waiting on the tables, shying away from human interaction and preferring instead to remain behind the scenes, cooking and washing up. It was a bit of a sweat shop – my sisters and I would later joke about 'child labour' – as we waited upstairs at night watching television, braced for the call to help when the restaurant got busy. We would then tie on our aprons with the resigned air of slaves descending into the galley for another round of enforced toil.

My siblings and I at first felt like fish out of water. It was easier for Debs and me, as we were always together and virtually inseparable. For those first 10 years of our lives, we had spent every waking and sleeping moment together. We'd always sat together at school and were absent together when we got sick. With our perfect synchronisation, we'd always won the three-legged race at sports days and we played epic games of Monopoly together – buying, selling, swapping property and robbing the bank blind – which went on for days and weeks because we didn't want it to end. It was the perfect fusion of two lives and profoundly shaped my attitude to friendships and relationships in future.

While Debs and I had each other, it was Julie, being the eldest, who bore the brunt of the change. For the first time we were split up and during the first year Deb and I went to Appleby Primary School with Russell, who was now four, while Julie attended the grammar school. She was put back a year, as Canadian education was deemed inferior, and this was to be a lingering humiliation for her and the start of a sometimes-difficult adolescence. There was occasionally a lot of anger and some violence in the cramped, overwrought space where we lived and once Julie kicked a hole in the front door during a particularly heated argument with Mum. Debs and I carried on in the lee of this emotion.

From the moment I'd arrived back in England I'd decided almost immediately that if I could have a horse it would compensate for what I had lost when we left Canada. Naturally, my parents were adamantly opposed. They had no money to underwrite the expense, no land to support it, and had three other children to consider. These minor impediments notwithstanding, and on the clear understanding that I was on my own, I focused all my energies on achieving this single objective. The horse became my driving obsession in life. I worked in The Potlatch during the summers and throughout the winter crocheted scores of hats and fingerless mittens for my aunts' gift shops in the Lake District. I toiled away nights and weekends and saved money like a miser, keeping minute accounts of everything and making endless lists and detailed financial projections. Over the next two years I chipped away relentlessly at my parents' opposition.

Debs shared something of this passion. We collected postcards of horses and stuck them on the walls around our bed and could identify every single breed in *The Observer's Book of Horses and Ponies* at the random opening of a page. We had learnt to ride in a very basic way when we lived in Canada and we continued riding in England, albeit rarely, and our first holiday away together was to a riding school in the Lake District. We rode at local stables near Appleby whenever we could afford to but it was all very haphazard and we frequently fell off. I assiduously cultivated friendships with people who had horses and it was in this way that I had a chance meeting with a lady called Eileen Chadwick in the village of Murton, four miles from Appleby at the foot of Murton Pike, the highest of three distinct conical hills running along the western edge of the Pennines. Miss Chadwick was grazing one of her horses by the roadside and, as I stopped to stroke it, we struck up a conversation. She was a short and rather dumpy woman with untidy, mouse-coloured hair and soulful, drooping eyes like her two spaniels. I immediately warmed to her.

Miss Chadwick had a small house and outbuildings with a single, one-acre paddock which was badly over-grazed and often reduced to a mud bath in the depth of the wet winters. There were stalls for five horses and another little disused building across the paddock which had been used to house pigs many years before. To generate an income, Miss Chadwick had set up a riding stable and hosted paying guests for riding holidays. After this first chance meeting, Debs and I cycled the four miles out to Murton every Saturday morning to help Miss Chadwick with her stables and in return she occasionally took us riding. After 18 months or so, Debs stopped coming out but I resolutely carried on.

In spring 1974, after two years of saving, I bought a six-month-old foal at the horse auction in Penrith for a hundred guineas. As I was only 12 and still at school, I charged Miss Chadwick, who was a certified judge of Fell Ponies on the show circuit, with the task of sourcing the right foal. Fell ponies are the dark, rugged breed native to the fells of the north of England, and the foal she selected was a pure-bred Fell pony who came from an illustrious line of champions. His registered name was Townend Victor II and, before his arrival, I had arranged with Miss Chadwick to keep him on her property in the outbuilding where the pigs had lived. Over successive weekends, I excavated two feet of accumulated black mouldering pig dirt from the floor, scrubbed and whitewashed the walls, and filled the stall with a thick bed of fresh straw, in preparation. Victor was delivered to Murton in a horse box and was already inside his little stable the first time I set eyes on him. I approached the door in an agony of anticipation and cried with pure joy when I saw him. He was a scruffy little thing, still in his shaggy winter coat, with the long mane and tail and heavily feathered feet which are characteristic of the breed. He stood quivering and hesitant, his lovely dark head and large, lambent eyes gazing back at me in the half light, as if he too had been expecting me.

From that moment, Victor was all the world to me.

It felt like we were destined to be together, my escape from an increasingly claustrophobic atmosphere at home. Little did I know that our time together would, cruelly, be all too brief.

Victor

WE had been brought back to England for our education and a good part of the reason for settling in Appleby was because of its old established secondary school. Before we darkened its corridors, however, Debs and I had to navigate our way through the local primary school.

Fortunately, we made several friends quickly and hung out together as a group of six. Almost immediately I could tell my best friend was going to be a girl called Carol. She, too, was something of an 'offcomer', as her father was German and had been a young paratrooper at the end of the war. He had been captured and sent to the north of England as a prisoner of war and put to work on the land. In what must have been a highly unconventional romance at the time in that most conservative of places, the German paratrooper married the Cumbrian farmer's daughter.

Fiery by temperament and gifted with a fine intelligence, Carol was a bit like a yearling thoroughbred – slight build and all legs, with a thick mane of straight, tawny hair and enormous dark grey eyes, which flashed with humour or indignation as the mood took her. Fate had thrown Carol and I together and it wasn't long before we became like twins. Her friendship would prove to be the most significant and enduring of my life.

Carol's family had a dairy farm just a couple of miles south of Appleby and, like me, she had long harboured a desire to own her own horse. Although her parents put up similar stubborn resistance to mine, eventually, after much exhortation, they reluctantly consented to Carol getting a foal, which she named Sherry.

In my early days with Victor, while he stayed with Miss Chadwick, he was able to join a herd of fell ponies on Murton Pike where they could roam freely in what was their natural habitat. I often hiked up to find him and could spot the herd from a mile away. As I whistled into the wind one of the black dots broke away from the group and cantered down the fellside towards me, mane and tail flying. I would catch my breath at the loveliness of this vision. It was like a scene from *Black Beauty*. When Victor grew old enough to take my weight, I climbed onto his back and wiled away many happy hours talking to him and weaving daisy chains through his mane.

For a year we carried on like this but, as he approached the age when I could start to train and ride him, I had to find a new home for him and I became dependent on other people for keeping Victor in return for a weekly fee for his livery on their land. Eventually, Carol's family agreed he could join Sherry on their farm – an ideal solution, as far I was concerned.

When the time came to start at Appleby Grammar School I soon discovered that, culturally speaking, it was another universe from McConnell Creek. Although a state comprehensive, the school had retained its historic name, first recorded in the 15th century and confirmed by Elizabethan charter in 1574. Its alumni included Augustine Washington and his two sons Lawrence and Augustine junior, who all attended the school in the early 18th century. Their half-brother George narrowly avoided the same fate; the sudden death of his father in 1743 meant that he stayed at home in Virginia and carved out a different career without the benefit of an Appleby education – becoming the first president of the United States.

Despite the somewhat normal family tensions, there were many fantastically happy times. There has always been a high degree of buoyancy in the family – and no shortage of opinions – and this often made for lively dinner conversations and much hilarity. I had a lot in common with my father; we were similar in nature and were interested in the same things – books, painting, photography and politics. As a family we hiked the fells of the Lake District every Sunday in all weathers and over the next few years we scaled all the main peaks and most of the minor ones as well.

In the summer of 1978, Debs and I turned 16 and, with our O Levels completed, had reached a watershed moment. For my twin that was the end of school forever, while Carol and I braced ourselves for two more years of A Levels.

Before we had to worry about that, however, Debs and I had a six-week holiday in Canada to look forward to. We had been saving for over a year and one of our fundraising efforts was opening a Christmas stall at the street market where we sold a range of handicrafts we had made along with bags of home-made toffee and fudge.

This time we travelled by air – my first time on a plane – and I gripped the arms of my seat in nervous excitement and held my breath as we accelerated down the runway, mesmerised by the sight of the wing trembling and flexing and the smoke-like vortices spiralling off the trailing edge as we left the ground. Then came the vibrating, roaring ascent through the clouds and breaking suddenly into the sunlight above.

We took it in turns to sit by the window but, a couple of hours into the flight, I was out of my seat like a jack-in-the-box when the captain invited passengers to come up to the cockpit. From this unrivalled vantage point, I gazed with wonder as we passed above the icecap over Greenland seen through veils of cloud, the stark black edges of rock breaking the surface of snow and ice like razor-back whales, and the dark spread of the Arctic tundra as we flew over northern Canada. From the very beginning, what I most loved about flight was the view.

We were met at Vancouver airport by our old friends, Gerry and Kathy O'Sullivan. They had lived up the road from us at

McConnell Creek, did not have a family of their own but did have horses and dogs, which was the dream ticket for Debs and I.

Their home was our base and we moved around seeing various other friends in Vancouver and on Vancouver Island. Gerry endeared himself to us forever by treating us like adults and we drank whisky every night over dinner with opera blaring through the house. Each day we rode out on the horses along the trails he had cleared through the woods and he let us drive his big sports utility truck even though Debs could barely reach the foot pedals and neither of us had a licence. The three of us packed up with the dogs and went on a three-day camping trip into the interior. It was the most intoxicating freedom we had ever known.

Many of my parents' old friends were extraordinarily kind to Debs and I, and notable amongst these were Christine and Christopher Potter, both called 'Chris' for short and both were English. Christine was, and remains, one of my all-time favourite people – a warm, generous, wonderfully engaging person, she was my father's secretary when he worked in Vancouver with Maclean-Hunter and went on to forge her own very successful career as a journalist and travel writer.

Chris helped connect me with all the things which would later define my adult life. When I casually mentioned to her I had seen a sign at the side of the road advertising an introductory flight at an airfield near Fort Langley for 15 dollars, she immediately offered to take me there. What would normally have been a 15-minute circuit around the airfield turned into a whole glorious afternoon of flying. After the first flight the pilot, an affable Austrian, agreed to let me come with him on a charter flight to Vancouver Island. We took off again in a bigger Cessna and tracked out to the coast and the Austrian made a scenic tour of it for my benefit. I didn't get back again until three hours later and as I stepped out of the plane I was walking on air. Poor Chris had been waiting the entire time back at the airport getting more and more anxious about my whereabouts. It didn't occur to me that we could radio back to the base to relay a message to her. It was to be five more years before I could afford flying lessons in very different circumstances, but this experience in Canada was a game-changer.

As with most journeys, Debs and I returned from Canada subtly altered by our experience. We had a brilliant time together and renewed something of our old unity. Soon after, Debs left home to do a City and Guild course for hotel reception in Kendal and was deliriously happy to be leaving Appleby. Julie, at age 17, had already left home the previous year. She had headed straight for London to work as a receptionist at a hotel in Oxford Street while also attending college for the same. In retrospect, it is incredible that the career advice to girls at our school was so limited and unimaginative that both my sisters left school to become hotel receptionists. It was a complete waste of my sisters' talents and eventually they would both get themselves re-trained for what they really wanted to do. Out of the four of us, only my brother Russell would pursue the conventional academic course, studying medicine and eventually becoming a doctor.

With Julie and Debs gone, it was just Russell and I at home with Mum and Dad, which created a very different family dynamic. Suddenly, I had a bedroom to myself and somewhere private to study. The often charged, hormonal atmosphere of our predominantly female household disappeared and we settled down to a calmer life. By the summer of 1979, Victor had reached maturity and looked magnificent with his summer coat burnished to a dark mahogany and his tail sweeping the ground. Carol had decided to sell Sherry so I moved Victor to the Bainbridge farm on the western side of Appleby a couple of miles out of town. I thought all was going well but just a few months later, in March 1980, my world collapsed.

Carol and I were at school and, having just finished the

morning break, were in the sixth form common room when to my surprise Debs suddenly burst into the room.

'Tracey, you need to come quickly,' she said, her face ashen. 'Something's happened to Victor.'

For a second I was rooted to the spot, overwhelmed by a wave of sick, hot panic but then shot out of the room after her and together we raced down the corridor and out to the front of the school where Dad was waiting in the car.

As we sped down the hill, through the town and out on the Colby Road to the farm, Dad explained that Mrs Bainbridge had phoned to say Victor was lying in the field and didn't appear to be moving.

We pulled up at the gate by the road and immediately I could see Victor lying flat out on the far side of the field. I vaulted the gate, screaming his name as I ran towards him.

At the sound of my voice, he staggered to his feet and for a fleeting second I thought everything was going to be all right. But by the time I reached him it was clear he was in a terrible state. He was shaking badly and breathing with difficulty, evidently in acute pain. Debs came running with a rope halter and I managed to walk him very slowly to the small stable block by the farmhouse, 100 yards away.

A vet arrived half an hour later and diagnosed colic, most likely caused from eating frozen grass or a thorny bramble branch. The digestive system of a horse is such that it cannot throw up so colic is a common ailment. In writhing around on the ground, he may have twisted his intestine or bowel, the vet speculated, and was now in danger of developing pneumonia as well.

It didn't look good but the vet was reluctant to put him down as there was still a chance he might pull through. He left shortly after and promised to come back in a few hours, but he never did. By some unimaginable cruelty of fate, the weather deteriorated as a freezing weather front moved in like a dark shadow. The temperature plummeted several degrees below zero and the roads froze with black ice in a matter of hours and by late afternoon they were impassable. I have never seen anything like it before or since. And so it was that the vet was unable to make the final visit that would have put Victor out of his misery.

Dad and Debs had returned home when the vet left, leaving me alone with Victor and as the long hours ticked by, he got steadily worse. I tried to keep him standing, as the vet had advised, but he staggered and fell down time and time again. At times I had to jump clear at the last second to avoid being crushed and every time he fell, I tried to coax him back up on his feet.

Sometime later that evening a thick white fluid started streaming from his nostrils and I thought, 'Ah, this is the pneumonia.'

I knew then that Victor would be spared nothing in this final struggle. He died an agonising death by my side – and a part of me died with him.

One way or another, it would all have come to an end as I would have been forced to sell Victor when I left home. That awful prospect had loomed over me the last year like the proverbial sword of Damocles and, according to the legend, that mythical blade was held in suspension by a single hair of a horse's tail.

In the end, fate resolved the dilemma for me and delivered a terrible kind of fait accompli. So total was my grief, I didn't think things could possibly get any worse. I was wrong.

The End of Innocence

ON any other March day, I might have marvelled at the sight of snowdrops dotted among the trees, the first lambs in the fields or the excited chatter of birds preparing their nests, but I was oblivious to any signs of spring and new life. As far as I was concerned the world around me consisted only of death and decay.

Two weeks on from the tragedy and I still felt hollowed to the core. Debs came home at the weekend, specifically to comfort me, and it was at her insistence that I agreed to take a long walk with her out of town to Flakebridge Wood. For nearly three miles we'd ambled arm-in-arm but now, as the road approached the trees and the March air cooled, the silence stretched between us.

I thought at first it was a desire to fill the aching vacuum of grief that prompted her to speak but as soon as she started talking I could tell she was trying – with great reluctance – to hint at something serious, something other than Victor.

Then, maddeningly, she clammed up. Even though she hadn't said anything, she feared she had said too much.

I protested and held her arm to prevent her walking on.

'What is it?' I pleaded. 'Tell me.'

We faced each other in the middle of the road.

I could tell from the look in her eyes it was something dreadfully personal – and painful.

I was not remotely prepared, however, for what came next.

Out it came in a crying torrent of anguish.

It was Dad. Our father. Over several years he had been subtly but insidiously grooming my precious twin sister and had then sexually abused her.

In my innocence, I couldn't comprehend the full physical and psychological horror of what she was telling me.

I could only stammer in shock and confusion: 'What? What do you mean? What?!'

She hadn't wanted to tell me. And she didn't intend to when we embarked on our walk. But in that intensely charged emotional atmosphere between us she felt compelled. It was like she could see what was destroying me and said, 'This is what has happened to me. This is what has destroyed me.'

She wanted to share it with me because the burden on her was so great. But she also knew that I was sharing her damnation because that was how she felt. She was stricken.

We were like babes in the wood, so innocent in a lot of ways.

I could scarcely believe what I was hearing – but seeing the pain in her eyes I knew it was true. My poor, poor Debs. How was it even possible that I had not known?

I had been so consumed with Victor I'd paid little attention to anything else and since his demise I had been gripped by the solipsism of my own struggle with grief.

The sad truth was that over the last year, Debs and I had lost a lot of our intimacy. After our Canadian holiday, which had brought us back together, we had once again diverged. Carol had become the one central to my existence – my other twin. And, as Debs developed more rapidly than me and was more interested in socialising and doing the things normal teenagers do, I had been immersed in my own little world.

She swore me to secrecy and for the rest of our walk did not go into any detail about what happened. That only came when we were much older, when it emerged Dad had been grooming her from around the age of 12.

Eventually, I realised that explained why they were together on the day Debs came to get me from school. At the time it hadn't crossed my mind.

Immediately, however, I could sense our relationship recalibrating. So it would prove. The burden of the terrible secret we shared renewed the bond of our twinship.

I felt a terrible guilt that I hadn't noticed or been able to help her, but the sin was my father's. I don't know what allowed him to believe that what he inflicted on my sister was an act of love, but from that moment on he became a stranger to me. It was a betrayal of everything we had been as a family, or everything I thought we had been. We were spared nothing in our shared realisation of the false family myth.

Debs predicted there and then that it would destroy our family, and she was right, of course. By degrees, this aberration would drive the departure of our entire family to the end of the earth.

In the immediate aftermath, however, I couldn't process it in my grief and shock. I was poleaxed. Nothing was ever the same again and it made my last few months at home almost unbearable.

I could never tell my father that I knew, yet, with my sisters already gone, I was the one stuck at home. Our parents weren't getting on and Mum tried to talk to me about the marriage because she saw me as some sort of conduit who understood my father. It was a dreadful position to be in and I felt very protective of my little brother. But I couldn't wait to escape.

I continued to work in The Potlatch most nights but was increasingly resentful of the obligation, especially while I was trying to study for my A Levels. I decided against going to university and even four decent grades didn't change that decision.

In our family the priority was not academic attainment but getting out to work and earning a living. We didn't grow up with any sense of deprivation but we had to pay our way and there was a tremendous impetus to fly the nest at the earliest opportunity.

It never occurred to me to pursue flying professionally, simply because there was no route into it. The RAF did not take female pilots until 1990 and, to my knowledge, there were no scholarship programmes for women that might have facilitated a career in civil aviation.

I spent months casting around for a job and one day Dad drew my attention to an interesting advertisement in *The Guardian*. A London-based company called the Central Selling Organisation was recruiting trainee diamond graders and sorters. It immediately struck a chord as I'd always had an interest in gemstones. I immediately dashed off a letter and was duly invited to Charterhouse Street for an interview. Six weeks later I was overjoyed to learn that I had been successful. It felt like a fantastic bit of luck.

As soon as I finished my A Level exams, I left on the night bus to London to join Julie.

Whether I was running from or escaping to something I wasn't sure. I only knew I had to get away.

Esprit de Corps

SORTING and grading rough diamonds required close visual inspection of each stone and for this we wore optical equipment, leaning over a workbench sifting through small piles of diamond crystals with tweezers.

It was monotonous work and very hard on the eyes. After a day of intense focusing, I was barely able to read at night. To relieve the strain one afternoon, I pulled off my headgear and sat rubbing my eyes for a minute before striking up a conversation with my instructor, Mike Scott, who was sitting nearby.

'That wouldn't be Scott of the Antarctic, would it?' I said, tongue in cheek.

'Yes,' he said, very matter of fact.

I was gobsmacked. Mike turned out to be the grandson of Robert Falcon Scott of the ill-fated British expedition to the South Pole in 1912. From that moment on we became firm and long-lasting friends.

For the 18 months I lived with Julie in her small bedsit in Earl's Court we had a fantastic time, gallivanting around London, cruising down the Thames, visiting museums, walking in the parks, dancing into the small hours at various nightclubs around town and eating a lot of McDonald's. Julie had moved on from her hotel reception job and was now the manager of Richoux in Mayfair – an elegant restaurant and coffee house with three branches around London. When I'd needed a temporary job to tide me over before starting at De Beers I waitressed at Richoux in Piccadilly. A month after I'd arrived in London, in summer

1980, Debs came down to join us and the three of us camped in the tiny bedsit just like old times – the Three Mrs Greens back together again.

Debs had fallen in love with a six-foot six Kiwi called Simon who also worked behind the bar at the pub in Tirril. After a year at the pub, Simon flew home again and Debs was determined to join him – in part, I suspected, to run away from life here and all the pain associated with it.

After six months I left my diamond sorting job to join the British Diplomatic Service as a clerical officer in Whitehall. I'd applied before starting at De Beers as I was passionately interested in geopolitics and had high hopes of working overseas. It had taken a year to get through the rigorous interviews and full security vetting before I was finally offered a job as a Grade 10 Clerical Officer and I accepted this because I hoped it would lead to a posting in Africa within two years.

My fascination with the Dark Continent went way back to reading *Tarzan* comics and watching the television series *Daktari* as a child in Canada. Later, I was captivated by the story of Elsa the lioness in *Born Free*, with its wonderful signature tune. In my teens I read more seriously about the early exploration of Africa and devoured the novels of Wilbur Smith. More than anything else the continent represented something primordial and unknown, a land inhabited by the most beautiful and exotic animals in the world and imbued with the promise of great adventure.

Those dreams were temporarily put on hold, though, as I was assigned to the Mexico and Caribbean Department and allocated the countries of Mexico, Cuba, El Salvador, Costa Rica and Haiti. The registers were great leather-bound files, one for arrival documents and one for dispatches to the various capital cities. My job was to record and file all the documents, diplomatic reports, correspondence and media articles relating to these countries.

I reported directly to a charming and funny chap called Geoff

Cowling and I have a fond memory of Geoff cantering into the registry office late one afternoon, mounted on a broomstick mocked up as a horse with a bit of impala skin tied around the brush, announcing with great pomp that a coup d'état had taken place in Gambia and we were all invited for gin and tonics in their office to mark the occasion – exactly the esprit de corps one expected of the British Diplomatic Service.

The thrill of roller skating to work through the London parks and the camaraderie I shared with characters like Geoff, however, were not enough to compensate for the mind-numbing tedium of filing, which was essentially what the job entailed.

Previously, clerical officers were considered for overseas postings after two years in Whitehall but budgets had been cut and the period was extended to four years, thus thwarting my chief ambition to travel. After only eight months in the job, I handed in my notice out of frustration and boredom.

To raise some more funds, while I formulated a plan to go to Africa the following year, I had taken on a part-time waitressing job three nights a week at Wolf's famous hamburger restaurant, in Basil Street, behind Harrods. When I quit the Foreign Office, I worked there full-time.

I felt conflicted, however. As much as I wanted to be in Africa, with Debs in New Zealand and seemingly intent on marrying Simon, I wanted to visit her out there, to make sure she was making the right decision, for the right reasons.

Wolf's attracted many customers from the Middle East and I got to know one regular, Ali Al Khalifa, of the Bahrain royal family, who had been educated in Britain and worked for the Metropolitan Police. He believed waitressing was a demeaning job but when I told him I was saving to visit my twin sister in New Zealand he revealed his family owned a travel agency in London and offered to give me a first-class return air ticket. I didn't think he was serious but, when he repeated the offer three times in as many days, I finally accepted. Ali offered to pay for my whole family to go with me but that seemed a bit over the top. In the end, Mum agreed to come with me, despite my father's disapproval.

We had the most brilliant trip together, stopping off to see Ali in Bahrain, then flying on to Singapore for three days before continuing to Sydney and Wellington.

Debs and Simon rented a small unit which they shared with their cat in a suburb of Palmerston North, a town on the agricultural flatlands of the Manawatu region. In a country blessed with jaw-dropping scenery I was amazed that Deb had ended up in such an ordinary place. As it turned out, I couldn't influence her in any way whatsoever in terms of what she decided to do. I tried to persuade her to come to Africa with me to no avail. Her mind was made up.

Mum could only stay away for three weeks and after the first week with Debs we went off on our own and toured around Rotorua for a few days, visiting the famous 'Champagne pool' at the Whakarewarewa geothermal site and cycling around the Blue and the Green Lakes. When Mum went back to Palmerston North for her last week I headed to the South Island on my own.

Standing in the visitor information centre in Queenstown, I was looking at a brochure on white water rafting when a voice behind warned against this as two tourists had drowned the previous week. I turned around to find one of the locals, casually dressed in a cream jumper, chinos and flip flops, with straight black hair, and cool, grey, laughing eyes. He introduced himself as Lindsay and over the next few days took me sailing on Lake Wakatipu, hang gliding in the hills above Lake Hayes and into the gold-bearing hills of Skippers Canyon near Arrowtown. I was completely captivated, not just with the scenery.

Still innocent, in many ways, I fell headlong into my first serious love affair. Those days with Lindsay were as extraordinarily intense as anything I'd read in a romantic novel. He was an architect, with very definite views on living in three-dimensional space and a delightful sense of humour. His penchant for witty one-liners had me in gales of laughter and this has ever since proved to be my weak spot with men, an almost fatal attraction.

After five halcyon days in Queenstown with Lindsay I dragged myself away to continue my journey to the far south to see Fiordland and the hauntingly beautiful Milford and Doubtful Sounds. As I got off the bus in Te Anau, I was surprised to hear my name being broadcast on the public address system, asking me to report to the office. It was a message from Lindsay: if I came back to Queenstown he would drive me to Christchurch. So, I turned around and went back. Our idyll continued as we drove in his old maroon Mercedes, tiptoeing through the Lindis Pass and out the other side into the spectacular Mackenzie Country and on across the Canterbury Plains. We eked out the time together until the very last minute, when I finally tore myself away, boarding a train at Christchurch station heading north. Our parting was straight out of a movie; my hands pressed against the glass as the train pulled away.

'What am I doing?' I wondered as he disappeared.

I had to go home of course, but I felt a terrible wrench; not just because of my feelings for Lindsay but also for Debs. I wanted to be with her.

The question now arose, what next? Do I follow my dream and go to Africa or head back to New Zealand so I could be there for Debs and continue the love affair with Lindsay?

When the Lion Feeds

AS luck would have it, Wolf's once again provided me with an unexpected opportunity.

One of my colleagues was a charming South African girl called Louise Kimber who was over in the UK on a sabbatical. We became good friends and before she left to go home, towards the end of 1981, she urged me to come over and visit. Louise's polo-playing family were in Pietermaritzburg, in the south-east of the country, but she was going back to live in Johannesburg.

'You can stay with me and we can work it out from there,' she said.

It was all the invitation I needed and I figured I would go there for a year and travel around the country. In January 1982, as soon as I saved up enough money, I bought a ticket to Johannesburg and phoned Louise to let her know of my imminent arrival.

She had recently become engaged to a wealthy industrialist and knew everybody in that rarefied world. She shared an apartment in Rosebank with another girl, who was equally as welcoming, and I slept on a mattress on the floor in their guest room. As soon as I arrived, life became a whirlwind of parties and socialising. Their male friends, a hedonistic bunch, circled like vultures on me, the fresh bit of talent in town. Given Louise's friends were predominantly English South Africans, it was something of a paradox that I fell in with an Afrikaner lawyer called Anton, just two weeks after my arrival. I was at a party and he made a beeline for me.

Since I'd left New Zealand, I'd continued to correspond with Lindsay. In one of his customary amusing letters, he said he'd even consider joining me in Africa, quipping that he'd be happy walking in my wake, fanning me with a palm leaf, but doubting whether he could keep up. I was conscious of building a bridge back to New Zealand at some point in the future but in those first few weeks, being in Africa, I was just swept along as Anton and I plunged into a full-blown affair.

As my relationship with Anton developed, I moved in with three of his friends, all Afrikaners, all lawyers and all fantastic fun. I often met Anton at his legal chambers in town and attended court hearings with him, where, as a criminal barrister, he would defend black Africans pro bono, to build up his experience. At this time, the death penalty was applied and, in his most harrowing cases, two of his defendants were sentenced to death. I sat in the courtroom as the verdicts were delivered with chilling finality.

Anton also took me with him into Soweto, the sprawling black township to the south of Johannesburg. It was a dangerous place to visit back then if you were white but I wanted to witness the effects of the apartheid system and see for myself what it really meant to live with such segregation. It was as shocking and soul-destroying as I'd imagined.

He also took me to Sun City, not the luxury casino resort in the country's North West Province but a prison of the same name just outside Johannesburg. Anton was investigating the death of a prisoner, who had apparently jumped to his death from an open window. We were allowed to see his cell. As soon as we entered, I recoiled in horror at the dark blood stains splattered up the wall. There, too, was the window from which he had apparently jumped. It was a macabre scene. Evidently, the man had been tortured before his death and the 'suicide' allegation merely a convenient alibi for cold blooded murder. Yet, how Anton would be able to prove this in such a place, I could never imagine.

As much as I loved many aspects of life in South Africa and toyed with the idea of staying on, I could not reconcile myself with the horrors of apartheid. The inequality and injustice were inescapable.

After several months, as I began to wonder how I would get home, I heard about a company that offered epic overland trans-continental trips. For around £1,500 you could buy your passage on a truck that took you on a five-month journey, crossing borders, from south to north and eventually on to England. You were only allowed one item of luggage, plus your sleeping bag. Blimey, I thought, this is what I wanted – to see the real Africa.

My Afrikaner friends were appalled at the thought of me travel-ling across land and, though they held a grand farewell party, tried to talk me out of what they considered a perilous undertaking.

When the southbound truck arrived from England it appeared their warnings were well-founded.

The tour company had been held up at gunpoint near Bulawayo, Zimbabwe, by hostile militia and four of the passengers, all males, were forcibly removed from the truck and murdered in the bush. Their bodies were never found. The driver and the two girls were allowed to go free and they were understandably deeply trauma-tised when we met them briefly in Johannesburg.

On hearing of the tragedy and seeing the bullet holes in the truck, several of the people booked on our trip dropped out.

The rest of us, however, including me, took a more philosophical approach. Convinced of our own indestructibility, we regrouped, resolved to continue as planned and set about patching up the bullet holes on the truck.

An American girl called Jill Rippchen was on the trip and we became close friends. Jill had broken her back in a car crash in California when she was 19 and lived in a state of constant, excruciating pain. The rugged conditions across Africa brought unimaginable agonies for her but she never let that stop her. I admired Jill's indomitable courage and ability to retain her sense of humour amid everything. We teamed up and shared a tent, although mostly we just hung our mosquito nets from a tree or a bush and slept out in the open. We drank like fish and howled with laughter the whole way.

Over five months, we travelled through east Africa to Dar Es Salaam on the Tanzanian coast, drove west through the heart of Africa and right across the Congo basin on to Cameroon on the west coast before tracking north through the Sahara Desert. We drove up to 12 hours a day on the worst roads I had ever seen, some little more than impacted earth and rock which just crumbled away like dry pastry under our tyres.

We crossed rivers on rickety old pontoons which looked as if they would disintegrate in the currents. We had a day's hunting with the pygmies in the Ituri rainforest of the eastern Congo and washed away weeks of accumulated grime swimming for hours in a hot mineral river in Nigeria.

We pressed on through the empty, sun-baked wilderness of the Sahara and through the Hoggar Mountains. There, we slept in a cave one night to shelter from a sandstorm and woke to find ourselves half buried, rubbing our bloodshot eyes in the bleached white dawn.

Throughout it all, the continent's vast and varied wildlife were around us in abundance. I marvelled at the sight of lions, cheetahs, elephants, giraffes – animals I'd only read about or watched on television – there before my eyes.

The experience was life-changing and the most profoundly moving part was the African people. We engaged with them at every opportunity, drinking banana beer with them in their houses and sundry roadside bars. We lingered to watch the singing and dancing in the villages and spent the entire trip waving to them as we passed. They waved back to us, smiling and laughing in spontaneous joy in that most basic of human transactions. The Africans had the most extraordinarily generous spirit and I left that continent with my first real sense of humanity.

Until that adventure, I had always been a bit reserved and found it hard to relate to people, but I returned to England invigorated by their infectious spirit and joie de vivre.

This wild and magical place would forever hold a special place in my heart and I knew one day I would return.

But I had more pressing matters at hand. While I had been in Africa, Debs had written to me saying she had gone ahead with the wedding, without any of the family there. I was heartbroken for her. It had been a muted affair at the Dugald Mackenzie Rose Garden in Palmerston North. On the morning of her wedding, she had got up at dawn to mow the lawn and had broiled three chickens for the lunch, which sounded vaguely ominous. When she finally got dressed, she had been overwhelmed with sadness and had shed a few tears. If there was a honeymoon, she made no mention of it. I felt I needed to get out there.

On arriving back in London, I landed a job as a waitress in a newly opened casino and in four months earned enough money to fly out to New Zealand again. I looked forward to reconnecting with my beloved twin sister and my first serious love. I had a presentiment, however, that it might not be quite so simple to pick things up from where we left off.

Love Lessons

MY plan was to go for a year – but quickly I discovered things were going to be very different this time.

Debs and Simon had moved to the small, rural town of Dannevirke, 125 miles north of the capital Wellington, and although it had been a struggle for her to carve out a new life on the other side of the world at just 18, she had put the bittersweetness of her wedding day behind her and was contented enough and settled with Simon.

I was happy for her but could not say the same for my relationship with Lindsay. He picked me up at the airport in Auckland when I arrived and we drove to the Coromandel Peninsula for a few quiet days together. Although we tried, we could not recapture the magic of our first meeting. Almost from the outset I felt inexplicably nervous, as if I were with a stranger. As we drove south to Queenstown we stopped off to see Debs. Simon was away working so it was just the three of us and as we sat talking and drinking, Debs and Lindsay got on famously well and there was an easy rapport. At some point I stopped drinking while they continued and although nothing untoward happened, as the evening wore on I had a growing sense of unease, as if I was on the outside of something. Those first few disorientating weeks in Queenstown only served to reinforce this impression.

Lindsay and I limped on for another few weeks but the end was inevitable. After little more than a month I packed my bags and moved out.

Determined to stay on in Queenstown, I found myself a job and discovered that the local airport had a flourishing aero club. It had been five years since my first flying lesson in British Columbia and now, with a little money still saved from my casino job, I started to learn to fly.

In addition to that first epic flight in Canada, the other great inspiration to me was *Those Magnificent Men In Their Flying Machines*. I remember vividly watching this film starring the delectable Stuart Whitman, James Fox and Terry-Thomas, which perfectly captured the romance and adventure of the early years of flight. Set in 1910 in Edwardian England, it featured the first international air race from London to Paris over the English Channel. The aeroplanes were a gaggle of implausible flying machines – bat-winged ornithopters, box kites with 'hairdryer' engines behind the pilot, sundry monoplanes, biplanes and triplanes with open-truss fuselages, laundry-basket seats and pram wheels for landing gear. It was a wonderful pastiche and after my first viewing I must have watched it at least 20 more times, laughing as heartily each time as I did when I first saw it. It not only reinforced my desire to one day pilot my own plane but sparked a fascination with old aeroplanes. I simply loved how they looked.

My instructor in Queenstown was a tall, sandy haired Kiwi called Bruce Kerr. He taught me all the rudiments – straight and level flight, climbing and descending, medium turns and basic stalls. I couldn't have been happier. Up there in the blue yonder flying against the backdrop of the Remarkables mountain range and the hills around Lake Hayes where just over a year before I had been hang-gliding with Lindsay, I felt completely free and detached from any relationship woes or the drudgery of life on the ground. I had the overwhelming sense that this was where I belonged.

I befriended a local farmer, Roy Murdoch, who had his own light aircraft – a nimble little AirTourer painted bright red. I joined Roy on several flights over the Southern Alps to the rugged west coast where he landed on the beach, deftly side-slipping the aircraft to lose height on the approach and touching down on the sand still wet from the ebbing tide. We dropped off mail and supplies to remote communities and loaded up again with fresh crayfish and whitebait.

Roy taught me how an altimeter works, with 30ft of height representing one millibar of pressure on the setting, and introduced me to mountain flying. He gave me my first taste of inverted flight when he flipped the AirTourer upside down and I gasped involuntarily as I found myself hanging in the harness with bits of straw and dust falling from the upended floor of the cockpit. Craning my head backwards to peer through the Perspex bubble canopy, I had the queasy sensation of looking up at the ground.

Before the year was out I secured permanent residency in New Zealand and, now able to pursue more interesting employment, worked for a time as a photographer taking candid photos of people on the local ski fields, before dropping the films off so they could be developed in time for the skiers to view when they'd finished on the slopes. When the winter season ended, I covered other sporting activities which went on throughout the year.

One evening, a friend and I were waiting to be seated at a restaurant when we couldn't help noticing the tall, blond man sitting opposite. He bore a passing resemblance to the late Duke of Edinburgh and was reading a book by Jean-Paul Sartre. I found him completely intriguing and couldn't resist making some passing comment. We struck up a conversation and he introduced himself as Dr Xavier Maniquet. It was clear, as his choice of reading material suggested, that he was a French intellectual and I was so fascinated to know more about him, we invited him to join us for dinner. We spent an evening engaged in stimulating conversation and when we parted a plan was made to meet again the next day.

There was no suggestion of any romance – as he was about 20

years older – but we hit it off so well I spent the next couple of days showing him around Queenstown.

He invited me to join him on a yacht that was returning to New Caledonia the following week. I was tempted but turned him down. Something didn't feel quite right but we parted company on good terms and as far as I knew he was on his way back to French Polynesia.

Barely 48 hours later, the Greenpeace flagship *Rainbow Warrior* was blown up in the Port of Auckland. A photographer drowned when the ship sank and the bombing sparked international outrage. The environmental activists were on their way to protest a planned nuclear test in French Polynesia and it was obvious this was retaliation.

As soon as I heard the news I felt a chill to my core. I knew immediately my mysterious friend was involved.

Two French secret service agents, Dominique Prieur and Alain Mafart, were subsequently arrested for terrorism and manslaughter but the spy master doctor disappeared without trace. When I Googled his name recently I was stunned to read that he was a specialist in aviation medicine and had died in 2009 at the controls of a light plane on a glacier in the French Alps. Death by misadventure, it seems.

What a lucky escape, I thought, that I had declined his invitation to join him on his yacht.

I might have dodged a bullet that day – but the next time I agreed to set foot on a boat I wasn't quite so fortunate.

What Lies Beneath

BLASTING along one of the wider channels of the Taieri River in a high-powered jet boat, sporting a new pair of sunglasses to protect from the blinding glare of the midday sun, I had to admit this was fun.

I'd had my reservations when my friend Liz Morrison suggested a day of jet boat racing with her rich American friends but allowed myself to be persuaded. We all drove down together towing the sleek white jet boat behind us to South Otago, not far from Dunedin where the Taieri river widens into a spectacular series of braided channels, where the racing took place. Before the main event, however, participants were allowed two practice runs. Ralf Brown, a tall, well-fed American in his mid-seventies, was the boat owner and driver and, by all accounts, highly experienced at racing them. After inviting Liz – a petite blonde with movie star glamour – for the first run, she waved excitedly as Ralf revved the engine and performed a series of dramatic turns as a warm-up before heading off down the river.

I settled back in my deck chair basking in the sunshine and chatted with Ralf's friend, Earle, who made up our foursome. Other jet boats idled in the water before us as other crews prepared before roaring up another section of the river. Twenty minutes later, Ralf and Liz came back, flushed and animated from the ride. Now it was my turn.

Into the front seat I climbed, not even looking to see if there was a seatbelt or harness.

'Enjoy!' Liz called as we pulled away from the bank. Ralf headed out into the deepest part of the river and then hit the gas. We cut through various channels with the boat banging the surface of the water with unexpected violence as it accelerated. Gripping on with both hands and squinting into the sun, I suddenly spotted an ominous dark ripple in the water 30 yards ahead of us. Something was submerged just below the surface.

'Look out!' I yelled.

Too late. The submerged object was a log which we hit at full speed. The jet boat took off into the air and Ralf and I were catapulted out towards the shore.

I smashed onto the beach on my chest and face, and such was the momentum that I was propelled several yards up the shingle before I finally ground to a halt. The jet boat slammed down close by and careened off into the scrub.

It took a split second to register I was still alive before I started convulsing so violently I thought I was having a heart attack. I was badly winded but the shock numbed any pain. Somewhere out of sight Ralf also hit the ground hard, his left arm impaled on the branch of a dead tree. People rushed to help and lifted me to my feet where I was finally able to catch my breath. With no medics on site, we were loaded into a vehicle and driven to the home of a local doctor who seemed irritated at being disturbed on a Sunday afternoon. He took the most cursory look at us, bandaged Ralf's arm and cleaned the cuts on my head and face before sealing them with surgical tape. Even though I was seeing double and the dark bruising spreading across my abdomen signalled internal bleeding, that was the extent of our treatment.

It was over two months before I could walk properly again. The bruising from my neck to my knees turned into ugly, hard black haematomas and I was so incapacitated I ended up losing 14 pounds in weight. What I didn't know until years later was that I had nearly broken my neck and I discovered that several vertebrae had been displaced by the impact.

Compared to Ralf, however, I got off lightly. Although he tried to brush off the extent of his injuries, he tragically died prematurely the following year. I never did find out if the wounds he suffered that day in the accident were a contributing factor.

That traumatic episode is one reason why I consider boats infinitely more dangerous than aeroplanes. I never seem to be lucky with them.

Fortunately, through time, I eventually recovered enough to get back on my feet and embrace life once more. And, as summer arrived in 1985, with it was just the tonic I needed.

Flying Solo

SITTING on a low wall by the lake in front of Eichardt's, in Queenstown, I knew as soon as I heard the noise of the engine it was them.

Sure enough, when a blue Mini careered down the road with two dishevelled blonde heads hanging out the windows, arms waving madly, music pulsating from within and a pair of bright, green tights tied to the aerial and streaming out behind the car like a windsock, my heart leapt with joy.

It could mean only one thing … the Three Mrs Greens were together once more.

I broke into involuntary laughter as Debs and Julie tumbled out of the car with sundry bottles, chocolate wrappers and crisp bags following in their wake. After a rapturous reunion, we immediately withdrew into the bar for the obligatory round of drinks.

We had a lot to catch up on. In the intervening years, Julie too had left London, working briefly for Gulf Air as a stewardess before bailing out to follow her passion for cooking. She embarked on a Prue Leith cookery course and worked in Italy and then as a cook on a luxury yacht in the Caribbean before finally making it out to New Zealand to see us.

We had further cause for celebration when Debs announced she was pregnant. Julie and I were thrilled at the prospect of being aunts and laughed uproariously at my twin's sly reference to Cinderella and the two ugly unwed sisters.

Julie stayed on with me for an extended holiday and then went back to England with the intention of flying on to America to meet her boyfriend. All this fell apart, however, and soon after she returned to New Zealand and for a time we lived together in Queenstown. Before long, Julie started working in a little café in Arrowtown and we had nearly a year together before I once again moved on.

After three years in Queenstown, I realised that outside of the tourism industry, job prospects were limited. I'd met a rather glamorous airline pilot called Duncan Beck while working on the ski fields and, although there was no romance at that stage, when he encouraged me to come to Auckland, I agreed.

I departed Queenstown with just a few clothes and books stowed in a large black bin bag and Duncan could barely disguise the look of horror when he came to pick me up from the airport in his white Lotus sports car.

I moved in briefly with Duncan, who had a big house in the leafy suburb of Epsom that he shared with some friends, but in a few weeks I found my own flat. For the first few months I worked at a photographic lab and then as the house model for a company called Bendon Industries, who made underwear. Despite my initial hesitation, it proved to be huge fun and very well paid with a bounty of free bras and knickers. I worked closely with the design and marketing teams, and several of them became close friends. Although I didn't think I'd stay long, I ended up working for Bendon for nearly three years.

In early 1987 Duncan introduced me to Ardmore airfield, near Papakura, around 20 miles south of Auckland and we dropped into the Ardmore Flying School to meet Liz Needham. Liz was immensely likeable and a first-rate pilot who, in addition to running her own flying school, had recently become one of the first women to fly for Air New Zealand, the national carrier. It was a three-year gap since I had last flown, so it was like starting again. I signed up for the ground theory course and resumed my flying with a weekly lesson, which was all I could afford.

On April 28, a particularly fine day, I pitched up for my lesson with Jeremy Mackie, my instructor, as usual. We did three circuits in the little red Piper Tomahawk, flying a rectangle around the airfield: taking off, climbing turn crosswind, then into the long downwind leg before the descending turn onto base leg, then the approach to land and repeating the pattern again.

When we landed for the third time, he told me to taxi to one side and then to my alarm, unlatched the door and climbed out.

'Right,' he said, 'you're on your own. If you screw up the landing, go around again.'

Immediately, my heart was in my mouth – precisely the reason why many instructors tend to disguise the day you go solo as the nerves might kill you.

This was it.

My hands were shaking but we'd been hammering the basics for the last few weeks and I just had to remember what I had been trained to do.

I took off again, momentarily startled by the way the aircraft sprang into the air with the lighter load. As I carefully banked in the climbing turn and then levelled off downwind, I felt such a surge of adrenaline I couldn't help bursting into operatic song. Montserrat Caballé I was not but such was the ridiculous sense of euphoria that my rendition of 'Just one Cornetto' to the tune of O Sole Mio filled the cockpit.

Every pilot remembers their first solo. For me it was a perfectly crystallised moment of joy, something I had dreamt about for years but had never quite believed would happen.

The landing, executed with painstaking care, was thankfully near perfect and I taxied back to the school where a little group had gathered to congratulate me. I jumped out of the plane laughing with delight and relief. They had tipped Duncan off so he was there too, with a bottle of champagne. From that moment on I just wanted to fly as much as possible.

After six months and logging 57 hours of flying, I completed my private pilot's licence. It wasn't long before I had a Cessna 172 rating, an aerobatic rating, and learnt to fly 'tail draggers'. I bought into a Piper Cub syndicate to learn to fly these old-style traditional aeroplanes which have a small tail wheel at the rear end of the fuselage that gives the plane the distinctive high nose, tail down attitude, hence the name. I was now working towards my commercial pilot's licence and logging hours. It felt like slow progress but I just kept chipping away. As flying increasingly came to dominate my time, I combined several part-time jobs to pay for it – modelling, restocking health supplies in supermarkets and waitressing several nights a week.

One evening in the autumn of 1988 I had my first taste of the New Zealand Warbird Association, an organisation that preserves and flies Second World War aircraft. They had a huge hangar on the central apron at Ardmore housing the collection of aeroplanes, including a North American P-51 Mustang, six North American T-6 Texans, which the Kiwis called 'Harvards', and a Dakota DC-3. They often flew on weekends at Ardmore and it was always a great spectacle. Most of the aircraft were syndicated and, as a Warbirds' member, it was possible to buy into these for a few thousand dollars and fly at subsidised rates.

The Warbird clubrooms were situated in a low, prefabricated building attached to the hangar, and these were decorated with flying memorabilia and old photographs from WW2. One Sunday evening in September of that year, another pilot friend, Sarah Caldwell, invited me to go with her to the club and the two of us rolled up at the bar. We quickly found ourselves surrounded by a throng of predominantly male club members, all flying enthusiasts, many of whom had flown for the Royal New Zealand Air Force. They swamped us with drinks and we had the most fantastic evening.

It was also the night I fell madly in love.

Flying High

STEVE Taylor – 'Taylor' to his friends – was tall with spiky, thinning blond hair and a ruddy complexion which emphasised his steely blue eyes. When we first met I could hardly hold his gaze, it was so direct and relentless. A car dealer with a sardonic sense of humour and a biting wit, he could be extremely funny but also intimidating.

Steve had learnt to fly at 16 and started selling cars purely to fund his flying habit. He was a gifted salesman and what had begun as a summer job eventually led to a partnership with the owner of the car yard, which grew into three more dealerships across Auckland. Steve had a master's degree in mathematics and prided himself on being the best educated car dealer in New Zealand. He had achieved his life's ambition to own a classic warbird fighter before the age of 40 with the acquisition of a Hawker Sea Fury, with his friends John Greenstreet and Robbie Booth.

A week after our first meeting, Steve invited me for a date at Ardmore airfield to take me flying in one of the Harvards. This was no ordinary joyride, however. We took off with John in a two-ship formation, climbed to altitude and then launched into a hair-raising 'tail chase', a simulated dogfight where the lead aircraft, the one being chased, tries to throw off his adversary with erratic and evasive manoeuvring. I had never experienced anything like it and it was by turns wildly exciting and utterly terrifying as the planes swooped and dived around the sky, one behind the other, as they closed in on each other for the imaginary kill. It was *Boys' Own* stuff and I was blown away by the machismo of it, which no doubt was the intention.

Both Steve and John were seriously good pilots. Neither were military trained but they both flew for the Roaring Forties, the Warbird Association's five-ship Harvard display team. John, tall and dark with a quietly commanding manner, was vice president of Warbirds and a successful businessman. They were close friends and John, in turn, became a good friend of mine.

Suddenly, my life was on a clear upwards trajectory. I was gaining altitude in every sense and felt happier than I had ever been. Three months on from our first date, Steve asked me to marry him. He might have been nine years older and still living with his mother at the time but I didn't have to think twice. Steve had been married before to a Finnish lady he met working in a pub in London on his first overseas experience in his early twenties. She had joined him in New Zealand and they married so she could stay but the union failed within two years.

Before I met Steve, I was working towards my commercial pilot's licence and when I sat the theory examinations that autumn and passed all the technical subjects in one go, he sent me a huge bouquet of long-stemmed red roses. We often flew together and he taught me the rudiments of aerobatic flying in a Slingsby Firefly. It was a fantastic love affair.

Seven months later, in March 1989, we were married, in a low-key open-air ceremony at Mission Bay, Auckland, by the old stone Mission House on the waterfront, followed by a cocktail party. The site of the first flying school in New Zealand, it was where the first two Boeing seaplanes, the 'B&Ws', had operated a nascent air mail service in 1919. Where we lived in Canada, near Mission City, was where Russell was born, so the name and the location had rich historical resonance for me.

Steve and I bought a very pretty town house on the southern slopes of Remuera, one of the older suburbs of Auckland. Tucked away down a drive, the house featured a wide wooden deck fringed with red bougainvillea and beyond was a sweeping view of exotic native bush on the opposite side of the valley.

Flying was my life and our social life revolved around our flying friends. There was a whole cast of characters. Keith Skilling was the chief flying instructor for Warbirds and led the Roaring Forties display team, and we were particularly close to him and his English second wife, Vanessa. Eric Schroder, a man of small stature but potent character, who had an accountancy company, oversaw the Warbird finances and lent everybody money to join the various syndicates, including me. Eric's second wife, Susie, was also English by birth, and she and I became a tight team organising the two biannual hangar balls to raise funds for the association. John Lamont, like Keith, was ex-Royal New Zealand Air force who took over the running of the Roaring Forties, and we got to know him and his wife Bev well.

The boys were also members of the Officers' Club in Auckland for retired service people, notable for its lack of female members. Julie took over the catering concession at this club and had the dubious pleasure of waiting on the Warbird men during their weekly dinners. The boys would congregate every Tuesday night for drinks and dinner and on very rare occasions, the wives would be invited to join them. But the girls showed up in force for the Warbird fly-ins and air shows. There were weekends away with the aeroplanes and the best one took place at Hawera during the summer of 1989.

On that Saturday morning, we all piled into the Harvards and the DC-3 with great gaiety and flew down to the Taranaki region, stopping off at the Ohakea air force base on the way for morning coffee.

Debs lived not far from Hawera and came over to join us. Steve took her flying in the Harvard, which she breathlessly declared on landing to be the most exciting thing she had ever done.

The boys flew all afternoon, performing displays and taking members of the public up for paid joyrides before we tucked into a barbecue that night and danced and drank into the small hours.

The following day, Steve and I once again took off in the Harvard accompanied by John Greenstreet in his, and we roared off together for a local scenic flight before heading for home. Steve tucked into position behind John's right wing and together they flew a perfect formation loop right over the top of Mt Egmont, yet another of New Zealand's spectacular volcanoes, before sweeping down the side of the mountain and heading out over the coast. We flew very low over the water, still in formation, and then John dropped down even lower, to barely 20 feet above the waves. Steve remained slightly higher and dropped back slightly. John was competitive by nature and a born risk-taker; even then it seemed that he always had to take things to the extreme.

We continued our warbird flying on Sundays in the meantime. I sold my share in the Piper Cub syndicate and bought into another one which owned an Se5a replica. These single-seaters were considered by many pilots to be the best British fighter of the First World War.

For my first attempt at aerobatics in this little single seat biplane, I drove out early one morning to Ardmore, keen to get airborne before the airfield got too busy. I climbed to 5,000 ft overhead the airfield and then did a sequence of rather inexpert, egg-shaped loops, rapidly losing height and slightly fearful that the engine would cut out with the inverted flight. I landed half an hour later, elated.

Life felt pretty damned exciting and I had the sense I was really living. Which is why it was even more shocking how quickly and brutally everything started to fall apart.

Diminishing Returns

ON a Sunday towards the end of February 1990, I was at Ardmore Flying School, preparing for the flight test for my commercial pilot's licence the following day.

I completed a final practice flight and spent a couple of hours tallying up my logbook and reviewing my notes. Once finished, I wandered outside into the late afternoon sunshine and sat, with a glass of wine, relaxing on the lawn in front of the school. Steve and the rest of the Roaring Forties team were scheduled to do a practice formation display at 4pm for a forthcoming air show, so I waited for them to appear. Soon, the five Harvards taxied out and roared off down the runway in a streamed formation take-off. With its big Pratt and Whitney engine, the Harvard makes a very distinct and penetrating sound as the propeller tips go supersonic at full power and I plugged my ears.

They headed north to join up and a few minutes later came charging back over the airfield in a Vic formation, making spectacular white smoke trails behind them. They went through the usual routine with stall turns and loops and then pulled up vertically for the final manoeuvre, the Prince of Wales' feathers.

John was flying the box position, tucked under and behind the leader, and he had to rotate through 180° to fly out the back of the manoeuvre. But as he did so, he cork-screwed wide and, to my horror, hit the aircraft out to the left. Fragments of aeroplane suddenly exploded into the air and John's inverted Harvard dived almost vertically from 800 ft straight into the ground.

It was like watching the sky falling in. I leapt to my feet and raced 150 yards towards the fallen aircraft, pausing only at the runway to let the other damaged Harvard make an emergency landing with part of its wing missing.

I was first on the dreadful scene but found only a large smoking crater with twisted strands of metal poking out of the ground – all that was left of the wings. The engine and fuselage were buried 15 feet into the ground and John had died on impact.

The airfield fire truck pulled up with the crew from Ardmore Flying School and one of them took my arm and practically dragged me out of the hole. It was in the bleakest of moods that we all walked slowly back to the clubrooms and faced the awful job of breaking the news to John's wife.

The following day I was due to sit my commercial flight test. Still inebriated from several shots of whisky and eyes swollen and bloodshot from crying and lack of sleep, I somehow completed the test but everything was a blur. What had seemed of supreme importance the day before, the culmination of two years' effort, turned to dust in a matter of seconds.

Things started to unravel in short order after that. The New Zealand car industry was deregulated by the government and seemingly overnight the value of stock halved, a catastrophe for Steve's business. With mounting financial pressure, he and his partner had a serious falling out and the dispute led to a year of litigation. Steve was out of a job and, with no income, we were forced to sell the house. More money was lost in the fire-sell process and we found a little unit to rent. It was all horribly stressful but Steve used the time to study for his Air Transport Pilots Licence with a view to applying to the airline for a flying job. When the legal case was finally resolved, Steve was able to set up his own car dealership with the out-of-court settlement. He began travelling to Japan every month to buy cars directly and slowly started to rebuild our resources. Two years on, Steve was tipped off about a repossessed house for sale in the suburb of

Kohimarama and bought it at auction for a knock-down price. It all happened so quickly that I couldn't see the house before the sale, but it was a nice place with a distant view of the sea from its elevated position on a hill.

It had been a constant struggle to pay for my flying and I had depleted my reserves paying for a commercial licence. I decided to do an instructor rating and Steve generously pitched in to pay for this additional training. When I qualified as a flying instructor in July 1990 I started working full time teaching people to fly and lecturing on the ground theory courses.

With more than 600 hours in my logbook, I now considered whether I should try to do a multi-engine instrument rating with a view to applying for the airline. This was the hugely expensive next step in the flight training and I was very uncertain about what to do. In the end, I decided not to pursue a career in airline flying for several complicated reasons. I was approaching 30 and time was running out for an airline job. I still had relatively low flying hours for my age and, apart from the big financial commitment, I needed to get a job flying twin-engine aircraft to get the 1,500 hours or so that I needed to qualify for the airline. Most of the young single instructors went and worked with small regional airlines in the Pacific Islands to achieve this but it was not viable for me to do that.

After three years working at the Ardmore Flying School, another flying friend, Barbara Thompson, offered me a fantastic sales job. She was only the third woman pilot to join Air New Zealand and was also the part-owner of an aerial photography and mapping business called Air Logistics. I drove all over the country visiting district and regional councils and government agencies, co-ordinating the photography with our flying base in Nelson while the digital mapping and ortho-rectified imagery was produced in Auckland. I loved the work and enjoyed my colleagues so much I ended up staying for five years. It was the most fulfilling job I ever had. And I kept my hand in with part-time instructing and flying warbirds at weekends.

Meanwhile, things were fomenting in my family. In the latter part of 1989, Russell came to Auckland to do his three-month elective medical term at Auckland Hospital and for one of the rare times in our adult lives the four of us siblings were together in the same place.

The following year, my parents sold The Potlatch and moved to New Zealand, leaving Russell behind to complete his medical degree at Newcastle University. By this time Debs' marriage to Simon was floundering and in the mid-nineties they separated. She moved to Auckland with the girls and quietly started again on her own, eventually training to be a social worker. Julie continued with her catering business at the Officer's Club and then set up her own café and delicatessen on the North Shore.

Debs and I had very mixed feelings about our parents' move to New Zealand. When Debs had become a mother for the first time, she had flown back to England with the newborn Sarah so they could meet their first grandchild. While there she told Mum about what Dad had done to her. She went in a spirit of reconciliation and her baby was offered as a kind of olive branch, but it only caused deeper divisions. Now they were coming to New Zealand there was a terrible undercurrent of anxiety.

Once Mum and Dad arrived, for a while at least, there was a semblance of normality and a few family gatherings passed without incident, but it wasn't long before the whole charade erupted.

In a confrontation with my father, I gave him an ultimatum: apologise to Debs and leave and, if he was unable to do that, then not only would he not see her again, but he wouldn't see me either. He chose the former option, leaving soon after to head to the South Island. Eventually, he found an old derelict homestead in the Dovedale Valley near Motueka, which was eerily like

McConnell Creek. He set about restoring it, living like an old pioneer without electricity or running water, and this became his home and his occupation for the next 25 years. He never returned to England.

In time, my mother came to see that she had been set free. With the lion's share of their modest resources, she was able to buy a small unit and lived within a mile or so of us all in the eastern suburbs. She worked for Julie and slowly rebuilt her life and started doing all the things which she had been denied for so many years while shackled to the restaurant in Appleby. She took up tennis again, went ballroom dancing every week, swam in the sea nearly every day and made a lot of new friends.

For my birthday in 1993, Steve gave me his share in Harvard 1078 and taught me to fly it. The North American T-6 Texan, the single-engine advanced trainer aircraft used by the United States Army Air Forces and British Commonwealth air forces during the Second World War and into the 1970s, was the most advanced aeroplane I ever flew. But, as with driving, husbands should never teach their wives to fly. Steve was impatient and easily bored and I never flew particularly well with him.

The best training I received in the Harvard was with Dr Ross Ewing, an ex-Royal New Zealand and Royal Air Force fighter pilot, whose flying career was cut short by a terrible car accident. He was one of the few people to survive a partially severed aorta and when he lost his professional flying licence for medical reasons he retrained as an aviation doctor. Perhaps this unusual combination of experience made him such a brilliant instructor. His manner was gentle, sympathetic and precise. I made several flights with Ross and, under his tutelage, developed a fair degree of proficiency. After one particularly good session of aerobatics, Ross climbed out of the cockpit and declared that he could yet make an ace of me – rare praise in that rarefied world of highly accomplished male pilots.

But while I was reaching new heights with my flying, life at home was becoming strained.

Steve had shown remarkable resilience to get back on his feet career-wise but on a personal level the stressful events of the past few years had taken their toll and he completely withdrew emotionally.

I tried my best to bridge the growing chasm between us but he increasingly shut me down.

Steve and I had never discussed having children before we married and, by mutual agreement, we didn't want them. He didn't want me to get a dog either but I ignored him and acquired a three-month-old puppy, smuggling him home one weekend while Steve was away on business. He was a little whippet I named Louis, after recently watching the film *The Immortal Beloved* about Ludwig van Beethoven. When I first took him to a park, a little girl pointed at him and exclaimed 'Mummy, look there's a fawn!'

Louis became not just my constant companion but probably saved my sanity and when somebody commented that he was a 'child replacement', I replied: 'More of a husband replacement, actually.'

Steve worked every Saturday and often on Sundays and took time off during the week to practise his aerobatic flying. During the mid-nineties he became the New Zealand unlimited champion, a title he retained for two years running and set his sights on competing in the world championship. He practised relentlessly and I saw less and less of him.

Something had broken between Steve and I, and I was conscious of a sinkhole of despair at the centre of my existence. Unhappiness is a pervasive thing and it seemed to spread through every aspect of my life. Any further illusions about our relationship evaporated one evening when I brought up the subject of our joint estate. I didn't have a will and wanted to make provision for Debs in the event of Steve and I getting killed together in an aeroplane.

To my astonishment, he said the 'bricks and mortar' belonged to him and nothing was going to my family.

Not long after, Steve went to the US and purchased a state-of-the-art aerobatic plane for an eye-watering price, which he only told me about afterwards.

That was the straw which broke the camel's back. After 14 years in New Zealand, I cut the rope. It was the most difficult decision I have ever had to make. In one fell swoop, I left my marriage, our home, our respective families, my friends, the best job I ever had and, effectively, my flying.

I was returning to England to start again from ground zero. Louis was the only thing I took with me.

Return of the Native

ARRIVING back in England, it was like I didn't exist. After 14 years away I had no credit history so even things like opening a bank account and getting a mobile phone proved problematic. I wondered whether I had done the right thing and there were times I was immobilised with fear about the future.

I needed to find work so I registered with an employment agency and did a succession of grim jobs working at a concrete factory and cold calling for the Register of Expert Witnesses.

London seemed too much to take on at this stage so I rented a small cottage in Newmarket, in Suffolk, where I had some friends in the horse racing industry.

I made friends with a couple, Anthea and Ian Davidson, who lived just outside Newmarket in the village of Dullingham. Anthea also had a dog and we started painting together in her studio, she with her acrylics and me with my oils, in what would become one of the most brilliant friendships of my life.

I registered with the British Racing School and had a few lessons riding jockey-style, practising the crouch position with shortened stirrups on a mechanical wooden horse bench. My friends introduced me to one of the local trainers, Alec Stewart, who kindly invited me to ride out with his string on one of his own hunters.

Within months of moving, I considered again trying to fly for a living. I signed up for the theory course for an airline transport pilot's licence in Oxfordshire and sat the exams but still faced the overwhelming problem of how to afford a multi-engine instrument rating. The clock was ticking. I was now in my mid-thirties and felt like I was 10 years too late. In the end it came to nothing, but my interest in old aeroplanes continued unabated.

Another reason I chose Newmarket was its proximity to Duxford, the legendary Second World War Spitfire fighter base immortalised in the film *The Battle of Britain*. Disbanded as an air force base in 1961, Duxford eventually became the home of the Imperial War Museum in the mid-seventies. A decade later, several private warbird operators also congregated there with their aircraft, starting with the Hannas and their family business, The Old Flying Machine Company. Stephen Grey, with his Fighter Collection, followed a year or two later. I had met all these people in New Zealand when they came down for the southern summer to fly, like migrating birds. The most notable of the New Zealand air shows was Warbirds over Wanaka, established in the late eighties by Tim Wallis, who was later knighted for his services to aviation. In 1989 we flew the entire Warbird fleet from Ardmore to the South Island for the first Warbirds over Wanaka and after that the show became a biennial event. This was where I first met Ray and Mark Hanna, renowned warbird pilots and handsome father and son double act, who performed a thrilling dogfight with their famous Spitfire MH434, and a Messerschmitt Me-109. Ray was a Kiwi and had left New Zealand in 1949 to join the RAF and led the Red Arrows for three seasons in the mid-sixties.

The Hannas introduced me to Tim Manna when they organised an air show at Cranfield in summer 1998. Tim, a tall, good-looking American of Italian extraction, was an all-round good guy and I was instantly smitten. Nicknamed 'The Moose', due to his big, square frame and long, antelope-like legs when he played for the Harvard University football team, he was recruited by the US Navy, trained as a pilot, and spent several years flying a Lockheed P-3 Orion on maritime surveillance and anti-submarine operations during the final years of the Cold War. An ardent Anglophile, Tim had lived in London for several years working in fund management and, as a fanatical warbird enthusiast, had his own diverse collection of aeroplanes, including both piston and jet aircraft and sundry old military helicopters, all of which he could fly.

Tim and I struck up together that summer and after a year-long hiatus I was back flying again, albeit infrequently. I started flying some of Tim's aeroplanes, including his Piston Provost and a De Havilland Chipmunk. We did frequent trips to New York together for his work and for a while considered the possibility of moving to America. We remained in England, however, and the following year Tim bought a beautiful, renovated barn in a village west of Duxford where we lived happily for a while.

Another friend of Ray Hanna was Stephen Grey, who I had met in New Zealand in the early nineties. Back then, Stephen flew a Spitfire in a three-ship formation with Steve, my husband, leading in the Hawker Sea Fury he co-owned with John Greenstreet and Rob Booth. Stephen had set up his own warbird operation at Duxford which became 'The Fighter Collection', the largest collection of Second World War fighters in Europe, and between him and the Hannas, they hatched the idea of starting their own air show. This was the Classic Fighters Air Show which eventually morphed into Flying Legends, one of the best warbird air shows in the world.

When I lived in Newmarket that first year I occasionally dropped by to say hello to them all and I was elated when Stephen offered me a job helping to organise Flying Legends. Having never organised an air show before, I was rather thrown in at the deep end with only six months to prepare for the 1999 event. As it was effectively a private show by the Fighter Collection within the strictures of the Imperial War Museum management, the logistics were challenging, with even the advertising and ticket sales handled internally, and everything was done on a shoestring.

The very best of it was Flying Legends in 2000 when several

famous aces from the Second World War took part, including the wonderful Johnnie Johnson, the highest scoring British ace in the European theatre, and that year Stephen had his Mark XIV Spitfire painted in Johnnie's colours as a tribute. It was absolutely electrifying to watch this Spitfire, brilliantly flown by Paul Bonhomme, tearing down the airfield in a series of low, fast passes. Johnnie was thrilled and so was the audience.

As I was too busy working, I wasn't doing much of my own flying at this point but I did a couple of flights with an old friend from New Zealand, Sir Ken Hayr, a retired Air Chief Marshall who'd had a distinguished career in the RAF. At the age of 66, he was now enjoying his retirement, living in New Zealand for six months of the year and the rest of the time in England. When I came home in 1997, Ken was one of the first people to make contact. He looked very much like the actor David Niven, with the same dapper charm and quick humour. I hugely enjoyed his company and loved flying aerobatics with him.

In the run-up to the Biggin Hill Air Show in 2001, I had been flying with Ken and he invited me to fly with him during the event. I declined because Tim and I had friends staying that weekend and Ken took an engineer instead.

During the air show, on June 2, Ken flew a De Havilland Vampire but on his final pass the jet was flipped upside down by the vortices from the lead aircraft in the formation. Ken was unable to recover in time at the low altitude and slammed into the ground five seconds later. Both he and the young engineer were tragically killed in the crash.

When Ray Hanna phoned me with the terrible news just minutes after the accident I was completely shattered. I could hardly believe it but air show flying has a unique set of pressures and, however experienced the pilots, they are still fallible human beings flying fallible machines.

Early the following morning, I drove to Biggin Hill and met

with the coroner and the stricken family of the young engineer who had also died. Ken's sons were too distressed to come to the airfield. The sole comfort was the reassuring presence of Stephen Grey and two of the Fighter Collection pilots, Paul Bonhomme and Guy Bancroft-Wilson. They were there to participate in the flying display that afternoon and I sat with Guy in the pilots' tent with his leather flying jacket over my shoulders, clutching a cup of black coffee.

Early that afternoon I was due to meet with the media and we were preparing for an interview in a building near the base of the control tower. I heard the distinctive growl of a piston engine overhead as the flying display continued but it sounded terrifyingly close. I felt an involuntary spasm of panic, an echo of the old recurring trauma from John Greenstreet's crash of 11 years before.

A minute later we stepped out of the building, just as there was the ear-splitting roar of an over-speeding piston engine and, barely 100 yards away, a plane hurtled vertically into the ground, exploding into a huge fireball. It was like a war zone. A huge pyre of flames and churning black smoke rose into the sky, as people and vehicles raced in all directions across the apron with sirens blaring. It was complete chaos but there was really nothing that could be done.

Speechless with shock, we retreated into the building.

The news then came through that it was Guy, a Fighter Collection and former Red Arrows pilot, who had died. He was 43 and left behind three young sons under the age of 10.

I was still wearing the flying jacket he had kindly lent me when he crashed.

Lady Icarus

WHEN I finally limped home that evening, I was exhausted and numb with shock. The rest of the flying display had immediately been cancelled but such was the jam of people and cars trying to leave the airfield it had taken me many hours to get away. Throughout that time, I had tried to call Tim several times but the mobile phone network was overwhelmed by people trying to do likewise.

I was met with a very cool reception from Tim, who was upset that I had been away for so long without calling. It was an extraordinary reaction in the circumstances and so fantastically unsympathetic that suddenly his attitude seemed symptomatic of a much bigger problem. We split up shortly afterwards. As one chapter ended, however, another started.

I began to spend an increasing amount of time at the Shuttleworth Collection, the oldest aeronautical and automotive museum in the world, in Bedfordshire, where I'd first visited on my trip to England in 1995 and had been mesmerised by ever since. Founded by aviator Richard Ormonde Shuttleworth in 1928, it is a mecca for the restoration and preservation of historic aircraft and vintage cars.

Every time I visited I felt like I was stepping back in time to the 1920s. The original grass strip was a paddock nestled in trees with an old 'blister' hangar where the engineering workshops were housed. Several more hangars had been added over the years and these bore the legendary names of all the early British aircraft designers: Avro, Sopwith, De Havilland, Vickers, Gloster. The

71

place, much like the people who worked there, was old fashioned, slightly eccentric, genteel, charming, modest and understated. The Shuttleworth Collection was underpinned by engineering brilliance and the engineers – exceptional in their quiet dedication to these lovely old aeroplanes – were a world away from the macho, ego-driven, intensely political environment of Duxford.

When my old friend Carol brought her young family to meet me there one Sunday, she instantly declared that it was *Flambards*, the book we had read as youngsters, and Shuttleworth became my flying home for the next nine years.

It was around this time I met a Belgian banker named Alain Grisay, who had a great passion for classic cars, and we started meeting in town for the occasional lunch or dinner. Alain was very charming but with a rather formal manner. A native French speaker, he was a lawyer by training but had never practised and had spent his career in finance. In his conventional corporate guise, Alain was almost invisible and I once walked straight past him at an airport when he came to meet me. Without his trademark glasses and business suits, however, he was a different person and possessed the clean-cut, classic good looks of an older David Beckham, with exceptional emotional intelligence. Alain's life was complicated though. He worked and lived in London but spent most weekends in Brussels, where his family was based. His wife, from whom he had apparently separated, lived in Brussels with their two teenage sons.

We bonded over a shared interest in old cars, old aeroplanes and Africa and when, in 2002, friends in New Zealand invited me over for several months to help organise an air show in Blenheim, I didn't hesitate, hoping our time apart would give Alain the time he needed to get divorced.

After eight months away, I returned to England in spring 2003 and moved in with Alain – and into another world.

Alain had a stable of classic cars and over the next few years we participated in several classic rallies together, including the Mille Miglia in 2005 and the Peking to Paris two years later, re-tracing the route first driven by Prince Borghese in 1907. It involved driving for six weeks through northern China, the Gobi Desert, across Russia to the Baltic and on to Paris. I'd given Alain a compass not long after we met but he had no aptitude for navigation. We made a good team, however, and the rallies were the most fantastic thing we did in our nine years together.

Alain's greatest gift to me was a 1941 Ryan Recruit aeroplane he bought in 2005, which I kept until 2022. Built by TC Ryan, the brilliant aircraft designer who created the *Spirit of St Louis* for Charles Lindbergh, it was the prototype for the PT-22 military trainer and this version was developed from one of the most beautiful civilian planes of the 1930s, the lovely Ryan STA Sports Trainer.

The Shuttleworth chief pilot, Andy Sephton, arranged for me to hangar the Ryan at Old Warden and for several years it lived alongside the rest of the aircraft in the collection. This was the start of an intensely happy period where I learnt to display the Ryan at the Shuttleworth shows and became close friends with many of the engineers, pilots and volunteers. I spent countless hours buzzing around the countryside of Bedfordshire and Cambridgeshire in my Ryan, taking people for joy rides or just flying on my own for sheer pleasure.

I also undertook an intensive course in formation flying – something I'd only tentatively done in New Zealand – with a company called Ultimate High, who were based at Kemble airfield and employed a team of ex-military instructors. After that, I was able to practise regularly at Old Warden with the help of Frank Chapman and Rob Millinship, two of the Shuttleworth Collection pilots. Rob took me under his wing and we flew many hours together practising formation flying. I grew in confidence and it wasn't long before I gained my display authorisation as both

formation lead aircraft and wingman, flying in multi-ship formations.

At Shuttleworth one afternoon in summer 2009, somebody
casually asked what my greatest ambition in life was.

Without thinking, I replied: 'To fly Africa in an open cockpit
biplane.'

Even as the words left my mouth, I was seized by an almost
psychic certainty that it would really happen.

In a vague, nebulous way, I had wanted to fly Africa ever since
watching the Academy Award-winning film *Out of Africa* in
1985. In one scene, a little yellow Gypsy Moth biplane takes off
from a clearing, rising above the trees before tiptoeing over the
Ngong Hills and along an escarpment before descending into the
immensity of the Rift Valley. Flying low over herds of elephant,
zebra and wildebeest, it skims over the surface of a lake where
flamingos take flight in a pink haze below. The biplane then
climbs up among the clouds, ascending higher still, until flying
straight towards the sun.

That extraordinary flight was one of the most achingly beautiful
things I had ever seen and left an indelible impression.

At the heart of the flight was a great love story. The pilot was
Denys Finch Hatton – Robert Redford in the film – and he had
bought the plane to show Karen Blixen Africa from the air. This
was her first flight and she would later write: 'I knew then, without
reflecting, that I was up at a great height, upon the roof of the
world, a small figure in the tremendous retort of earth and air,
yet one with it.'

Charged with eroticism, the flight was the ultimate consum-
mation of their long love affair and signified something infinitely
greater. The scope, freedom and epic grandeur made it a spiritual
ascent into some purer element.

It was the realisation of exactly how I wanted my life to be.

When I made the decision to fly Africa, the celebrated inter-war flyers Amelia Earhart and Amy Johnson were well known to me. However, until I took a German visitor to Shuttleworth flying in the Ryan, there was one name I knew nothing about. As a thank you for the flight, my guest gave me a copy of *Lady Icarus* by Lindie Noughton – a biography of Lady Mary Heath.

Here was a woman considered the original Queen of the Skies, at one stage one of the best-known women in the world during the golden age of aviation, yet largely neglected by history. She was the first woman in Britain to gain a commercial pilot's licence, the first to make a parachute jump and the first British women's javelin champion. She also scandalised 1920s society by smoking Turkish cigarettes, dressing in furs and marrying three times.

The more I read, the more I was captivated.

In 1928 Lady Heath made global headlines as the first person to fly solo in a light aircraft from South Africa to England. In the same year she spent a few weeks as a volunteer co-pilot with civil airline KLM but attributed her failure to secure a permanent appointment to male prejudice.

Her fame spread to the US, where she was dubbed 'Lady Lindy'. She acted as agent for Cirrus aero engines in the States, became a lecture circuit celebrity and considered applying for American citizenship when, in August 1929, she was injured in a crash just before the opening of the notoriously dangerous Cleveland National Air Races. She reportedly hit a cable while flying around a chimney stack and her aircraft went crashing through the factory roof below. Her passenger managed to jump clear but Lady Heath was strapped in and fell through two floors with the aircraft and had to be cut out of the wreckage. She survived with severe head and facial injuries, which left her permanently disfigured.

After three failed marriages, she became beset by alcoholism and depression. She disappeared to London for weeks at a time and there were several court appearances for public drunkenness.

It was in east London in May 1939 that she fell down the steps of a tram, struck her head and died in hospital in Shoreditch. The post-mortem stated the cause of the accident was not alcohol but a blood clot, probably a consequence of the 1929 Cleveland crash.

Press reports of her death noted that she was a 'pioneer airwoman', but Mary had been largely overshadowed by the next generation of female aviators, notably Amy Johnson. The key aspect of her strange life that remained untarnished, however, was her passion for flying and remarkable talent. She was a trailblazer: a modern woman, ahead of her time but still painfully dependent on men. Her obituary in the *Weekly News* remarked: 'She never knew fear, and was daring to the point of recklessness.'

When I finished reading I not only marvelled at her achievements, but her story had added a new dimension and purpose to my Africa flight.

I wanted to track back through history and follow Lady Heath's epic flight, telling her story through a documentary film to restore her to the pantheon of aviation pioneers. I resolved to work as hard as I could to make that dream a reality.

Initially, Alain was very supportive, but our relationship floundered when I discovered that he had been living a double life. Throughout our time together – all those years when I was waiting for him to get divorced – he had not only remained married but had collected a string of other women, just as he did classic cars. I had no option but to move out of Alain's London mews after a truly dreadful scene.

Devastatingly, an even greater love quietly passed away that spring, when I lost my beloved whippet, Louis, just short of his 15th birthday.

A month later, at Shuttleworth, on the first day of May, I was cleaning the Ryan when a Cessna landed and parked up some distance away. A tall, fair-haired man alighted and approached in long, graceful strides. He was dressed rather formally for flying in a dark blazer with a loose neck-tie and as he strode up, he greeted me and asked if I could direct him to 'ops' so he could sign in. I smiled slightly at his manner and said there was no such thing at Shuttleworth, but if he went down to the greasy spoon 'caf', gesturing over my shoulder, they should be able to help him out there.

This was Robert Marshall. We got talking and made a plan to fly together.

I didn't know it then but, after all the recent heartbreak, a heady season of thrills and adventure lay ahead.

Gone With The Wind

FROM that first chance meeting at Shuttleworth, Robert and I had the summer of our lives.

The following week I took him flying in the Ryan and afterwards we had a picnic in the Swiss Garden at Shuttleworth and lazed around under the trees talking. I'm not one to express myself in French as a rule, but it seems the only way to describe what happened which was, quite simply, a *coup de foudre*.

Casting all else aside we tore around in aeroplanes, enjoyed long dinners at the pub, riotous nights out in London and dancing into the small hours, all in a heightened state of euphoria. I had more fun in those few months with Robert than in nine years with Alain. Unlike my previous relationships, Robert and I were the same age and in lots of ways considered ourselves 'two peas from the same pod'. I had only ever used that expression in connection with my twin but, when Robert made the comment, it seemed apposite.

Like me, Robert was extracting himself from a long and difficult relationship but through the sadness of this break-up the one positive outcome had been a daughter.

For me, finding Robert was like breaking out of the cloud into the sunlit uplands as life took on a spectroscopic brilliance. I was delighted to learn of his own blood connection with Africa. His maternal grandparents had been in Tanzania with the colonial service during the 1940s and, after returning to the UK, had settled, by an almost freakish coincidence, in the north of England, just a few miles from Appleby.

Robert, the scion of a prominent Cambridge family steeped in engineering and aviation, had gone to Eton College, then Cambridge, and was himself an engineer. Wonderfully bright with boundless energy, he had a savage innocence about him, like a young lion.

Robert asked me to marry him and, towards the end of that memorable summer, I organised a little soirée at Shuttleworth for the last sunset air show of the season. I invited all my old friends and with a prime view of the airfield, we set up camp with our picnic paraphernalia: folding tables, deck chairs, a large hamper and a chilly bin crammed with bottles. There was a lot of laughter and joking around as we settled down and cracked into the wine and it had all the makings of a very jolly evening.

This was the first time I was going to meet Robert's teenage daughter. We had deliberately not rushed into it, given the sensitivity, and this seemed like the perfect occasion with a few friends around in a fun, informal setting. Robert and his daughter were late arriving and I began to feel slightly anxious. An hour later they finally turned up and I jumped up to meet them as they walked towards us. As I introduced them to the group, however, everything suddenly felt charged with tension. Robert's daughter was dressed in a bright red designer coat with a ribbon through her blonde curls and a small, pale blue fabric flower wilting over her left eye.

When I spoke with Robert later that evening I shared with him my concern about building a relationship with his daughter. Robert rented a house in Cambridge on his own where he could spend time with his daughter. He took her on several overseas holidays and I encouraged these trips, hoping they would help them after the family split. The following year, Robert and I bought a house together, which proved to be a huge and expensive undertaking. It needed extensive renovation and landscaping and we spent many months co-ordinating the work with a team of builders, plumbers, electricians and gardeners, but over the next year the Bee House, as we called it, morphed into something fabulous. It was a large bungalow with two conservatory wings off a central octagonal room and a little tower on top resembling a lighthouse. We had dark oak floorboards installed throughout and by the time I had furnished it with large tropical palms, rugs, big paintings and my cherished collection of tribal artefacts, it looked like a kind of Africa house. It was the dream home, for me at least. Sadly, however, Robert's daughter didn't like it and always resisted coming there.

Against this background, I focused on my Africa flight and Robert was hugely supportive. Together, we approached several Cambridge companies to augment the sponsorship and Cambridge Airport was going to be the home base for my flight. To promote the airport, I called the expedition 'Cape to Cambridge', which resonated nicely with Lady's Heath's 1928 'Cape to Cairo' route.

My first challenge, though, was to find a suitable aeroplane, one robust and reliable enough to cope with the heat and high-density altitudes of Africa. I also wanted it to be spectacularly beautiful. I had always loved the Boeing Stearman and, from the outset, I knew it would be the perfect aeroplane.

Stearmans are big, handsome, classic biplanes, designed by Lloyd Stearman in Wichita, Kansas, during the early 1920s. The Boeing Company took over Lloyd Stearman's aircraft business and built thousands of Stearman as basic trainers for the Second World War and hence they became known as the Boeing Stearman. Famously strong, the aeroplane could withstand any amount of mishandling by young student pilots who often 'dropped' them on the ground from 20ft in the air as they learnt the rudiments of landing. After the war, the surplus Stearmans were sold off and mostly used as crop-dusters.

Initially, I looked at hiring a Stearman and there was one based at Stellenbosch, near Cape Town, which looked promising. I flew to South Africa and had a trial flight but it had a big 450 horsepower engine, which felt very nose heavy, and it became clear the fuel consumption would be too high. Sourcing aviation fuel was going to be one of our most serious challenges in certain parts of Africa.

I went to look at another Stearman in America but that too proved unsuitable. Another then came up for sale in Liverpool, so my friend, Derrick Gunning, and I flew up with one of the Shuttleworth engineers to take a look. However, the aeroplane was in terrible condition and with the owner demanding a huge price, I returned home disappointed and irritated.

Sometime after this, Derrick phoned to say that he had found an engineering company in central Europe which specialised in the restoration of Stearmans. I tracked down the owner, Ewald Gritsch, and had several long phone conversations about the technical specifications. A week later, I jumped on a flight to Vienna to meet him.

Ewald's workshop was based at an airfield in Hungary, just a few miles over the border from Austria. He employed a team of Hungarian engineers, most of them ex-military, as one might expect in a former communist Eastern Bloc country, and I was hugely impressed with the whole set-up.

Talking things over with Robert when I got back, he said that of course we should commission the restoration of a Stearman and stop messing around. I always loved his enthusiastic and impulsive approach but it was a big financial undertaking at a time when we were already heavily committed with the house. We agreed we would buy the plane, then sell it after the Africa expedition to recoup the money. I immediately phoned Ewald to confirm we wanted to proceed.

It was a ground-breaking moment – I finally had my aeroplane.

In 2011, I was introduced to Geoffrey Matthews, to bring some impetus to the expedition. Geoffrey looked a bit like Hugh Bonneville, the actor who plays Lord Grantham in *Downton Abbey*. After a stint in the army, he had worked with The Prince's Trust, had helped to organise the benefit concert for Princess Diana at Wembley in 2007 and Prince Harry's Sentebale charity in Lesotho. After a productive first meeting, Geoffrey came on board as my project manager.

At this early stage, we were still not sure what the business model would look like and variously explored how we might support a charity with the flight and raise money for the expedition at the same time. We had several meetings with the wonderful Cambridge based charity, Camfed, which was dedicated to educating girls in sub-Saharan Africa and in the previous 25 years had sponsored over a million and a half young women through secondary education. I loved the idea of joining forces with them but by any calculation, this was going to involve us having to raise several million pounds to generate enough commission to underwrite the flight. It was a frustrating conundrum and for many months it felt like everything was on ice.

The other dimension to the expedition was the route planning and logistics. I had been recommended a chap who specialised in this and had considerable experience in Africa, albeit with modern light aircraft. He had never dealt with a vintage aeroplane before. His name was Sam Rutherford and his company was called Prepare2Go. Sam was based in Brussels but his background was British establishment. His father had been a vice admiral in the Royal Navy and Sam had been privately educated, before attending the Royal Military Academy at Sandhurst for officer training. He joined the army, went on to fly helicopters and had served in Northern Ireland. Sam seemed exactly the sort of person we needed to provide our logistical support and security in Africa and this was important to reassure potential sponsors.

Geoffrey and I first met Sam in September 2011 at St Pancras Station. I was slightly surprised by Sam's small stature, somehow expecting someone taller. Dressed, safari-style, in khaki chinos with matching shirt, he walked with a slight swagger, had a very confident manner and a ready answer for everything. Geoffrey liked Sam immediately. As is often the case with men of a shared military background, there was an instant 'band of brothers' rapport.

We commissioned Sam to prepare a basic route plan and budget for the expedition and I paid him an upfront retainer.

Shortly after this, we also had a break on the filming front. Geoffrey met Annette Porter at a dinner party and it emerged that she had a small film production company. When Geoffrey mentioned my project, she wanted to meet me as soon as possible. Annette was a big, dynamic, blonde American with a cracking sense of humour and we immediately hit it off.

Annette had attended Columbia Business School and forged a successful career as a management consultant; and she was also wealthy and prepared to put up some of her own money for the project. Annette had set up Nylon Films with a close friend, Helen Morrell, who had worked as a production assistant with the BBC for many years. They had made several corporate videos but never a feature documentary of the kind we envisaged. Annette immediately loved the idea of emulating Lady Heath's journey and she wanted to start filming straight away.

While filming some of the restoration work on the Stearman in Hungary, we connected with Ingrid Strahammer, who lived near Vienna and was from the well-known Parkinson aviation family in Nairobi. The Parkinsons had set up Phoenix Aviation during the 1950s and operated aircraft all over Africa.

Ingie's brother, Steve Parkinson, now ran the family business and became the solution to our last big problem – the support aircraft. Steve brilliantly offered to provide a big, safari-style,

Cessna Caravan at a reduced rate which would ultimately allow Annette to bring an expanded four-man film crew.

The logistical elements were falling into place. I still had no sponsors, however – and without that there would be no expedition.

While this was going on, I immersed myself in another flying project – a plan to fly an old Antonov An-2 biplane with a Russian crew from Siberia to South Africa, as a kind of dry run for my own flight. My involvement in this unlikely jamboree came by way of an introduction to a South African businessman who ran a company called ExecuJet, which had a base at Cambridge Airport. Niall Olver had a great friendship with the chief executive of Utair, the biggest regional airline in Russia, and together they hatched the plan for Utair to donate one of their An-2s and provide the crew, while ExecuJet provided the logistical support using its operational bases across Africa. The aircraft would then remain in South Africa for humanitarian purposes. I did a type rating in Europe that summer and the British Civil Aviation Authority provided a temporary endorsement on my pilot's licence which enabled the Russian authorities to issue me with a crew licence to fly a Russian registered aircraft.

For this expedition, we needed someone to organise our refuelling stops across Africa and, as Sam Rutherford claimed to have a network of contacts across the continent, I thought he would be ideal, so introduced him to the project.

However, as things were progressing with both expeditions and 2012 slipped by, my homelife took a devastating turn. Robert was under so much stress something seemed to break – I just didn't realise it was us. I tried to support him with his life and the issues he was dealing with. Robert had been away on an overseas business trip and was forced to return early for various reasons.

We had been engaged for two years when he said he had something to tell me. His divorce had come through months before but he had felt unable to share this with me. He had other matters to attend to and could only give them attention by ending our relationship. That was it – an abrupt and brutal termination. I was so stunned I could barely utter a word. It was like being shot through the heart at point-blank range.

I flew to New Zealand a few days later but was so traumatised I couldn't bring myself to tell my family what had happened. The photographs from this time tell their own story. I look gaunt and distraught but if anybody noticed they didn't say anything. I stayed for just two weeks before flying home again.

A few days later, I flew to Ukraine to join the Russian crew who were already making their way across Siberia from the Arctic Ocean. Arriving in Kyiv, where the temperature was -20°C and the city lay buried under three feet of snow, I found myself alone in a strange, frozen, Dante-esque world, seemingly disconnected from anything that had gone before.

Only a single, solitary idea throbbed in the darkness of those interminable nights like a heartbeat.

In the tight, dark pit where I found myself, two words echoed in my head like a mantra: 'Aviator. Avatar.'

It was strangely comforting and I took it as a sign.

I was now free to become the aviator I truly was, and in so doing I would become my own avatar.

The Grapes of Wrath

WHILE the expedition from Siberia to South Africa settled any residual doubts in my mind that I could handle a long-distance, multi-stop journey across continents, it also highlighted some of the pitfalls of not having the required logistical support in place on the ground.

Not only did we get stuck in Port Harcourt, in Nigeria, for two weeks due to political and paperwork issues, by the time we ended up in Cabinda, despite having supposedly prepaid for fuel, the local agent tried to blackmail us for the Avgas we needed for the An-2's piston engine.

Cabinda is a province of Angola but is a separate enclave situated on the northern bank of the Congo River. It is entirely surrounded by the hostile Democratic Republic of the Congo apart from 56 miles of shoreline, which protects the rights of Angolan offshore oil rigs and one of largest offshore oil fields in the world.

As soon as we landed we realised we had a serious problem. The fuel which Rutherford had arranged was not there and his agent requested an extra payment of $15,000 for the three barrels we needed. The security situation was precarious and access to the airport was difficult. It was 30 hours' drive time from the nearest depot over sometimes impassable roads and a dangerous border crossing, so the fuel agent knew we were vulnerable flying in there and saw the opportunity to take advantage.

We were stuck for three weeks and largely confined to our hotel as we were warned not to leave the city. Militia groups were operating in the area and there had been several instances of attacks and kidnappings, including a visiting football team, so the danger was very real.

In the event, I managed to persuade the boss of our handling company, Nuno Pereiro, to pull some favours with the Angolan air force. After several more days they dropped into Cabinda in another Antonov transport aircraft and three barrels were rolled straight down the plane's loading ramp into the long grass at the side of the runway and then they took off again.

Without warning, our handlers came to the hotel and told us the fuel had been delivered. We scrambled our stuff together, and piled into a taxi back to the airport 20 minutes later. It was late afternoon and we had to get the fuel pumped from the barrels into the An-2 as quickly as possible because time was running out for us to get to our next stop before nightfall.

Once airborne, we flew straight out to sea for 20 miles, as we had been advised to do to avoid being shot at from DRC. The vast mouth of the Congo River glinted in the distance and when we finally turned south, still miles out over the water, a line of dark thunderclouds flashed along the coast. Nearly three hours later, as darkness fell, we landed in Luanda, the capital of Angola.

The whole thing was a huge adventure but it left me with serious concerns. If we got stuck on the ground in the same way with our forthcoming expedition, the delay and cost would be ruinous. We could easily grind to a halt with African bureaucracy or corruption and technical issues. It underscored the importance of logistics and having reliable supply lines for the fuel.

What also concerned me was Sam Rutherford – the logistical expert I brought into the project. I had some doubts about his African network and whether we could rely on him to deliver the required support. I shared this with Geoffrey but he waved away my concerns, having complete faith in Rutherford's military credentials. I had to put any reservations to one side, however, because there were more pressing issues.

I had returned home to a very different landscape.

Any kind of financial security had effectively gone up in smoke. I had a half-finished aeroplane, the bare bones of an expedition and was back to square one with the sponsorship. I also had to sell our home, the Bee House, where I continued to live on my own. Most of my money was tied up in the house and my priority was to put it on the market.

The break-up with Robert also forced me to make significant changes to the expedition. I had lost what was going to be home base and consequently it would no longer be 'Cape to Cambridge'. I kept my options open as I resumed the search for sponsors in earnest. I networked like mad, shuttling back and forth to meetings in London, writing dozens of emails and letters appealing to various prominent people and companies for their support. Mostly, these met with rebuttals or worse, complete silence. It was very disheartening but I doggedly persisted.

Boeing came to the rescue. I had met the Boeing Defence team at the Royal International Air Tattoo the previous year and told them about the Africa flight. As a global company, Boeing is very proactive about promoting women in aviation and my flight in a vintage Boeing Stearman and the Lady Heath story clearly struck a chord. They now came back and offered a generous donation to the flight and, in so doing, became my first sponsor. I could now say with immense pride that I had the biggest name in global aerospace behind me.

But I still needed a main sponsor and as the weeks wore on with no results it was approaching make-or-break point for the expedition. In early May things took the most extraordinary turn. A year earlier I had come across an advertisement for 'Artemis the Profit Hunter' in the *Financial Times*, which featured an illustration of a 1930s aeroplane with the occupants kitted out in pith helmets and safari suits. They were flying over hostile terrain hunting for 'profits' and, on closer inspection, these profits looked like prehistoric wingless birds. It was eye-catching and original, and I concluded that somebody in the company liked old aeroplanes.

Artemis Investments is a specialist fund management company based in London and Edinburgh and these 'profit' creatures were in fact a pictorial representation of their profit performance graph, which looked like a bolt of ascending lightning. Below the picture, the text read that they were looking for opportunities 'off the beaten track', in 'remote locations' … with 'calculated risk'. It sounded just like my flight. I had kept the advertisement for a year, almost too frightened to do anything with it. I knew I would only get one crack at it and wanted to make sure we had our ducks in a row before I made the approach. Finally, I plucked up the courage to write to the chief executive, John Dodd – one of the founding partners. Within an hour, John's personal assistant replied, saying he would like to set up a meeting. I was speechless with surprise.

Two days later, Geoffrey and I fetched up at the Artemis offices in St James. Feeling extremely nervous, I had no idea what to expect but Artemis's splendidly named managing director Dick Turpin – a delightful character with a warm, ready laugh – quickly put us at ease. Before long, John Dodd came to join us. Casually dressed and equally welcoming, he was nevertheless cool as marble and harder to read.

Geoffrey led our pitch in a very professional, if formal, manner but as time ticked on I grew increasingly desperate that our big chance to make a telling impression was passing us by. When John asked me what I thought I bit my lip and went for it – launching into a slightly incoherent but impassioned speech about what we were trying to do and, more specifically, what had happened to me which had so badly derailed things. I don't know whether I appealed to John's sense of gallantry – or he could sense my desperation – but I could scarcely believe it when he cut through all this and said, calmly, 'How much do you need?'

Half an hour later, as Geoffrey and I fell out of the Artemis offices, he said: 'Well, fuck me! Never, in 30 years of business, have I seen anything like that before.'

Three days later, John phoned me to confirm I really wasn't dreaming … Artemis Investments were indeed going to provide sponsorship, adding that the money would be forthcoming in a matter of days. Just like that. After I put the phone down, I sat for a full minute in astonishment, both hands over my mouth, before leaping into the air, shrieking like a banshee and galloping wildly around the house.

Another company we had approached about potential sponsorship was the Goodwood Road Racing Company – better known as simply 'Goodwood' – the estate owned by Lord March (now the Duke of Richmond), near Chichester, world famous for the Goodwood Revival, the Festival of Speed car-racing events and, of course, Glorious Goodwood, the annual horse-racing festival on the South Downs overlooking the airfield of the same name.

Having fallen in love with Goodwood since attending some early Revival events in the late nineties, I felt the synergy with our expedition was obvious. I had met Charles March on several occasions over the years and John Dodd also knew him well, so we all met for breakfast in London one morning to discuss possibilities and, shortly after, Geoffrey and I went down to Goodwood to meet their marketing team.

And so it transpired that Goodwood would be both the launch pad for the Africa flight at the 2013 Goodwood Revival and the finale for when, hopefully, I arrived back in England several weeks later. The expedition became known, thereafter, as 'Cape Town to Goodwood'.

The Stearman finally had a name too. I had long wanted to call it the 'Spirit of …' something, to evoke the *Spirit of Ecstasy*, with the figure of a woman leaning forward with her arms flung backwards like wings in the wind. In Greek legend, Artemis is the Huntress, but she is also Goddess of the Wilderness and of the Animals. I decided to call the Stearman the *Spirit of Artemis*.

It would be the latest incarnation for an aircraft originally built in Wichita, Kansas, in 1942. After starting life as a naval trainer during the war, it was most likely flown by a lot of pilots and, as a result, probably suffered a lot of mishandling. After the war it was re-configured for agricultural purposes and fitted with ugly loader tanks in the front cockpit, where previously the student pilots would have sat. It suffered the fate of many Stearmans when, loaded to the gunnels with fertiliser and flying low over crops, it crashed in the Midwest at some point in the 1980s. The wreck languished in a barn for many years before Ewald Gritsch salvaged it and brought it back to Europe.

Work on the ground-up restoration started in July 2012 and was completed a year later. Ewald and his team fitted it with a Lycoming R680 nine-cylinder radial engine with 300 horse-power, bigger than those in the original training Stearmans, most of which had Continental engines with 220 horsepower and wooden propellers. In addition to the bigger engine, mine also had a modified aluminium propeller with a variable pitch control in the cockpit and extra fuel tanks fitted in the top wing. Although it was an American aeroplane with a military history, I wanted it to look British and more 'period' for the civilian pioneering era I wanted to invoke. Initially, I considered an all-silver paint scheme which I thought would give it a classic art deco look, but then I saw another Stearman in Ewald's workshop with dark green fuselage and cream wings. It was so stunning I decided only the same would do for my aeroplane.

Thanks to Ewald, the Stearman came back to life again in July 2013. Flying in it for the first time was a deep and thrilling joy. For the first test flight, Ewald flew the aeroplane from the main cockpit in the rear seat. Sitting up front, I felt a wave of adrena-line as he fired up the engine and we taxied out onto the grass for the take-off. It was an extraordinarily happy moment. As I looked out at the wings, the top one spread above my head and the bottom one shining and pristine, it seemed I was looking out at the most beautiful thing in the world. As we roared into the air, the flying wires, taught and tightly stretched between upper and lower wings, vibrated like the strings of a Stradivarius in the hands of a virtuoso. It was as if I really could hear music, like a whole orchestra had struck up in my chest. We climbed up several thousand feet and Ewald put the Stearman through some basic manoeuvres to check the control handling and rigging. Then he dived steeply for the start of a whole sequence of breath-taking aerobatics – loops, stall turns, Cuban eights and barrel rolls. I clung to my seat and laughed deliriously. It was like a victory parade.

The test flight completed, we swapped seats and over the next few days we took it out several more times together as I became familiar with the handling characteristics and engine performance. I then spent many hours on my own with the Stearman, practising circuits with take-offs and landings, and just flying around the countryside for hours at a time running in the new engine.

With the initial test flying complete in Hungary, I prepared to fly the Stearman to England. There was a complication, however. I needed an American licence to fly a US-registered aeroplane through certain countries in Europe, including France. By the time I realised this, it was too late to arrange. Ewald was away with the airline so I needed to find someone quickly with an American licence who could come with me in the Stearman to satisfy the regulatory requirement. I cast around my various flying friends and one suggested a pilot called Richard Blain, who, even though we hadn't met before, was willing to jump on a flight to Vienna and join me as we flew the Stearman across Europe to Shuttle-worth in two days. During the trip, I closely monitored fuel and oil consumption to see how the new engine was bedding in and was shocked by how slow it was in a strong headwind for the first few hours of the trip. Suddenly the pressure was on. I planned to publicly launch the Stearman at the Royal International Air Tattoo, at Fairford, at the end of the week but now I only had two days to prepare.

Luckily, my formation flying buddy Rob Millinship and Rory Cook, one of the Shuttleworth engineers who had so often helped me with the Ryan, were waiting for us in the old blister hangar and they worked through the night, cleaning the Stearman and getting all the sponsorship artwork in place.

By the next morning, however, there was another problem. I had miscalculated the length of the 'Spirit of Artemis' print transfers and they were over a metre too long. Mercifully, the printer, Graham Talkes, of Artworks in Nottingham, ran off some replacements and I drove up to pick them up. Rob and Rory did a fantastic job and, right on cue, I lurched off in the Stearman to Fairford that Thursday morning with barely a minute to spare.

The Stearman was on static display for the show and I also entered it in the concourse for civilian aircraft, where it would be judged by a panel of 25 international judges. When they proclaimed my aircraft the best of show, I was thrilled beyond words and, collecting the splendid trophy at a glittering black-tie dinner on the Friday night, in front of the great and good of the aviation world, was one of the proudest moments of my life.

The whole weekend was a whirlwind of media interviews and pleasant surprises. The Duke of Kent stopped by to see the Stearman with Air Chief Marshal Sir Peter Squire and my donation of a flight in the aeroplane, to raise funds for the Royal Air Force Charitable Trust, incredibly raised more money than a ride with the Red Arrows. We were definitely on a roll.

I flew the *Spirit of Artemis* back to Shuttleworth and a few days later Ewald came over to inspect the Stearman. We were well through the initial test flying programme of 20 hours with no problems but Ewald wanted to do a full engineering check to see how everything was settling in. Having been such a big part of this, he had become a great friend and loved the Stearman almost as much as I did. His technical knowledge of the aeroplane was so complete, I asked him to join the expedition to provide engineering support, as the Africa flight was going to involve many hours of flying every day, and the plane would need constant care to keep it operating at optimum. Disappointingly however, Ewald was unable to commit at this stage as he was uncertain of his work schedule.

As July merged into August and preparations intensified, the flight requirements and film requirements seemed to diverge, as if two separate entities. Geoffrey started another job and handed over the project management of the expedition to Annette. Helen Morrell, her business partner, was engaged as the film producer and working on a detailed budget. Sam Rutherford was on board to provide full logistical support which included the flight planning, fuel positioning, overflight permissions and documentation, ground transport and hotels. He requested up front payment if possible which would provide a 'war chest' for him to reserve everything well in advance and negotiate the best rates. The film team had several meetings in London with Sam, which I was not privy to and between them they decided that an engineer was not necessary for the flight.

I was very concerned about this. Having been driven across Africa in a Bedford truck and flown the length of the continent in an old Antonov biplane, I knew how much maintenance old machinery required. With the An-2, the engineer, Alex, had toiled the whole time keeping the aeroplane going when we weren't in the air.

I was concerned our film people were making decisions about the flight without consulting me. Helen and I had a frank exchange of views during which I effectively told her to leave matters regarding my aeroplane to me.

To my great relief, the engineering issue was resolved when Ewald told me he could get leave from his other commitments and would be able to join us. Now there would be no compromises with the Stearman – or my safety for that matter – which really amounted to the same thing.

Ewald took charge of the Stearman preparations and in early September wrote a long email to Steve Parkinson at Phoenix Aviation, copying everybody in, laying out the technical specifications for the flight which urgently needed co-ordinating. This included an approximation of the weight and balance of the Cessna Caravan, which had to consider the full complement of seven crew, plus all the equipment – cameras and computers, the tools, spare parts and oil for the Stearman – as well as an overview of the logistics, the route and the navigation.

Sam appeared to take exception to this, asking Ewald not to contact Phoenix Aviation directly, as communications should go through him and that it was his responsibility to manage the Caravan.

Ewald replied that it didn't matter whose job it was, as long as it was done. His concern was that, with less than two weeks to go before the Stearman was shipped to South Africa, we needed to know what allocation of weight we had for the tools and spare parts. He also wanted to programme the Stearman's GPS with the route data before it was packed up.

It was the first sign of a gulf between what Ewald expected should be provided for an expedition of this nature and what was provided.

Another unexpected complication during that summer would have far-reaching consequences.

Trouble was brewing at Old Warden. I had always steered clear of the internal politics at the Shuttleworth Collection but couldn't fail to notice rising tension among both volunteers and engineers. Earlier in the year, Tony Haig Thomas, long-time Aviation Trustee of the Shuttleworth Collection, stood down and retired Air Chief Marshal Sir John Shakespeare Allison KC, CBE took his place. Sir John, in his 70th year – following an illustrious RAF career, a decade as Gentleman Usher to the Sword of State, and several years of involvement with Shuttleworth – became, in effect, the collection's chief executive and quickly stamped his authority as he set about making some serious changes. Various people told me Sir John was keen to run a close eye over the organisation and wanted to see every email and oversee every decision. Some of the ground crew seemed to be unhappy with Sir John's autocratic style.

I first became aware of Sir John Allison when he attracted publicity by crashing a Messerschmitt at Duxford in 1997. I didn't meet him until I was based at Shuttleworth with my Ryan from 2005 and had no personal difficulties with him. On the contrary, he very kindly offered to do some dual training with me in a Piper Cub to demonstrate the rudiments of display flying and I subsequently wrote him a testimonial for his professional coaching business at his request. I also introduced John to Alain and we invited him for dinner in London as a thank you.

I didn't have a formal role at Shuttleworth but, over my eight years there, I helped with fundraising and marketing, organised crew dinners and, one summer, stood in to help with the air shows while the display director was on maternity leave. While we were together, Alain also came to love Shuttleworth and we occasionally took the engineers out for dinner. In his capacity as chief executive of a major company, Alain had signed up to a three-year corporate sponsorship contract with Shuttleworth which I arranged and that contract continued after we split in 2010. Before retiring as Aviation Trustee, Tony Haig Thomas had invited Alain to be the financial director of the Shuttleworth Collection and he had accepted. I had mixed feelings about this appointment. On one hand, I knew Alain was well disposed towards the collection and would do a good job managing the finances but, on the other, he knew how close Shuttleworth was to my heart. He had been very bitter over our break-up and in the two years following had perversely shadowed me in a manner close to stalking. His involvement gave me a deep sense of foreboding.

I felt concerned enough to flag this up to Sir John when he invited me to a meeting in June 2013 to discuss how I might continue to support the marketing and promotion of the collection under his trusteeship. I was happy to help him and we also talked at some length about my Africa flight and how the Stearman might potentially generate some publicity for Shuttleworth. By then we had a scheduled date for departure from Cape Town of October 1. I would have to fly the plane back to Hungary immediately after the Goodwood Revival to get it back in time for dismantling and shipping to South Africa. My conversation with Sir John was very constructive and he invited me to keep the Stearman at Shuttleworth at no charge for the six weeks it was back in England for the public launch before it returned to Hungary. This was, he said, in recognition of what I had done for the collection in the past and I very much appreciated the generous offer.

A few days later, however, Sir John phoned. His tone had changed. He complained that our draft expedition brochure, which I had shared with him, made it sound as if I was one of the official Shuttleworth pilots. I was a bit taken aback but, as I had not written the brochure, I asked for it to be amended to remove any doubt. Sir John liked clear demarcation between the civilian pilots, who flew at Shuttleworth with their own aircraft, and the military test pilots, who flew the collection aeroplanes. I completely accepted that.

When I returned to Old Warden with the Stearman after the weekend at the Royal International Air Tattoo, I liaised closely with Tony Podmore, the Shuttleworth marketing manager over the media and publicity. He asked if the *Spirit of Artemis* could be on static display at the next air show the following weekend, and the air show director also wanted to include the Ryan as part of the flying display. I was scheduled to be in Ireland filming the Lady Heath story with Annette that weekend, but I readily agreed to both aeroplanes being used in the show in my absence.

All of that went without a hitch and we started planning for the follow-up air show two weeks later, at which I was now scheduled to fly a display in the Stearman. At this show, Tony also arranged for a crew from ITV to film and do an interview.

Just two days before the event, however, while I was on a train from London, he called me in a very agitated state. Sir John had cancelled my involvement in the air show, ostensibly because he was unhappy at the 'branding' on the Stearman.

I couldn't understand it. Only two weeks earlier, he had been happy to have the *Spirit of Artemis* on static display. As soon as I got home I rang Sir John and asked him, frankly, what was going on. Why was he now objecting to sponsorship for an international expedition that had already attracted national media attention?

I told John I felt his conduct was indefensible. He remained insistent that the branding was a problem and denied there was an ulterior motive.

In that case, I said, given he had cancelled my appearance at the air show, I had no other option but to remove the Stearman from Shuttleworth with immediate effect – and I vowed to take the matter further. After our terse conversation, I came off wondering whether Sir John had ever been spoken to like that in his life.

The next day, I contacted Richard Pleydell-Bouverie, chairman of the Shuttleworth Trust, and arranged to meet him at Old Warden. Una Watts, the long-time manager of the Shuttleworth Collection, came with me and corroborated the deteriorating situation with the engineers and volunteers. Over a two-hour meeting, I urged the chairman to come to the airfield to see for himself what was really going on, warning there could be a mass walk-out if things continued. I then flew the Stearman to Fowlmere Aerodrome, near Duxford, where the ITV filming and interview took place.

In the coming weeks the Shuttleworth engineers duly threatened their walk-out and Sir John left his role as Aviation Trustee after less than a year in the job. I was already in Africa by the time all of this played out.

Richard Pleydell-Bouverie also stepped down during this time and a new chairman took over. A couple of months later, I received a letter from Shuttleworth terminating my tenancy agreement to keep the Ryan at Old Warden. It struck me as petty and unfair, the fallout, seemingly, from challenging men in a position of power.

The sad end of my long association with Shuttleworth might have made a greater impact but the whole summer was such a frenzy of activity I didn't have the time to dwell on further heartache. I plunged headlong into a blur of meetings with sponsors, filming, accountants, et al. There were also discussions with the real estate agent as I was desperate to sell the Bee House before I departed, which meant viewings with prospective buyers and various niggling repairs to get fixed. There were licences and documenta- tion to sort out, flying and air shows and a plethora of lunches and dinners.

On the surface I might have appeared highly functioning, but inside I was crumbling. It felt like, and probably was, a nervous breakdown at some deep, subterranean level. In truth it was grief; the kind that sends a ship onto the rocks. The loss of Alain and then Robert was a terrible accumulation of conflicting emotion, and even though neither heartbreak killed me, I felt somehow weakened as if I had sustained a mortal wound. Other, more careful, people might have given up after this crucifying experi- ence, but I was determined to carry on. Not to do it was to give up on life. I had paid a huge price for my freedom, indeed my survival, and now I was determined to live it to the hilt. Such was the existential force of that romantic dream to fly Africa.

To my unspeakable relief, the Bee House sold at the end of the summer and completed in early September, just two weeks before I was due to leave. Robert and I could now finally conclude the separation of our financial affairs, the last vestige of that dead relationship.

On Friday, September 13, I flew to Goodwood for the Revival weekend, which was to be our send-off to Africa. If the date wasn't ominous enough, it was amazing how much happened that weekend, as if some inexorable law of convergence had taken control and determined a certain outcome.

First, I knew Alain would be there, taking part in the Freddie March Spirit of Aviation Concours d'Elegance with an aeroplane he had initially bought for me as a bribe to marry him but of course that never happened. With its soft shining silver fuselage and silver wings, the beautiful Ryan STA is pure art deco and one of the loveliest aeroplanes of all time. I felt sure it would do well in the judges' competition.

Then, late on Friday, the night before the press launch, I received an email from Robert. With consummate timing, he was writing to tell me of his intention to marry someone else. What's more, they were starting a family together. It was an extraordinary development, given what he had said before.

I put it all out of my mind, however, as I was up at dawn the next morning, dressed in my flight suit, to prepare the Stearman for the photo call with Zara and Mike Tindall, who were also sponsored by Artemis Investments. Zara, dressed in a chic 1920s black and white outfit with a cloche hat and high-heeled stilettos, wanted to come flying with me and I shuddered at the thought of how one false step in those vertiginous heels could destroy a wing in a second. Thankfully, this nightmare scenario was avoided because Zara was heavily pregnant and kept her feet firmly on the ground.

Our photo shoot, widely circulated in the press, was huge fun, however. Zara and Mike were a very happy charming pair and we had a lovely hour together.

Afterwards, Zara introduced me to Prince Michael of Kent, with whom I had an enjoyable chat, as I discovered he was an adorer of old cars who had done a lot of racing in Bentleys and a keen flyer. At lunch, I was starstruck when I found myself sitting next to the prince with Rowan Atkinson on my other side. Quite apart from my unfeigned enthusiasm for *Blackadder* and *Mr Bean*, Rowan too was a serious racing driver and a regular at the Goodwood Revival. When I told him about my forthcoming flight from Cape Town to Goodwood, he looked at me with that distinctive raised eyebrow and said quizzically, 'What, fly to Goodwood? But you're already here…'

Caroline O'Donnell, the marketing director from Artemis, joined me on Saturday night for the fancy dress ball, the pièce de résistance of the Revival weekend. The theme was 'Cowboys and Indians' but, being among the minority of people to eschew fancy dress and opt for formal black tie, I dressed in a full-length black ball gown with a gold metallic mesh overlay, which I fancied looked like an 'Artemis' dress. Theo Fennell kindly lent me some beautiful jewellery to accessories this and my hair was swept up into a high knot with loose curls tumbling down the back.

The party was heaving and when Caroline and I finally made our way through the throng to our dinner table we discovered we were placed next to Alain. I hastily pushed Caroline forward and with great stoicism she sat wedged between the two of us, meaning I didn't have to exchange a single word with him.

It was the last time I ever saw Alain. Just weeks later he died of a heart attack, aged 59.

As I felt sure it would, his Ryan won best in show.

The next day, Sunday, the weather cut a swathe through everything. An intense trough was advancing rapidly from the west and by 10am it was already darkly overcast and blowing a gale. It looked like it was going to be a washout for the classic car racing and everything else.

Ewald had flown into Gatwick first thing on a commercial flight to help me with the Stearman and our plan had been to spend the day at Goodwood and then strike out for France later in the afternoon. The looming weather changed all that, however. As I met Ewald at the entrance gate, he grabbed my arm and urged me to hurry. We ran through the gathering crowd, making our way to the enclosure where the historic aeroplanes were on display. The marshals helped us clear the aircraft out of the way and moved the fence to liberate the Stearman onto the active runway. We scrambled in and within minutes were roaring down the grass strip with a shearing crosswind. It was only once we were in the air that I realised that I hadn't filed a flight plan – a stupid oversight but I was beyond caring.

After the overwhelming few days, I was just so relieved to be in the air and leaving it all behind. We were blown along the south coast at a terrific rate of knots and turned to cross the Channel at Lydd with a 50mph tailwind. It made for a wild ride as the Stearman bucked around in the turbulence but it was deeply thrilling to look down at the furrowed waves and the white caps and to see the dark line of France in the distance. We stormed across Europe and arrived in Hungary two days later. Working around the clock, the Hungarians dismantled the *Spirit of Artemis* and just 36 hours after we had arrived it was loaded into a container and on its way to Hamburg and the ship that would take it to Cape Town.

My personal life seemed to be mirroring the romantic upheavals of my flying heroines and history records that most of their lives ended tragically. What was the price to pursue my dream? I had no idea.

I was technically homeless, but I had my aeroplane.

It was all I needed.

The Cape of Good Hope

WE peered into the darkness as the steel seal was broken. It was the moment of truth.

Prior to shipping I'd heard some nightmarish stories about containers being dropped, badly shunted or, in the worst cases, lost at sea after they were swept off the deck in storms. Now in Cape Town, we had to see if the Stearman had got through the voyage without damage.

Ewald, his Hungarian engineer colleague Istvan and I held our breath as the wings were wheeled out of the ExecuJet hangar on their jigs and then the fuselage was delivered tail first, like a breach birth, into the light. I exhaled a sigh of relief. Everything was unscathed.

Since I'd arrived in South Africa on October 12, a few days ahead of the rest of the crew, things hadn't exactly gone smoothly. I'd had an anxious wait before confirmation came through that the container ship had arrived and that its precious cargo had been safely transferred to the wharf amid howling easterly winds.

Then, just as I'd been relaxing in Stellenbosch – a town I'd last seen 30 years previously – I took a call from the freight company DB Schenker to say Customs and Excise were holding the container and demanding an immediate payment of nearly $30,000 in South African rand to release it. I hastily got a hire car and drove straight to their office in the hinterland of Cape Town's industrial area.

Much had been lost in translation. The load sheet for the container had detailed 'Boeing', which led to the assumption that it was part of an airliner fuselage, or the back end of a 737. I laughed in amazement when I heard this. Evidently, the agent had no idea it was a vintage aeroplane and when I explained this there was a stupefied silence. The team at DB Schenker then swung into action and, with the invaluable help of Etti Poggiore, head of ExecuJet South Africa, were able to arrange a temporary import licence for the Stearman to avoid the horrific customs tax.

Ewald and Istvan had arrived the following day but there was no sign of the aeroplane.

After two more nervous days of waiting there was still no news when the container would be delivered. We were driving to the airport when a container truck passed in front of us at a T-junction and we realised it was the Stearman. We all broke into an involuntary cheer and roared off after the truck like a pursuit scene from the Keystone Cops.

Now it had safely arrived in Cape Town, an enthusiastic young team of student engineers from a local technical college came to see it and help us with reassembling the aircraft. They had never seen a vintage aeroplane before and some of the press came to take photographs as we worked and I started doing the first of many interviews with local radio stations and other media.

It took three days of painstaking effort to reassemble the Stearman. First, the tail section had to be reinstated, then the heavy centre section of the top wing reattached on the four column struts above the front cockpit. It took several men to lift and bolt the wings into place: first the lower wings and then the top wings. The upright struts which separate and strengthen the upper and lower wings near the tips were locked into place and then the criss-cross of rigging with flying and landing wires were screwed on and tensioned. Plumb lines were suspended from the top wing to make sure the alignment and the symmetry were correct.

The Stearman was then ready for its inaugural flight in Africa. Ewald climbed in the rear cockpit as pilot in command and I took the front seat. We launched off from the international airport and cleared out to the east climbing to several thousand feet where Ewald did a few turns and stalls to check the rigging and to see how the plane was flying. Once he was satisfied with the handling, we flew on to Stellenbosch and landed so he could have a look at the engine and check the oil and fuel lines, to see if anything had come loose. We had a coffee at the aero club and then took to the air again. This time I flew with Ewald up front. I did a few circuits at Stellenbosch to get current again and then went on a tour of the Franschhoek mountains. The wind was calm and the sky an almost liquid, translucent gold and, as we soared along the rock faces barely a wingspan away, they glowed pink and gold in the evening sun. We then peeled away down the valley over the immaculately manicured vineyards and back to the international airport in a beatific mood.

Over the next two days we did two more flights, flying up the west coast north of Cape Town and back over Robben Island, the desolate rock atoll in Table Bay where Nelson Mandela was incarcerated for 18 of his 27 years in prison. There was a short grass airfield running down the middle of the island so I did one low pass so we could take a closer look, but there was nothing much to see beyond some bunker-like buildings and old fortifications. The island is now a World Heritage Site but it might have been better left to the ravages of the Atlantic Ocean and the seals who once made their home on those inhospitable, windswept rocks.

Next we flew around Table Mountain, which I'd last seen out of my airline window on my arrival, as we began our descent into Cape Town. The mountain seems to dominate not just the earth but the sky as well. It makes its own weather which can be a death trap for the unwary aviator. In certain wind conditions, severe vertical downdrafts develop on the lee side and dangerous rotor zones of turbulence can hurl an aircraft into the ground. Once, when I was driving in the city close to the base of the mountain in a violent easterly wind, a downward blast of air hit the roof of the car so hard I ducked at the force of it. It was like being hit by a solid object, as if someone had thrown a refrigerator off a 10-storey building.

From there we headed out to the Cape of Good Hope, the rocky headland lying on the Atlantic coast, marked by a lighthouse standing sentinel on its fractured ramparts. Contrary to popular belief, it is not the southernmost tip of Africa. That point lies 90 miles further to the east at Cape Agulhas and it is there that the Indian and Atlantic Oceans merge deep green and dark blue in a mass of churning white caps.

Nevertheless, the Cape of Good Hope still felt remote and atmospheric and it was slightly daunting flying just a few hundred feet above, getting tossed around in the wind as the sea exploded over the rocks below. After circling for a few minutes, we continued east towards False Bay and I dropped down low to fly along a wide and deserted stretch of beach. I suddenly became aware of huge birds sitting in the sand below, all orientated in one direction like weathervanes. They were looking straight out to sea and for a fleeting moment I thought they were albatross. On closer inspection they turned out to be ostriches and I rocked the wings of the Stearman in salute to those flightless birds before flying on.

With the Stearman back in the air, Istvan's job was complete and we had a farewell dinner before seeing him off on a flight back to Europe. The expedition crew now started to arrive in bursts. Annette came first and then the rest of the film crew, which included Matt Green, our cameraman, and Joao de Valle, our sound man. Justin Wood, our gopher and 'the kid' on our expedition, was just 18, very technically gifted, and his job was to manage the setting and downloading of the Go-Pro cameras on the Stearman and to operate the satellite communications kit, which Inmarsat had provided for the expedition. We weren't paying Justin, but we had to feed him, and if first impressions were anything to go by he would be eating like a horse all the way up Africa.

Matt and Joao were old friends and seasoned filming veterans, having shot many documentaries around the world, and had been in several war zones together. I had met Joao, a small, cuddly Brazilian with curly dark hair, liquid brown eyes and a lovely sense of humour, in England when we experimented with recording microphones in the Stearman. He had come flying with me on several test flights and was thrilled at the thought of flying up Africa. Joao was wonderful with people and, wherever he went, there were bursts of spontaneous laughter. I met Matt for the first time in Cape Town and liked him immediately. Tall, in his early fifties with a dry, laconic wit and an air of slightly cynical worldliness, his company was called Hungry Eye and he was never without a camera. He and Joao were perfect counterpoints to each other and Annette used to joke that they were like an old married couple.

The Phoenix pilots flew in from Nairobi in the Cessna Caravan. Johnny Beveridge and Gibran Chaudhry or 'Gibbs', as he was known, were going to split the flight between them. Johnny, a giant of a man at 6ft 6ins, with a laid-back, easy charm, was going to fly the first part of the expedition. He had left a successful career in banking, moved his young family out to Kenya in search of a different way of life, and became a bush pilot. Sam Rutherford also arrived from Brussels with another load of equipment, making up our full complement of eight crew and two aircraft. As we raced around the ExecuJet hangar making the final preparations, there was a lot of commotion and a great buzz of excitement.

Just as everything seemed to be coming together, clouds appeared on the horizon.

Sam had brought a contraption, which looked suspiciously like a child's playpen, that he said would go in the rear part of the Caravan cabin to hold all the luggage. This effectively blocked the exit and the space needed for the air-to-air filming. As soon as Matt clapped eyes on it, he said, 'Well, that fucking thing can go!'

And so it began.

Of more concern, it appeared to me there had been a lack of flight planning. We had been provided with landing plates for the airports and an A4 print-out for each leg, which was simply a line from A to B with no topographical information. The absence of low level sectional paper maps and terminal area charts was particularly concerning.

In our first flight briefing in Cape Town, Sam announced that he would be directing both aircraft from the front seat of the Caravan in the military-style 'chain-of-command', which he had already demonstrated, and would be sending me text message directions using a Yellowbrick hand-held GPS device.

However, the Yellowbrick was unusable in an open cockpit where there is nowhere to secure it and operate during hands-on flying. It wasn't viable for Sam to be directing my flight remotely from another aircraft when mostly we would be some considerable distance apart, as the Caravan operated at a much higher speed and altitude than the Stearman, for fuel efficiency. The only time we would actually be flying together was at pre-arranged air-to-air filming points; and when we were filming I would be talking directly to the Caravan pilot over the radio, not through a third party.

The Yellowbrick was fine for use in the event of a forced landing on the ground, but beyond that its usage was limited for our operation.

Ewald and I had no option but to formulate our own flight plan from scratch, gathering material together. I had borrowed a set of old 1:5,000 topographical maps from a flying friend, but what we now needed were visual terminal charts and the proper VFR (Visual Flight Rules) procedures into the airports where we would be landing.

We scrounged a few maps from the ExecuJet briefing room where we met with other pilots, got additional flight information from Johnny Beveridge, and in this way managed to improvise the navigation.

While Ewald and I were poring over the route with one of the local pilots, the three of us kneeling on the floor with the maps spread out before us, Sam came into the room and told Ewald that was *his* job, and that he should be outside loading the Caravan.

'Wow. What's his problem?' our South African friend said, as we all looked at each other, utterly bemused. I felt that Sam's behaviour was unacceptable and made the point to Annette.

We had come so far there was little we could do but make the best of the situation but, already I felt the team had been let down and we hadn't even left Cape Town.

As if to mark the shift in mood, the weather also deteriorated rapidly with the approach of an Atlantic front and the whole Cape was engulfed by cloud and heavy rain. The easterly winds, which had been strong before, now became gale force.

We held a big press launch in the ExecuJet hangar, with a red carpet laid around the Stearman for two dignitaries who came to see us – Helen Zille, premier of Cape Province and a woman who had dedicated her life to public service, and Dame Judith Macgregor, the British High Commissioner to South Africa. The three of us posed next to the Stearman and Helen was very keen to take a closer look at the cockpit. I think she thought the whole idea was completely mad, even remarking that she was glad I wasn't her daughter.

As Michel Foucault wrote in Madness and Civilisation: 'Navigation delivers man to the uncertainty of fate; on water, each of us is in the hands of his own destiny.'

The weather delayed our departure but November 2 dawned clear and we were finally good to go. Ahead of us lay the whole continent of Africa and beyond that, Europe. The challenge: 15 countries, 38 stops, 10,000 miles, in just seven weeks.

My adventure was about to begin.

Cape Town to Crete

WALKING around the Stearman doing the pre-flight, I felt a surge of something beyond happiness to be finally starting the flight, yet couldn't help but reflect on the four tempestuous years that had gone before.

Against all the odds, somehow, we had made it.

Having fuelled the night before and after checking the oil for the third time, I pulled the propeller through to clear any accumulated oil in the bottom cylinders, then climbed into the cockpit.

It was a beautiful morning with a stiff easterly breeze for our first leg from Cape Town to George, around 300 miles along the coast to the east. Press photographers were positioned out along the coast road by Gordon's Bay, which had elevated views from the cliffs, but I doubted I'd be able to get close enough to give them a shot because of the hazard of downdrafts. The first part of the flight was to be in the lee of the mountains and I had been warned about the likelihood of severe turbulence.

My maps, water and other paraphernalia carefully arranged in the cockpit side pockets, I secured the four-point harness, pulled my helmet and goggles on and went through the familiar checks, breathing fast as a cat. Fuel on, throttle set, mixture rich, engine primed and then the start up. With one last clearing glance behind, I raised the ignition engage switch. The engine caught first time, roaring into life with a dramatic burst of exhaust smoke. A small crowd of friends and supporters waved and cheered and the team from ExecuJet were all there to see me off. Once the tower gave permission to leave, I moved forward off the ExecuJet apron onto the taxiway. Matt caught a particularly good sequence of the Stearman weaving along the taxiway with an airliner on the runway behind, the perfect juxtaposition of modern mass air travel and a small biplane from the past.

I was held for several minutes while another airliner took off in front of me and the wake turbulence behind the jet dissipated – always a hazard for aeroplanes of any size, but especially light aircraft at an international airport.

The air traffic controllers were fantastically accommodating, agreeing to let Annette and the film crew up into the tower to film my take-off. The controller now directed me onto the active runway and I carefully lined up with the long centreline into a 15-knot headwind. With the final clearance to take-off, I pushed the throttle forward slowly and, as the Stearman accelerated, pushed the stick to raise the tail. A few seconds later we soared into the air. My heart was in my mouth as we climbed away and I did a left hand turn around the airport to position for a low pass in front of the control tower. I swept past waving to them, then rocked my wings in goodbye and headed off in a south easterly direction for the coast.

This was it then.

Completely absorbed in the moment, I felt a wild breathless excitement. All the things that had weighed with me on the ground vanished in an instant. All I could feel was the power and throb of the engine with the wires humming and the whole structure vibrating to the enormous aerodynamic forces of the biplane in flight.

Flying a tail dragger is very physical – right hand firmly gripping the joystick, left hand on the throttle, feet firmly planted on the rudder pedals. There is a basic fore and aft trim wheel below the throttle quadrant and this relieves pressure on the control stick in the climb or descent, but apart from that there are no control aids or auto-pilot. Out there in the elements, you must concentrate on flying the aeroplane and this gives an intense feeling of oneness with the machine, a feeling completely different to flying a modern aircraft.

As I picked up the shoreline, the sea was high with a thrilling flush of wind. I buzzed along at about a thousand feet and steered around the conurbations of Somerset West and Strand. What had been a relatively light wind on the ground was a good 25 knots of headwind up in the air and this dramatically reduced my ground speed to barely 55 miles-an-hour – slow going just 15 minutes into the flight. I climbed to 2,000 ft and now the turbulence started to kick in as I got closer to the mountains, the air violent and hard-edged. I tightened my harness and hunkered down in the seat, clutching the control stick with both hands to withstand the buffeting. While I remained in the lee of the mountains, things were only going to get worse, so I decided to head out to sea to try to find smoother air. A few miles up ahead, once I got around a great shoulder of a mountain, the Hangklip headland, which fell away steeply into the Indian Ocean, the conditions would ease.

Sure enough, rounding the headland was like entering a different hemisphere. I turned obliquely towards the shore and, dropping down again, picked up the beach, feeling a great wave of relief. Now, I really could begin to enjoy the flight. The sunshine was dazzling and out to my left a line of brilliant white surf separated the golden sands from the emerald water.

I flew along for some miles before suddenly I became aware of movement out to my right. I spotted a plume of spray, then another, before a long, dark fin broke the surface of the water. It was a whale. Immediately, I pulled into a tight, circling turn and to my delight discovered that it was more than one – a mother and calf basking in the green loveliness below. These were southern right whales which breed off this coast and seeing them from 30 ft above, as I craned over the side, was one of the greatest spectacles I have ever been lucky enough to witness. Mad with joy, I stayed with them for several minutes before continuing my way, feeling extraordinarily blessed. There was another larger pod further along and I had a lovely time wheeling around like a seagull above them, flying through a fine mist of salt and sea spray, and the breath of whales.

Soon after, I winged past the town of Hermanus and immediately recognised the harbour and the distinctive terrace of rock which sits above the water, making a perfect viewing platform. Years before, I had sat there, sipping wine and eating fresh shrimp while watching the whales just a hundred yards away – something quite different to see them from the air.

I stayed with the coast for as long as I could but then needed to cut inland from Cape Agulhas on a straight easterly track to George. This took me over marshland and dunes and low lying, scrub-covered hills with estuaries meandering through. I passed over a couple of airfields and tried calling on the radio but there was no response. It seemed deserted below and the sky too was empty. I didn't see a single aeroplane until further east, when I picked up the coast again, and the Caravan that had been tracking me on its radar system came into view and drew up alongside.

This was our first crack at air-to-air filming and initially Johnny positioned the Caravan slightly ahead of me and I tucked in behind his left wing, giving the crew a jaunty wave as I did so. I could see Matt with his camera at the window and Joao bobbing around next to him and they started to gesticulate for me to drop down or to ease further away. Johnny also relayed instructions over the radio and by degrees they filmed the first sequence of the Stearman in the air against the panoramic backdrop. We continued like this for the next 20 minutes and then the Caravan pulled away and disappeared into the distance. After three hours of flying, I landed at George. The Caravan had landed well ahead of me and the crew was there filming as I taxied up to the fuel pump.

A little red RV-6 sports plane was parked nearby, belonging to a flying friend, Dion Wraath, who had flown in specially to meet me. Dion was the son of a wonderful old South African airline pilot called Laurie Wraath, who had been introduced to me by his friend Flippie Vermeulen, and together they were the number one and number two most senior ranking pilots in the airline with over 100 years of flying experience between them. It was great to see Dion on the ground at George and when I took off again an hour later, he flew with me in a loose formation along the next stretch, the world famous 'Wilderness Coast', a spectacular, rugged rock face with a drop of several hundred feet straight into the sea. There is no beach to speak of, just boulders and rock-fall eroded from the cliffs by the wind and the sea. I had a fantastic flight cruising along below the level of the cliff with Dion hanging off my right wing, and every so often we would wave at each other in acknowledgement of the sheer joy of it all. He peeled away when we got to Plettenberg Bay, where he was holidaying with friends, and I rocked my wings in farewell and carried on along the coast.

The sun was already setting by the time I approached Port Elizabeth. A vast stretch of sand dunes runs for several miles to the west of the city and, here, I dropped down to about 30 ft and skimmed along the top with the sun behind me casting purple shadows on the rippled surface below. Suddenly, from out of nowhere, a JetRanger helicopter pulled up alongside off my right wing, looking so much like something out of *Hawaii Five-0*, and I could almost hear that distinctive soundtrack in my head as I roared along. I gave him a wave and then he too pulled away.

Shortly after, I arrived at Port Elizabeth and did one low pass down the runway before pulling up into a 'dumb-bell' turn and landed back in the direction from which I had come, pointing straight into the sun. I was completely blinded by the low solar position but plonked the Stearman firmly on the runway and taxied to the terminal where a small crowd had gathered to meet me and a small deputation of local media alongside our crew filmed the arrival. This would become a familiar ritual as we flew up Africa.

I was immediately surrounded but – as I pulled off my helmet and goggles and was conscious of looking perfectly awful with flattened hair and racoon-style rings around my eyes – what I really needed was the lavatory and a cold drink.

I had just flown for a further two and a half hours, totalling nearly six hours over the two legs, and was sunburnt, dehydrated and stiff from sitting so long. With the exposure and noise, open-cockpit flying is exhausting and I felt it now as I stepped down from the wing and into the throng of well-wishers and eager cameramen.

It was at this welcome reception at Port Elizabeth that I met Captain Phetogo Molawe, the first black female helicopter pilot in the South African Air Force, who came to the airport to meet me so that we could film an interview with her. Her father was a military pilot and had encouraged his daughter from a young age. Phetogo was delightful and very modest about her remarkable achievement. I couldn't help but hug her and told her that she was the most fantastic role model to women not just in Africa but around the world. Inside the airport terminal, a group of Xhosa dancers welcomed us and I sank into a seat with the longed-for cold drink to watch the performance.

It was beginning to feel like a very long day by the time we got to the guest house at 8.30pm that night. It was a basic place, which Sam had arranged, and there was no food in-house so we ordered a pizza delivery. This didn't arrive until nearly 10pm, by which time I was dead on my feet. The pizza was stone cold on arrival so I swallowed one limp slice and retired to bed.

November 3, Port Elizabeth to Durban

As it was an early start the next day, the film crew wired me up with a microphone over breakfast and we were out at the airport by 7am. Despite having slapped on a factor 50 block, my face was livid with sunburn and I kicked myself that I hadn't thought of bringing a stick of zinc or a proper nose shield.

As Ewald and I prepared the Stearman, we caught up on the events of the day before. I was annoyed to hear that there had been yet more tension amongst the crew in the Caravan for various reasons. I decided then and there that I would cut through this garbage and take Ewald with me. I wanted Africa to be a fantastic adventure and we were so bonded in our love for the Stearman that it felt like the most natural thing in the world to share it with him. We loaded up and were airborne by 7.40am.

My priority that morning was to find more whales and not long after take-off we came across a pod just half a mile off the coast. We lingered overhead for a few minutes and then pressed on for what was going to be another long day.

We were going to fly two legs again, the first to a little airfield near East London called Wings Park, around two hours' flight time away. The flying club had invited us to visit, so the plan was to stop for an hour for lunch, during which I would give a brief talk, before we flew on to Durban. I liked the thought of landing at small airstrips but this one wasn't such a good idea. It was several miles inland up an estuary through hill country and as we got closer to the field, the sky suddenly seemed to be swarming with aeroplanes as several enthusiastic club members flew out to meet us. I appreciated their interest but this was exactly the situation I was most keen to avoid – unbriefed, aerial reconnaissance with unknown pilots in unfamiliar surroundings.

I told Ewald to keep his eyes peeled for aircraft as the airfield was not that easy to see. The short strip was cut into the side of a hill and approached over power lines. Somewhat rattled by the distractions, my landing was rather rugged. The ground was rough and slightly boggy and dipped in the middle before steepening up the hill on the other side. We soon came to a halt and I taxied towards the little crowd gathered outside by the club building, who gave us a cheering welcome. The aero club members laid on a barbecue for the occasion and I was pleased we had made the effort to visit them. I gave a brief talk about the flight and then joined Ewald to refuel. We got away on schedule and embarked on a long four-hour flight to Durban.

On a map, the route should follow the coast but flying a straight-line track from Wings Park took us well inland and now we started to see small villages below and individual homesteads with roundel huts and livestock enclosures or 'bomas' as they are called. It was fascinating to see these and Ewald and I chatted away, pointing out and circling anything which particularly took our fancy. It is always a lot more fun having somebody along for the flight and I was glad of the company.

We landed at a small regional airport called Victoria Field in Durban, and the runway ran in parallel to the beach and had a light drift of sand covering the asphalt surface. It had been another long but enjoyable day and we were all in high spirits as we made our way to the guest house. A very personable Jack Russell terrier was there to meet us and I spent several minutes playing with him. There were lovely sea views from upstairs and after a session of flight planning with a round of cocktails we headed out to an Italian restaurant for an altogether more relaxing dinner than the night before.

NOVEMBER 4, DURBAN TO JOHANNESBURG

With Johannesburg 400 miles to the north-west of Durban, we planned to stop off at the Baragwanath airfield where Lady Heath had officially started her solo flight. Annette arranged to film at the aero club, where we would meet the president and several members. They had several old photographs taken in 1928 and other memorabilia from that time they wanted to show us.

It was another early start and we launched into the usual

round of preparations, resetting the four GoPro cameras on the Stearman, which was Justin's job at every stop. Ewald and I had done our best to wash the sea spray off the propeller and flying wires but, in just a few days, the corrosive effects of the salt on metal parts were all too apparent. I started the engine and ran through the checks in the cockpit when the carburettor heat cable snapped as I moved it, leaving it in the 'hot' position. This mechanism diverts heat from the exhaust into the carburettor at low power settings or in ambient conditions which might cause icing. As the application of carburettor heat uses engine power and causes a noticeable drop in the revs, it is best not to have it on during take-off when all the available power is needed to get the aeroplane safely into the air.

I was always curious as to why Charles Lindbergh elected to fly the *Spirit of St Louis* with his carburettor heat hot-wired on. Carburettor icing would have been a real and constant threat flying the Atlantic in cloud and rain, but first he had to get into the air and he nearly didn't make it. There is a film clip on YouTube of the *Spirit of St Louis* taking off from Long Island and, even though you know he makes it safely, it is nail-biting to watch. The famous Ryan aircraft was so heavily loaded with fuel it lumbered down the water-logged runway with excruciating slowness and bounced several times before barely staggering into the air, clearing the trees at the end by inches. Just getting the aeroplane off the ground was the first bit of genius handling by the pilot.

If we were to avoid the same take-off we needed to fix our broken carburettor cable. I shut down the engine as Ewald got to work replacing the cable but this delayed our departure by nearly 45 minutes and we now needed to crack on for the long flight ahead. We set off north-west, leaving the Durban coastline and headed into the interior through the province of KwaZulu Natal towards the town of Ladysmith, a place synonymous with the Second Boer War and the centre of British operations in Natal during that bitter conflict. We now flew in real African savannah, with the vast open plain and the distinctive towers and turrets of the Drakensberg Mountains out to the west. Progressing north, we gradually climbed and by the time we reached the high veld of the Witwatersrand, the ground was 6,000 ft above sea level. This escarpment of metamorphic rock, extending 40 miles in an east-west direction like a continental divide, is known as the 'Rand' or the 'Reef'. The name Witwatersrand means 'ridge of white water' and the runoff to the north drains into the Crocodile and Limpopo rivers while in the south it feeds into the Orange river. The Rand rises in a distinctive terrace and the city of Johannesburg is built on that reef of gold-bearing rock and is clearly visible from miles away.

We were three hours into the flight when the Caravan called us over the radio and instructed us to land at Vereeniging, a town to the south of Johannesburg. They wanted me to fly into Baragwanath on my own for the filming so we landed for them to pick up Ewald. We then carried on to Baragwanath, a splendid little airfield to the south-west of Johannesburg with a long tarmac runway. It is not the same place that Lady Heath visited in 1928. The original aerodrome was reclaimed by the mining company which owned it and the Johannesburg Light Plane Club, as it was then known, was relocated a few miles away to Syferfontein in 1981. Two gate guardians marked the entrance, a North American T6 Harvard and an Atlas Impala jet, both used by the South African Air Force.

The cameras were rolling as I landed and taxied up to the clubrooms. The club chairman welcomed me and took me on a tour of their little museum, which featured two fine paintings of First World War aircraft including a Se5a and an Avro 504, and several old photographs of Lady Heath. Club member Courtney Watson had kindly prepared a poster for me as a keepsake of the visit and in one corner of the club a strange wooden contraption – a cross between a baby's highchair and a rowing machine – caught my eye. It turned out to be an early flight simulator.

Two other club members requested a formation flight with me so, after briefing the sortie, we all got airborne together and I led the formation with an aircraft off each wing. We flew two circuits around the field with low passes past the club rooms and then I signalled them away and headed off on my own.

ExecuJet had a large, fixed base operation at Lanseria and I had been there just a few months before when the Russians and I flew into a red-carpet reception with the An-2. They had been the most splendid hosts and provided us with lavish hospitality and it was now a fantastic pleasure to see them all again. As we pushed the Stearman into the large and luxurious hangar, it was an immense relief to know it was in good hands. We then repaired to the local safari-style hotel just down the road from the airport and went straight to the bar to plan our flight for the next day.

NOVEMBER 5, BOTSWANA TO ZIMBABWE

For the next leg, 300 miles due north to Francistown on the eastern side of Botswana, I flew solo. With Johannesburg at 6,000 ft above sea level and an ambient temperature of around 28°C, the combined effects of the thinner air at this altitude and the heat, which further reduces the density of the air, meant that I was taking off at a density altitude equivalent to about 9,000 ft above sea level. As the Stearman was fully loaded with fuel, I didn't need the additional weight on board.

Flying over the eastern part of the Kalahari Desert, there wasn't much to see below, just a dead flat and virtually feature-less landscape. The ground looked dark and amorphous but, as the convective cloud started to build, it became mottled with the shadows they cast below, and it was extraordinary to observe how the land reflected the colours and patterns of light and shade. Strangely, it began to mirror the patterns of African animals as, for a while, the land resembled the rough and tawny coat of an old lion, then changed into irregular blobs like the markings on a giraffe.

Another atmospheric effect which is extraordinarily African is that the sky seems bigger. This isn't an optical illusion. The troposphere is twice as deep at the equator as it is at mid latitudes due to gravity and the Earth's rotation and clouds develop to much higher altitudes in that thicker layer of the atmosphere, giving a towering verticality to the cloudscapes. The effect is most noticeable with tropical thunderstorms which can develop up to 60,000 ft and more.

Flying through this vastness made me feel infinitesimally small. When Karen Blixen wrote of her own experience of flight as feeling like a small figure 'upon the roof of the world', that's exactly how I felt, but I knew that I was also upon the roof of my life.

Four hours later, I landed at Francistown feeling fresh as a daisy, to see the Caravan already landed with the usual bags and camera equipment spread over the tarmac under the wing. No transport was arranged so we had to find taxi cabs to get to the hotel. There was only one cab at the airport that afternoon so the rest of the crew loaded into this while Ewald and I stayed behind for the second ride. We managed to find a cold beer at a refreshment stand and sat outside the terminal drinking in the late afternoon sun, happy just to be in Africa.

Our plan for the following day was to fly to Bulawayo but we were still waiting for the film permit for Zimbabwe to come through. It still hadn't arrived by late morning. Delays were not only frustrating, but they could also potentially cause problems as our entry permits for each country were issued for a specific date. Zimbabwe was always likely to be one of the more difficult countries but just after 1pm Annette's authorisation arrived. We were on our way again.

I invited her to fly with me on this next leg to Bulawayo. She had flown with me several times before in England but this was the first time in Africa. After the usual rigmarole with bags, packing and cameras, the two of us strapped in and roared off down the runway. This time we headed north-east with around 120 miles to run for the crossing into Zimbabwe. We encountered lowering clouds and rain but weaved our way through the showers in reduced visibility. As we got closer to the airport we could see a dark thunderstorm over the field and held off a few miles away while it passed through. The rain made it noticeably colder and I was beginning to feel chilled as we flew around waiting for a clear run through to the airfield. When the worst of it was over, I positioned downwind to land and came in on a short, curved approach to get on the ground as quickly as possible. I had to skirt around a lot of standing water from the downpour before we taxied to the main apron in front of the control tower for a most unusual welcome.

The Matabeleland Vintage and Classic Car Club had brought its entire collection of old cars and trucks out to meet us and it was as if we'd stepped back into the 1920s. I left the locals admiring the *Spirit of Artemis* while I went off to inspect their vehicles. They let me drive several of these old bangers and I had great fun lurching around the apron, grinding the gears and jumping the clutch in my ineptitude.

A local couple, Neil and Ginny, very kindly adopted our entire crew and went out of their way to help us, arranging transport into Bulawayo and ferrying us around for the next two days – which was just as well as, once again, no transport had been arranged by our logistics manager.

Annette and I stayed at the lovely old Bulawayo Club which was in the grand colonial style and each had a palatial suite with deep baths and balconies overlooking the main street. The rest of the crew stayed down the road, joining us for champagne after we had spruced up.

The next day was a welcome break from flying and while Ewald headed out to the airport to do a day of maintenance and an oil change, the rest of us filmed at the Bulawayo Club. Annette had arranged for local historian and former Rhodesian Air Force pilot Bill Sykes to join us for an interview. Bill claimed to know the exact spot of Lady Heath's forced landing in the bush with her Avian. In one of the most dramatic incidents on Lady Heath's Africa flight, she took off from Pretoria and was aiming to fly 400 nautical miles direct to Bulawayo in time for a civic lunch in her honour. She didn't make it. Nearly six hours into the flight and with just 10 miles to run to Bulawayo, Mary was suddenly overcome by sunstroke. Seized by panic that she might faint at the controls and struggling to keep conscious, she crash landed in open bush. She woke up four hours later to find herself lying on the ground with her helmet off and her brow being bathed in goat's milk by three semi-naked local women. Her disappearance made the front page of the Rand Daily Mail and the South African Air Force prepared to launch a search party when the news came through that she had been found. With the help of the military, she resumed her flight a few days later.

Bill offered to take us to the spot so we planned to meet up early next morning to fly out and try to find it.

Before then, we had the rest of the afternoon for some sight-seeing so loaded up the cameras, piled into a minibus and drove out of town to the famous Matopos, the ancient boulder-strewn kingdom of the Shona and Matabele tribes. Lady Heath had flown right over this just before her crash landing but our afternoon was rather less eventful.

The vast natural amphitheatre, stretching over miles, was a haunting place. A wall of huge boulders marks the perimeter and more rocks and granite blocks, which rise to several hundred feet, are scattered through the inner area, giving a strange spectral quality to the landscape. Eroded by the elements, they form fantastical shapes, with rocks precariously balanced on bigger boulders called kopjes. Some seemed fashioned on an improbable scale by invisible hands into rounded pots and vase-like shapes with narrow necks, while others resembled the curving backs of whales. Ancient rock paintings had been found in caves along the terraces of rock and a human skeleton over 40,000 years old. In the centre of this rock kingdom sat a raised plateau of granite like an island, surrounded by a sea of acacia trees and wild aloe with pockets of denser bush. Somewhere in these lower thickets hid a small population of white rhinos, and leopards also lurked amongst the rocks. The park also boasted the highest concentration of black eagles in Africa.

It is on this central raised stone terrace that Cecil Rhodes was buried according to his last wish. His sarcophagus is embedded within the stone which forms a shoulder of sloping granite and has a grand elevated view across the whole area. Even in death, the old imperialist forced his presence on what was most sacred to the Africans.

After heading back and collecting Ewald, who had been working on the Stearman all day, we changed hotels, relocating to the Traveller's Lodge near the airport, and had dinner at a nearby restaurant with Neil and Ginny, before retiring to the pool in the garden for a last drink.

That night I lay awake listening to distant, rolling thunder and woke before dawn to the sound of rain.

By the time we reached the airport the weather had cleared to a bright and humid morning. Bill was there to meet us, but my heart was in my mouth as he climbed in – a haul for anyone, not least someone of Bill's advancing years. After teetering backwards and nearly losing his balance, he got in and we set off in search of Lady Heath's crash site.

Once airborne, I got the impression Bill hadn't the faintest idea where it was but it was a good excuse for a joyride so we buzzed off south for 10 miles and I did a steep descent with the power closed for the cameras to simulate what Lady Heath's plunge for the ground might have looked like from the cockpit.

The ground below was quite rough and speckled with small trees and bushes, but it may have been cleared grazing land back in 1928. I would have been hard pressed to land without hitting a tree and concluded that Lady Heath had done a very good job of landing her aeroplane, sustaining no worse damage than a bent undercarriage.

An hour later, after Bill and I landed back at the airport and a final round of goodbyes, we fuelled up and got organised for the flight to Livingstone. While we waited in the terminal to process through immigration, a schoolboy who was part of a group sitting close by asked what I was doing there. He can't have been more than about 12 or 13 and had a shock of unruly blond hair. His name was Luke Hay and he explained he had been born with a rare brain condition that caused nerve damage and resulted in him having more than 30 operations. Despite this, he was remarkably nonchalant about what had happened to him and had the kind of precocious maturity which comes with acute physical and emotional suffering. He cheekily asked me if I was married, to which I replied, 'No, Luke, I'm not. Are you asking me?'

He snorted, 'No!' and made a throwing up gesture, to which I grinned.

When the time came to say goodbye, I said I hoped we would meet again and to this day we are still in contact. He moved to America and is still thriving.

NOVEMBER 8, BULAWAYO TO VICTORIA FALLS

This was what I anticipated to be one of the most outstanding flights of the expedition – the leg from Bulawayo to Livingstone, a name synonymous with the early exploration of Africa. Dr David Livingstone, Scottish explorer, missionary and antislavery crusader who was the first European to explore this area in the 1850s, regarded the great rivers of Africa as 'highways into the interior' and the commercial development they facilitated ultimately saw the end of slavery, the dark heart of Africa. Although Livingstone originally set out to find the source of the Nile, it was his exploration of the Zambezi which was to be definitive and his greatest discovery was the largest sheet of falling water in the world – the Victoria Falls.

It was the prospect of seeing this epic view which gripped me now. We were airborne just before 11am for the two-and-a-half-hour flight north-west to pick up the Zambezi River and then upstream to the falls.

Andre, the South African pilot who had helped us with the flight planning in Cape Town, had given us a piece of advice about flying Victoria Falls, as usually the area is congested with tourist flights – sundry aircraft and helicopters – stacked in a holding pattern up to several thousand feet above the falls. I was concerned we would have to position above all this traffic but Andre assured us that this was the quiet season and if we planned our arrival for lunchtime then we should have it to ourselves.

Approaching from the east, the horizon appeared dead flat and the dark emerald Zambezi, snake-like in the gorge below us. I kept my eyes peeled for the only distinctive feature ahead, a puff of cloud resembling a 'smoke signal' – the vapour from the falls. When it came into view I trembled with excitement. During the wet season, when the river is at full flow, this rising spray can reach 1,500 ft, and is visible from over 30 miles away. As Livingstone wrote: 'No one can imagine the beauty of the view from anything witnessed in England. It had never been seen before by European eyes; but scenes so lovely must have been gazed upon by angels in their flight.'

At exactly 1.40pm, the *Spirit of Artemis* roared over Victoria Falls. It felt like the flight of angels and anybody looking up through a veil of mist and refracted rainbows and seeing those shining wings might have thought the same. Just as Andre had predicted, there were no other aircraft in sight; the only things flying apart from us were a couple of buzzards and these swerved away as we approached. We flew right along the edge, looking straight down over the 350 ft drop. My heart was in my mouth and I felt a wave of vertigo. Half the rock face was dry, resembling the edge of a huge tectonic plate but, even at relatively low ebb, the river made a fantastic cataract as it swept over the edge and hurtled into the deep chasm, throwing up billowing clouds of spray. It was a stupendous sight and we circled several times, just a couple of hundred feet above, to take in the splendour below.

At the head of the falls are two distinct islands, large enough to divide the curtain of water at full flow. At the base, the river split into several vertical gorges of petrified lava. The Second Gorge is spanned by the Victoria Falls Bridge and water entering this steep channel makes a sharp right turn and there, carved into the rock, is a deep pool called the 'Boiling Pot'. At low water the surface of this pool is smooth and deceptively benign but at high water it whips up into a maelstrom of whirling currents and white caps. Anything swept over the falls, even the occasional hippopotamus or crocodile, is frequently found swirling around there. It is where the bodies of two tourists, mutilated by crocodiles, were found in 1910 after two canoes were capsized by a hippo at one of the islands above the falls.

The airfield was just seven miles away from the falls and I took the precaution of climbing another 1,500 ft before making radio contact with the control tower. Confirming my position and height at 4,000 ft on the altimeter, there was a pause before the air traffic controller told me that I should be at 6,000 ft and requested me to climb to this altitude. I replied that I had visual contact with the runway and requested a straight-in approach from my current height given that the high ambient temperature would have made for a slow ascent. I was granted clearance and continued accordingly. As I landed, I squealed with delight at the sight of baboons racing with us in the grass alongside the runway.

While I taxied onto the apron, however, there was another radio call requesting me to report to the tower as soon as I had parked up. I groaned. Clearly there was a problem. Ewald came with me to the tower and, after being made to wait for some minutes in the corridor outside the control room, we were ushered into a large office. The head controller took a very dim view of our seeming ignorance of his airspace. Given we had deliberately flown low to see the falls, he had a point but we could hardly give this as an excuse.

I apologised profusely and said we got carried away by the spectacle but he brushed this aside and said, without a hint of irony, 'This sort of thing might be all very well in Britain, but here in Zambia we have health and safety regulations.'

Suitably chastened, I apologised again and he finally said we could go.

We reunited with the rest of the crew at the Livingstone Hotel, a mile or so above the falls on the eastern bank of the river – a late change of plan after Annette cancelled the original booking which was a grim little backstreet lodging with no facilities or internet. To the delight of the crew, she managed to book us into the more luxurious alternative.

Every night, it was routine for the pilots to sit down for a detailed briefing about the next day's flight plan. It normally took an hour and a half or so and we'd generally have a round of drinks and make a bit of a session of it, as pilots do. Joao, who was interested in flying, usually joined us and Matt, too, if we were discussing air-to-air filming. While at Livingstone, Sam complained to Annette he felt excluded. She was unsympathetic and told him that it was a situation of his own making. While that was true, we were not trying to make things unpleasant. He was still part of the

My parents with me on the left, aged four, with Julie in the middle and my twin sister, Debbie on the right in Winnipeg, 1966

Me at our home in McConnell Creek, British Columbia, circa 1970

Me, aged 12, with Victor as a foal in Murton, near Appleby in Cumbria, 1974

My first flying lesson at age 16, during a summer holiday back in Canada in 1978

My first open cockpit biplane, a replica Se5a WWI fighter, at the New Zealand Warbirds Association, Ardmore Airfield, New Zealand in 1991

Working as a flying instructor at the Ardmore Flying School in 1990. From left, Graeme Beggs, me, Paul Bryant and John Kendal

My wedding to Steve Taylor with Debbie on the left and Julie on the right, March 1989

Top left, with Alain Grisay in the Gobi Desert on the Peking to Paris Classic Car Rally, 2007 and, top right, climbing into the cockpit of a De Havilland Chipmunk at Kennet Aviation, Cranfield in Bedfordshire, 2001

Me with my adored whippet, Louis, and my friend and painting mate, Anthea Davidson with Digby, Dullingham near Newmarket, 2009 (Copyright: Rebecca Green)

With Zara and Mike Tindall for the launch of the Cape Town to Goodwood expedition at the Goodwood Revival, September 2013

With the Stearman loaded into a container, the four wings in jigs behind me for the shipping to Cape Town from Hungary, September 2013

Flying the Stearman off the south coast of England, July 2013 (Copyright: Rogier Westerhuis)

Lady Heath after her record-setting solo flight up Africa in 1928

The Stearman reassembled and back in the air for a
test flight off Cape Town, South Africa, October 2013

Overhead the legendary
Victoria Falls in Zambia

The Spirit of Artemis over the Masai
Mara in Kenya, note the wings on the
underside. (Copyright: Nylon Films)

Flying the Wilderness Coast in South Africa
(Copyright: Nylon Films)

The breathtaking immensity of the
Sahara Desert, South Sudan
(Copyright: Nylon Films)

Visiting one of the women's community
groups at the Lewa Conservancy, Kenya
(Copyright: Nylon Films)

Filming at October 6 Airport, outside Cairo
with the Cessna Caravan, our support plane
on the right. (Copyright: Nylon Films)

Champagne celebration on the beach at Mersa Matruh, Egypt, having reached the Mediterranean. From left: Matt Green, Annette Porter, Ewald Gritsch, Gibran Chaudhry, Justin Wood, me and Joao Valle

My rear cockpit with a GoPro camera mounted on the windscreen, the basic instrument panel, the top of the joystick in the middle and iPad on the right with routing information

The Spirit of Artemis flying over the Artemis yacht off the Needles on the Isle of Wight during the Cowes Regatta, August 2014 (Copyright: Gijs Kaars-Sijpesteijn)

crew and always welcome to join us but it was remarkable how often this led to an argument.

Such a situation arose when we discussed the next two legs of the flight, which would take us north to Ndola and across a narrow finger of the Democratic Republic of Congo which protruded into Tanzania and lay directly across our route. We did not have permission to overfly DRC and talked over the merits of flying over this area without it or flying around it to remain legal. Johnny was concerned about the possibility of having to force land in the event of an engine failure and was considering flying the Caravan around the edge of the area to avoid the risk. I was also in two minds about what to do in the Stearman. The diversion would involve another hour of flying and our schedule was already tight. Sam arrived in the middle of the conversation, dismissing these concerns and saying it was stupid and unnecessary to go the longer distance. He said he had done it before and there had been no problem. Johnny, a very unflappable character, said he would make up his own mind.

NOVEMBER 10, LIVINGSTONE TO NDOLA

From the southern border of Zambia, the next leg was to Ndola, halfway up the country – a long flight of around 350 miles, taking four hours.

I was desperately keen to see elephants and we now flew over open country with extensive areas of marshland scanning for these large beasts. Ewald and I could talk over the intercom but in fact we seldom conversed and just preferred the roaring silence and the spectacle of Africa. When we saw something interesting, though, such as some large distinctive dark shapes with trunks around a watering hole or black shadows lurking under a tree, we broke out in a flurry of excitement. I circled down to take a closer look and try for a decent line of sight for the cameras and Ewald made a note of the time to help Justin index the film downloads each night.

BIRD

We landed at Ndola to find cold beers waiting for us, compliments of Johnny Beverage. There was a little airport bar perfectly situated at the side of the apron, close to the aircraft, and pilots could literally park up and walk straight into the bar. I had taxied down to the fuel pump and, after refuelling, left it there while we walked around trying to find a hangar for the night. Once we had, Ewald went back to get the Stearman with the help of two local chaps, who eagerly stepped up on each wing and held on to the side of the cockpit while he taxied. The aeroplane was even more exotic than an elephant in this part of the world and the Africans were always excited to see it. They couldn't quite believe it when we told them that we were flying back to England and most of them thought we were mad. One African was bemused by the exposed radial engine and declared that it looked 'unfinished'. Our lodgings for the night were just down the road at Hotel African and there was a big football match playing on several huge screens in the bar. I hesitated for a minute to watch the action and was amused to see that it was Manchester United and Arsenal playing, the locals as fanatical as if they'd been at the Old Trafford stadium instead of a bar in the middle of Zambia. The crew joined them but, after a quick dinner, Annette, Matt, Joao and I slipped away for another filming session. It turned into a long night and the camera rolled for over two hours. The more I talked about Lady Heath the more upset I became at what had happened to her. She was brave and brilliant and yet, through a combination of misfortune, hubris and a terrible kind of fatalism, it had all ended in tragedy. By the time we finished, I was too wound up to sleep and the air conditioning in the room didn't work so it was a sweltering, fitful few hours until daybreak.

Lady Heath, now joined on her flight by First World War ace Captain Richard Bentley and his bride Dorys in a Tiger Moth, also routed through Ndola in what was then Northern Rhodesia and as they advanced north they had flown into bad weather. During extensive thunderstorms, they were forced to fly in heavy rain just a couple of hundred feet above the ground but pressed on into the vast wetland around Lake Bangweulu, which Mary described in her memoir as a 'vicious looking swamp'. The low flying biplanes spooked pods of hippos wallowing in the shallows along the lake shore as they buzzed on through the rain. Somewhere in that same swamp, 54 years previously, Dr Livingstone died of malaria and dysentery. His servants cut his heart out of his chest and buried it a few miles to the south-east of the lake. Lady Heath winged lightly overhead, seemingly untouched by this earlier history, but she recorded a burst of nostalgia as they approached the border of Tanganyika. This was where she had lived briefly with her first husband on land which he had been granted under the Soldier Settlement Scheme after the First World War.

November 11, Ndola to Kasama

Although we were only 10 days into the flight, it already felt as if we had been going for weeks. Ahead of us was another long day with two stops – Ndola to Kasama and then across the border into Tanzania to Mbeya. I flew the first leg over the narrow trajectory of the Democratic Republic of Congo (DRC) on my own. We had deemed it best that both aircraft fly the same route so we headed on a straight north-east track for Kasama. Johnny flew high in the Caravan to make sure he could glide clear in the event of an engine failure and I flew at 3,000 ft, sufficient to put me out of range of ground fire if there were any rogue militia below. It seemed devoid of life but one could never be entirely sure in Africa.

Having cruised across this finger of DRC without incident, I was intrigued to see vast plumes of smoke ahead, rising from a huge area of burning land and as I got nearer I breathed in the acrid stench and skirted around the worst of it. Amazingly, there were dozens of huge cranes with black wings and white heads spiralling in the smoky thermals, seemingly unconcerned by the polluted air.

As I flew along, the Caravan pulled up alongside for a few minutes before veering away to the east. It was another two hours before Kasama appeared in the distance. The runway was a gravel strip in flat open bush and I could see the distinctive bright orange of the exposed earth from several miles away. Matt and Joao set up the camera right on the threshold of the runway but it was impossible to see them over the Stearman's engine and I crabbed slightly to keep them in sight, landing well down the strip on what turned out to be a perfect wheeler landing. It was the first time I landed on a gravel runway and I was relieved it went well, especially with the camera rolling.

As I vacated the runway I saw two fire trucks and an ambulance on standby next to the control tower. They had obviously been prepared for the worst. I gave them a wave as I taxied past, 'Sorry boys, not this time!'

Beyond was a wide tarmacked apron and to one side was a little cluster of schoolgirls in blue and yellow uniforms. I taxied over to meet them and as I climbed down from the wing, they came surging towards me with outstretched bouquets of frangipani, tropical white flowers with egg-yolk yellow centres which smell like the sun. I buried my sunburnt nose into their whiteness and breathed deeply. These little girls had never seen an old aeroplane and most of them had never been flying. They were amazed that a woman could fly and one commented resentfully that only boys got to do that sort of thing. I assured them that girls could too and hoped they would all have that opportunity in future.

From that unexpectedly sublime moment, I was then subjected to a wearisome pantomime for the purpose of the film. A local, by the name of Ewart, advised there was no fuel on the airfield and we needed to drive into town to collect some. I duly climbed into the back of Ewart's old flat-bed truck and Matt came with me with his camera. It was noon and getting very hot as the truck lurched into town along the heavily pitted roads, spewing out a cloud of black diesel smoke. As we skidded around one corner, Matt nearly fell over the side, hanging on by a knee with both hands support-ing the camera. We stopped to refuel the truck at a garage, but there was still no sign of any Avgas and I was conscious time was dragging on. We finally pulled into the yard of a private house and there were our two barrels of fuel. We loaded these up, along with three trays of eggs, and I stopped to pat the various dogs milling around the yard – a very friendly boxer who reared up on his back legs, a terrier and a sausage dog – before returning to the airfield. We now had the job of hand-pumping the fuel from the barrels into the top wing of the Stearman.

Even in normal circumstances it takes two people to refuel, one up on the top wing while the other hands up the nozzle first on one side of the engine and then the other to access the two side tanks in both wings. Ewald was there waiting to help but, while I had been away, Sam wanted him to let me struggle alone with the fuelling, ostensibly to enhance the drama for the film. Sam had brought his own hand pump from Brussels for this refuelling from barrels but the seals were broken, causing it to leak, and the gauge to determine fuel quantity was also broken. Evidently the pump hadn't been serviced in a long time. We then had the problem that the pipe attached to the pump was too short to reach the top wing of the Stearman.

To resolve this, we moved the truck with the barrels to the front of the Stearman and with this added height the hose pipe could reach the fuel tanks – an impossible task for me on my own.

It was now even hotter and took us around 45 minutes to refuel. I just wanted to get flying but it now transpired that Sam had arranged for a sit-down lunch at a restaurant in town. We still needed to clear immigration and another two hours slipped by. I was now getting anxious that we were running out of daylight time and, with it, any margin of safety for our second leg to Mbeya.

It was only when we were back at the airport that Sam announced that we needed to change the flight plan. We were now flying into a new airport at Mbeya as he had just discovered the old one had stopped operating six months ago.

I was seriously irritated by all of this but, as soon as I got airborne with Ewald, my mood lifted.

We had 170 nautical miles to run, mostly over low-lying hills which made blue shadows in the setting sun. As the light started to fade, even Ewald began to get worried, but we pressed on, slowed by a 10-knot headwind. It was still some distance to the airport and now the hills became mountains. Down the valley to the east was the huge menacing shadow of a thunderstorm and if it moved west by just a couple of miles the airport would have been engulfed and we would have been in deep trouble. However, we landed right on dusk and taxied to the apron where the Caravan was parked to find there were no facilities and no obvious means of securing the Stearman. Ewald spotted some blocks of broken concrete a short distance away in the scrub and the whole crew hauled these over. We anchored the Stearman with ropes to prevent it moving or blowing over if the wind picked up in the night.

There was no transport arranged so we got the airport bus for the hour-long trip to the hotel, which was back at the old airport, as per our original flight plan.

It was nearly 10pm by the time we got there and I was already beginning to feel unwell, with a sore throat and a stinker of a headache. The hotel kitchen was closed so, with no chance of food, I grabbed my key and stomped off to my room.

In the morning, perhaps due to my worsening cold, I couldn't face the breakfast on offer, so left on an empty stomach to find another gruelling exercise to get fuel when we got to the airport. The site was under construction and there were no fuelling facilities. We ended up heaving the Stearman along a dirt track to a locked shed where they stored barrels of fuel but an airport official drove up and told us we shouldn't be there.

I was now thoroughly hacked off, as we pushed the Stearman back up the track, but was grateful for the African construction workers who helped us push. The barrels were then brought to us on the apron and we went through the same laborious process of hand pumping the fuel into the top wing.

No doubt these situations made the eventual film more interesting but, from my point of view, they were an annoying distraction from the flying. By the time I strapped into the cockpit, exhausted from the heat and dripping with sweat, I had to mentally switch into flying mode which wasn't easy. By contrast, the film crew could settle into the Caravan, crack into their plentiful supply of food and drink and sleep until landing.

NOVEMBER 12, MBEYA TO MWANZA

The first of our two legs was a three-hour flight to Tabora and as Ewald and I approached the airport around noon I was momentarily confused by a familiar voice over the radio, ostensibly from the control tower, requesting us to make a low pass. Johnny had hijacked the air traffic controller and was speaking over the radio. Accordingly, I swooped down and roared past the control tower, as Ewald waved to the crew who were at the same level. We landed but didn't stay long on the ground. The message that I wasn't hanging around had obviously got through as Annette handed me a muesli bar for lunch, as we refuelled and got ready to fly on. Even in those few minutes, the sky darkened and the wind picked up which could only mean one thing – thunderstorms. Several huge cumulonimbus clouds were building up to the west and I wanted to get away before the rain started. The wind was now erratic and gusting and I took off with a stiff crosswind, unable to stop the Stearman veering across the runway despite booting in full opposite rudder.

We had a two-hour flight to Mwanza on the southern shore of Lake Victoria, where Lady Heath enjoyed one of the highlights of her flight – a buffalo shoot with the district commissioner and his wife. They stalked a herd of buffalo for several hours with Mary blasting away at several of them with a heavy rifle, and after feasting on buffalo steaks that night, she declared it one of the best days of her life, on the ground at least.

The hunting party had steamed back to Mwanza the next day and, as Dorys Bentley took to her bed with heat exhaustion and stomach problems, Mary headed up the Gulf of Mwanza to track kudu and leopard. Over four days, she trekked more than 80 miles in tropical heat and on one day covered 20 miles before breakfast. Her physical endurance was exceptional, like everything else about her.

My own experience in Mwanza 30 years before on our overland trip was more akin to Dorys Bentley's experience. We had stayed in a monastery on a rare night of civilisation after weeks of camping in the bush. Lulled into a sense of security, tired and dehydrated, I drank from the bathroom tap and within hours became ill with suspected typhoid, running a high fever and every joint and bone in my body ached. Then the stomach problems began. I had excruciating, bowel-burning dysentery but there was no chance of recuperation, we had to keep moving. It was grim to say the least and nearly three weeks before I started to feel normal again.

How different our arrival in the *Spirit of Artemis*. We caught our first view of Lake Victoria glinting in the distance through the hills like a vision of paradise. The tropical forest below blazed with colour, giving way to fruit tree plantations and homesteads as we approached the lake. The airport was right on the lake shore and I positioned wide downwind to land but was then requested to orbit by the air traffic controller to give priority to an airliner on a 10-mile final approach to the runway.

On the ground, the hot humid equatorial air was like a sauna as we stripped off our helmets and climbed out. It was still quite early in the afternoon, so we all piled into a little open-air taverna at the airport for lunch of cold drinks and hot barbecued chicken. In the bar that night we congregated for what would be the last supper with Johnny Beverage and drank some very expensive French wine to celebrate. We were sorry to be losing him as we had all got very attached, but Johnny had to get back to Nairobi. Gibrain Chaudhry was going to be our pilot for the rest of the trip. Gibbs had flown in on a commercial flight that afternoon – he may well have been on the airliner I'd given way to – was in his late twenties, Kenyan born, and had an unassuming and charming manner. He immediately fitted in with the team. Gibbs had flown for Phoenix Aviation for several years and was a first-rate pilot with a lot of bush flying experience, which was exactly what we needed for the next part of the expedition.

November 13, Mwanza to Arusha

Today was going to be an *Out of Africa* flight over the Serengeti and we had a long briefing to discuss the intercept point of the aircraft and formation flying for the air-to-air filming. For the purposes of the film, I was going to fly this leg alone and I took off and headed east over the hills and then picked up the lake shore again as it curved to the south.

The huge brooding shadow of a thunderstorm loomed over the lake but, as it was still several miles away, I continued east along the shore before heading inland and into the vast sweeping plain of the Serengeti. From my open cockpit, what a view I had of scatterings of wildebeest and gazelle below, while the occasional safari vehicle blew up dust clouds on the gravel roads that cut white lines across the plains. I reached the rendezvous point a few minutes before the Caravan circled into view and I climbed up to meet it and closed in on Gibbs' left wing.

Ahead was one of the great sights of Africa – the Ngorongoro Crater, the world's largest extinct volcanic caldera, which, when active two and a half million years ago, would have been a similar height to Kilimanjaro. With one almighty explosion, the volcano collapsed in on itself leaving an uneven 'pie crust' rim 2,000 ft above the crater floor and enclosing an area of nearly a hundred square miles, now teeming with wildlife. The crater was voted one of the Seven Natural Wonders of Africa and I climbed to 8,000 ft to get over the rim, watching Gibbs in the Caravan a mile or so ahead of me. He descended into the crater and then started to ascend the other side.

Staying high, I flew along the rim and was amazed to recognise the camp where we had pitched our tents 30 years before with the Bedford truck. There was the steep, zig-zagging road leading up to where we'd pushed and heaved the truck for 12 hours in the rain when the differential broke. Jill and I had woken at dawn the next day to find fresh elephant droppings steaming in the early light barely two feet away from our tent. A herd must have tiptoed through the camp in the small hours and soundlessly departed again.

It was all just so beautiful I flew it in a kind of rapture, catching a strong updraught of air as the wind swept up the outer side of the crater which sent the Stearman billowing upwards for several hundred feet. I poled forward on the stick, surfing down the air like a boat, before heading over the lush forest on the eastern slope of the crater. I now headed to a dirt strip at Lake Manyara for a short break with the crew. We were on the ground for five minutes when Sam told us we had to leave immediately. We grabbed a quick sandwich and then caught sight of a little souvenir stand off to the side. Annette and I couldn't help having a look but Sam badgered us to hurry up. I bought a carved ebony candle holder with three stooping African figures following each other round in a circle as a memento before we headed off. Later that evening, Annette wondered what all the rush had been about. I wasn't sure but I suspected we might not have had permission to land.

We now had a short 50-mile flight to Arusha, and this time Annette joined me. The strip was on an elevated terrace and as we flew over the sheer edge the ground fell away sharply. I turned steeply to the right to pick up Lake Manyara and dropped down to 30 ft to track the shoreline. The lake was like a mirage, shining a pale, airy blue and surrounding it was a wide, bleached salt pan, where a herd of several hundred goats scattered like marbles as we buzzed overhead, while the Maasai goatherds, clad in their red cloaks, looked up and waved. Turning away from the lake, heading towards Arusha, we flew across the arid bush and spotted several zebra and giraffe, the latter startled into a slow-motion canter as we circled overhead, and further along a small group of elephants sheltered from the sun under a large baobab tree. It was all utterly magical.

An hour later, we landed at Arusha and, as Annette set out to find hangarage, I tried to find a fuel man who could activate the pump. The Caravan landed a short time later and Ewald immediately came to help. In the meantime, Annette had found Mr Kabuki, a delightful man who was thrilled at the thought of having the Stearman in his hangar for the princely sum of $10-a-night.

We stayed for the next two nights at a lovely little boutique hotel called Christina's, who was also our host. Originally from Rwanda, Christina had been running her little hostelry for 20 years. Mango and banana trees filled the garden and purple hibiscus and crimson bougainvillea festooned the walls and railings. Annette and I had rooms on the second floor leading from the deck, which housed a covered lounge area and it was there we all collapsed at the end of the day.

We had a 5am start the next day for an air-to-air filming sortie with a helicopter Annette had booked for the crew but when we arrived at the airport we found early morning fog prevented us from flying. We were having breakfast in the cafeteria and were all sitting there chatting when Caroline O'Donnell from Artemis strolled into the terminal in a flowing skirt and dashing straw fedora, looking very cool and chilled out. I sprung to my feet and we hugged and rocked around laughing together.

We drove back to the hotel and I slumped onto the deck and hardly moved for the rest of the day. I still felt lousy so it was a relief just to drowse and sleep in the shade of that peaceful terrace, while the rest of the crew went into town to another hotel which had internet and a swimming pool.

We enjoyed a big dinner that night, which Christina prepared, and Caroline came to join us. It was also Gibbs' birthday so we had a lot of toasts to celebrate the occasion. During dinner, our hostess told us she had escaped the Rwandan genocide in the 1990s and had an ugly scar the length of her thigh from a machete strike to show for it. It puts life into real perspective when you see things like that. When we drove through Rwanda in 1982 it struck us then as one of the most beautiful countries in Africa, prosperous and idyllic with heart-warming people. It was therefore deeply shocking that 12 years later, the country was cleaved apart by tribal division with one million Tutsi murdered in cold blood by machete-bearing Hutu. Christina was one of the lucky survivors.

NOVEMBER 13, ARUSHA TO NAIROBI

It was another pre-dawn start for our second attempt at the helicopter filming sortie and this time, on a beautiful, liquid clear morning, we got away as planned and I took off with the chopper alongside me. The door had been removed for the filming and Matt was there, slung in a harness, with his camera sticking out the side. We climbed to a thousand feet and the helicopter hovered while I flew around it and then made several passes flying directly below it. This footage – used in *The Aviatrix* documentary – was one of the loveliest scenes, perfectly capturing the *Spirit of Artemis* flying into the dawn and towards the horizon and Mount Kilimanjaro, which is where I headed next.

It was a 20-minute flight to Kilimanjaro Airport at the base of the mountain and, after landing, we processed through Tanzanian immigration and crossed the border into Kenya.

Ewald had so much wanted to do this flight and had given me an old map of Kilimanjaro in the hope of that eventuality but, alas, I had already invited Caroline to join me, which is why she came to Arusha. Caroline had flown with me in England in both the Ryan and Stearman and loved it so much she was considering learning to fly. The rest of the Artemis team, including John Dodd, Dick Turpin and Mark Brandis from the Libertine Agency, who had designed Artemis's distinctive advertisements and the artwork on the Stearman, had also flown in to meet us. Helen, our film producer, was also there waiting for us at Wilson Airport. Another reason this flight was special was my chance to meet up with Steve Parkinson in the air and the crew were going to film us flying together over Lake Natron. With Steve in his Piper Cub was his sister, Ingie, my friend from Austria who had also come over for the occasion. It would be quite a party once we landed in Nairobi.

With Caroline strapped in, the first part of the flight was through the Rift Valley, a primordial landscape with towering cones of extinct volcanoes, ancient lava flows burnt red and white into their steep slopes. Winging our way through this lunar landscape, we could see in the distance the soda lake which was to be our intercept point with Steve and Gibbs in the Caravan.

The strong alkaline waters of Lake Natron give it an astounding deep, dark red colour, with swirling pink foam on the surface like a strawberry milkshake. You could almost believe you were on Mars, so alien is the effect. After the crew finished filming, Gibbs peeled off in the Caravan to make his way to Nairobi, while Steve and I flew on together in a low tail-chase to Lake Magadi, around the steep banks and into narrow inlets and small bays. Tucked away in these hidden pockets, we found the odd zebra and giraffe, before we climbed and spaced out a bit, while I dug around in the side pockets to find my little flight plan sheet for the radio frequencies into Nairobi. Just as I retrieved this paper, the wind snatched it out of my hand and it flew out the cockpit. Steve was close enough to see this and laughed over the radio and I told him to guide me in as we proceeded to Wilson Airport.

A crowd including several local schools and a deputation of local dignitaries came to Phoenix Aviation to welcome us.

I was still high as a kite and launched straight into a succession of media interviews with local television stations but, really, I was desperate to drink something and dying to go to the bathroom. As usual, it was difficult to get a few minutes' respite and after an hour of this, Ingie spirited me away into the Phoenix facilities to get sorted out. All the girls of the expedition – Annette, Helen, Ingie and Caroline were by now long overdue to join John and Dick for lunch but we piled into a vehicle and made our way to Carnivores restaurant and proceeded to get absolutely plastered, as predicted, on mojitos. I sat next to John and we talked and laughed and it was more fun than I had had in months.

NOVEMBER 16, LEWA

Pronounced 'Lay-wah', the wildlife conservancy in the heart of Kenya is a very special place. Even the name sounds like an incantation. Covering an area of nearly 100 square miles, it lies to the north of Mount Kenya and the landscape is quintessential Africa with undulating savannah, low-lying hills and spreading acacia trees. Elephants, rhinos and zebras graze upon the grasslands and giraffes wander amongst the thorn trees picking at the high foliage.

Lewa is spectacularly beautiful. Set up in the early 1980s by the Craig family, who were some of the early white settlers in British East Africa, it was originally a cattle ranch but is now dedicated to the preservation of the indigenous black rhino. Tens of thousands of these magnificent, almost prehistoric animals roamed the plains of East Africa but they have now been poached for their horns to the edge of extinction. Only a few hundred survive and a significant number of these live at Lewa. I had hoped to meet the legend that is Ian Craig when I first visited Kenya in 2006. By this time, my old friend Carol, her husband Adam and their three children were living in Nairobi. Adam, then on a four-year posting with the BBC as East Africa Bureau Chief, had met Ian several times, but unfortunately we weren't able to get together but it was on this occasion that Carol took me to see Karen Blixen's house. Wandering through the cool dark rooms together and sitting on the lawn under a great bower of purple bougainvillea, gazing at the Ngong Hills, Appleby was a long way from our thoughts.

Now, I wanted to make Lewa the centrepiece of the expedition. Artemis Investments was also a keen supporter of both the Lewa Conservancy and the Tusk Trust, a British non-profit organisation also set up to help protect African wildlife, particularly elephants. Our plan was to stay at Lewa for two days and film their ground-breaking conservation work with rhinos. Dick, Caroline and Mark were also going to join us there so it was to be a very convivial couple of days.

After that first night in Nairobi, we left the next morning for Lewa, 120 miles to the north-west. As we got closer to Mount Kenya, the land below with its richly dark volcanic soil, intensively cultivated with dark green terraces of coffee plants, maize crops and banana groves, eventually gave way to denser forest.

We hugged the forested lower slopes to avoid the large military zone to the west and a layer of cloud which had settled around the top of the mountain obscuring the peaks.

Steve, outbound to some remote place, also flew this narrow corridor in a twin-engine King Air and nipped past us with a jaunty wave. The aviation community in Kenya is small and very close-knit and Steve was good friends with Ian Craig as well, often dropping into Lewa to ferry guests and VIPs.

Lewa had its own little airport with a gravel landing strip and it was late morning by the time we arrived overhead. We landed in radiant hazy sunshine with the lightest of winds and the Caravan parked up on a wide verge by the runway. A short distance along the strip was a dirt road leading to a row of open sided shelters with corrugated tin roofs where aircraft could park for the night. We pushed the Stearman into one of these and Matt laid his camera down for a few minutes to help chock the aeroplane. Suddenly, he yelped in pain and jumped around clutching his bare knee which now sported a tell-tale red welt. He had been stung by a small black scorpion, cunningly concealed in the sand – a palpable reminder that predators, even small ones, were never far away.

Ian Craig came out to meet us at the airfield and, in his habitual khakis and driving an open Jeep, he looked just like one of the heroes from *Daktari*. Ruggedly good-looking with cropped fair hair and fine blue eyes, he had a modesty and gentleness about him which belied his formidable reputation as a man of action. Here was a man in his true element and perhaps his most remarkable quality was an intensity which came from living his life's passion to the hilt. Mike and Sarah Watson were part of Ian's team. Mark was the chief executive of the conservancy and together they worked tirelessly on the day-to-day operations. The Watsons lived and worked at Lewa with their two young children and Sarah told how on one occasion she had been stung several times by a swarm of black scorpions and had to be airlifted to Nairobi suffering from anaphylactic shock. I related that story later to Matt when he was still nursing his solitary sting and told him to man up.

We stayed in one of the Lewa safari lodges, open-sided with a high-pitched thatched roof, which opened out onto a patio and a wide stretch of lawn with a gentle fringe of acacia and eucalyptus. Beyond that lay an enchanting vista of open plains and animals. The crew slept in the main lodge and I was happy to find myself in a little thatched cottage standing on its own across the lawn, a little Karen Blixen house, or so I liked to think.

After lunch, we went to film with one of the women's groups which make up part of the surrounding Lewa community. We met around 30 women of all ages, with one or two of the older ones in traditional Maasai dress with layers of beads around their necks. One old lady, with rheumy eyes and a broad smile, while chattering away in her native tongue, lifted one of these necklaces over her head and gave it to me. It was an astonishing and moving thing to be given such a gift knowing how little these people have – an act of real and spontaneous generosity and I couldn't resist hugging her with something that was more than gratitude. We were blessed with a beautiful golden evening when we loaded into two Jeeps and threaded our way through the trees and out into the open to look for wildlife. The most spectacular sight was a huge black rhino with the whole plain lit up behind him as he advanced slowly but resolutely down the dirt road like a tank, oblivious to our vehicles and seemingly in a world of his own.

The following morning, Annette wanted footage of the Stearman flying with Mount Kenya in the background and Dick Turpin generously offered to pay for the Lewa JetRanger helicopter as the camera ship, with Mike Watson piloting. We took off together and headed south to the mountain climbing up the slopes into the hazy morning light. I got to 10,000 ft on the altimeter but was only flying about a thousand feet above the rising ground. The twin peaks of the mountain stand at 18,000 ft, which was beyond the capability of the Stearman's aspirated engine, but we could see the two pillars of Nelion and Batian shining in the distance.

Ian Craig was there to meet us when we landed. He was going to come flying with me in the Stearman and Joao wired us both up with microphones to record our conversation. Without further ado Ian climbed up into the front cockpit and strapped himself in. I then taxied out and took off. Ian was also a pilot so, soon after, I gave him control with a wiggle of the joystick, exhorting him to show me Lewa. With the wonderful intimacy that comes with this kind of flying, we headed off over the plain and around the hills, and all the time Ian was pointing things out and explaining everything. We flew low over several small groups of elephants, all of which he knew almost by name, and flew at tree-level along a river, scattering gazelle and zebra along the banks. Further on, over flat, arid bush, Ian pointed out the decaying carcass of an elephant which had been killed by poachers a few months before. We tracked on around the hill, the vegetation formed a low bush line of trees which seemed marine-like, all leaning the same way as if in some invisible underwater current. We roared through a dry, rocky gully and below us were two rhinos, the first I had seen from the air. I was ecstatic as we made our way back towards the air strip and winged past Ian's house, on an elevated terrace on the side of a hill looking towards Mount Kenya. On the adjacent hilltop, he pointed to a site where his best friend was buried. I didn't ask what happened to him but it reminded me of another grave in the Ngong Hills where Denys Finch Hatton, Karen Blixen's lover, was laid to rest after the fatal crash at Voi in his yellow Gypsy Moth.

When we landed I hugged Ian, laughing in the joy of the moment. It was quite something to see Africa in this way. Ian and I were still chatting about the flight when there was a slight commotion behind us as Justin went to unload the GoPro cameras on the Stearman. He swore violently as he realised that he hadn't turned the cameras on for the flight. Although it was rather embarrassing, Ian graciously took it in his stride and said he was happy to repeat the exercise that evening. So, we met later and I was secretly thrilled at the chance to fly with him again.

Ewald now cracked on with engineering work while I went to join Annette, Matt and Joao who had been filming Sarah Watson with a little group of baby rhinos. Sarah looked after these little orphans, whose mothers had been killed by poachers. As I approached, I couldn't quite believe the scene before me. Sarah sat with a little rhino lying next to her, snoozing in the sun like a large, leathery puppy. I sat down alongside and stroked him. He had a stubby little tortoise head and the merest snub of a horn on his nose. His wrinkled grey coat was rough to the touch even though he was just a baby. Matt and Joao filmed us together and Sarah spoke eloquently about the terrible annihilation of these animals and their efforts to save them against almost overwhelming odds.

Two more little rhinos were milling around with some of their African keepers and one of these flopped down in the mud by the water hole and rolled around in evident bliss, like the proverbial pig in shit. The other one, slightly larger, was blind, his eyes veiled by a pale membrane which gave him an eccentric and slightly mad appearance. We were all completely entranced by these little animals and Matt filmed a lovely sequence of one of them lifting his nose to sniff the extendible boom microphone which Joao was dangling above his head to record their snorting and snuffling.

I could have stayed at Lewa forever. I wish I had been born in Africa and that I had grown up in this environment close to these wonderful animals. In another life, I would be a bush pilot, or Sarah Watson.

When I saw Ian again the next morning, his eyes were bloodshot and his face ravaged with anguish. Seldom have I seen such desperate fury in a man. He had been up most of the night and paused for just a few minutes to speak to us as he pulled up in a Jeep. I felt my own tears start as I watched him and listened with silent horror to what had happened.

Poachers had come into the reserve in the night and mowed down a young female rhino with a machine gun. It happened very close to the village we had flown over and when the villagers heard the rapid gunfire in the small hours, they knew it could only mean one thing. The alarm sounded and the whole place erupted into action. Mark Watson had immediately taken to the air in the helicopter, in a frenzy of rage, trying to catch the murderers and teams of armed trackers were mobilised with specially trained bloodhounds.

The poachers knew exactly what they were doing though and these killings are well planned. It takes seconds to kill the animal and barely a minute to butcher its face. Then they disappear into the night on motorbikes and the bleeding horn from this horrific amputation is transported to Nairobi in a matter of hours and smuggled out of the country to markets in China and the Far East. It is appalling beyond words. I felt a deep and visceral loathing for the ignorant and barbarous people that prize the horns and tusks of these vanishing African animals for their spurious potions and killer ornaments. The horn is made of keratin – it is not Viagra – and consuming it is like feasting on your own toenails.

They took me to see the dead rhino, escorted by a team of security guards all dressed in military fatigues and carrying guns and ammunition belts across their shoulders like heavily armed soldiers. As we advanced slowly up the steep slope towards a rocky gully the silent, mournful air made it feel like a funeral procession. I remarked to the African ranger that trying to protect these animals was *like* a war. He immediately corrected me – it was not like a war, it *was* a war. A fight to the death.

Suddenly, she came into view. The rhino had plunged several yards down the side of the gully and lay awkwardly on her back with her legs jutting into the air. For such a big animal, she looked small and vulnerable in that unnatural position. There were several oozing red bullet holes in her side where she had been sprayed with machine-gun fire and her lovely face had been hacked away in one savage slash, leaving a livid red expanse of flesh still wet with blood. At this awful sight, I completely lost the power of speech. It was the most barbaric and shocking thing I have ever seen and I sat down on the rocks for a few minutes with my hand on her side, crying helplessly. The dead rhino had been pregnant and she had also had a young calf with her which had run off into the bush and whom the search teams were now trying to find.

I came away with an even greater respect for the work that Ian and the Lewa team so bravely undertake every single day of their lives. It takes extraordinary dedication and courage to do this work and they are some of the most remarkable people I have ever had the honour of meeting.

November 18, Nairobi

Meanwhile, the problems with our logistics continued. No advance preparations had been made to position fuel and we had ended up having to buy a barrel of Avgas at Lewa.

Annette, Helen and I had a meeting at Lewa to discuss our predicament. I was so disenchanted by this point that I thought we should dispense with Sam's services. That wasn't so easy, however. Ahead of us lay some of the most difficult countries and Phoenix Aviation cautioned us about dismissing Sam as this could jeopardise the fuel and entry permit arrangements which had been made along the rest of the route, potentially delaying us for two to three weeks, a scenario we could not afford. In the circumstances, we had little choice but to press on with the status quo but none of us were happy about it.

BIRD

NOVEMBER 20, NAIROBI TO ENTEBBE

Our five-day stay in Kenya at an end, we were now flying north-west from Nairobi, across the Rift Valley and over the Maasai Mara back to Lake Victoria. We took off over the suburbs and continued the climb as the ground rose steadily towards the eastern rim of the Rift Valley. We needed to get up to 9,000 ft to clear the Kijabe escarpment and we flew in parallel to the ridges to ride the warm updraughts that would carry us the last few hundred feet over the top.

This was exactly the place where Lady Heath also struggled to gain height in her overloaded Avian and resorted to throwing some of her belongings overboard to lighten the aircraft. Her tennis racket, several books and a pair of shoes were cast over the side and she cleared the edge with barely 20 ft to spare. I told Ewald that he would be thrown overboard as 'extraneous kit' if there was any issue, but we sailed over the ridge and over several villages in the high hills.

The Maasai Mara is the largest national game reserve in Kenya and is really the northern extension of the Serengeti which starts in Tanzania. The area is famous for the Great Migration where over a million wildebeest and hundreds of thousands of zebras, topi, eland and gazelle pour into the Mara from the south every year in search of fresh grassland. This mass movement of animals is rated one of the Ten Wonders of the World and occurs in July, but there were still plenty of wildebeest and zebra sprinkled across the plain as we swept over in a low wide arc.

The direct track to Entebbe from Nairobi was 275 nautical miles in a straight line and this cut across the north-eastern part of Lake Victoria. This famous tropical lake is like a vast inland sea. You can't see to the other side; it just disappears into a blue haze. With this vast surface area of water and the extreme equatorial heat, it is intensely atmospheric and Lake Victoria has the highest occurrence of thunderstorms in the world. The water vapour rises off

the lake and ascends at a terrific rate, condensing into huge cumulonimbus clouds and releasing huge amounts of heat energy into
the sky. These clouds or 'CBs' (Charlie Bravos), as they are known
to aviators, are the power cells of thunderstorms and they can
bubble up over the lake in a matter of minutes. I shuddered to
think of getting caught out over the water in one of these as it
would have been a death trap. Flying in cloud, without reference
to the horizon, it takes less than half a minute for a pilot to become
disorientated and lose control of an aircraft. Over water, the
horizon is even more difficult to distinguish from sky in reduced
visibility. Before taking off, Sam suggested we cut the corner of
the lake and fly over the water to save time but we deemed it an
unnecessary risk and elected instead to go the safer and more
scenic route following the shoreline. This added another 80 or 90
miles to the flight but gave us somewhere to land in the event of a
sudden thunderstorm or engine failure.

The lake was a hive of activity as we barrelled along. We flew
over several fishing villages and out on the water were any number
of red, blue and green fishing boats with nets trailing over the side.
Small steamers and ferries chugged off into the distance on their
scheduled services around the main ports of Mwanza, Kisumu,
Bukoba, Entebbe and Jinja. Islands with dark lush vegetation
dotted the way and water hyacinth spread in a bright green fringe
around the inlets and bays. Lake Victoria also has a thriving population of crocodiles, hippopotamus, giant perch and otters.

As we buzzed around the lake we flew abeam the town of
Kisumu, one of Lady Heath's stops, and half an hour or so later
crossed the border into Uganda. We were now heading in a
westerly direction along the northern shore of the lake and, as the
afternoon wore on, individual towering cumulus clouds built up
around us and Ewald suggested that we climb up and fly amongst
them. I had rarely had the opportunity of doing anything like
this and it was irresistible in this phenomenal equatorial atmos-

phere. We climbed up several thousand feet and flew through the white chasms marvelling at the verticality and slightly dazzled by the light. I dipped the Stearman's right wings into the billowing surface and felt a jolt of turbulence from the thinner air density of the cloud. Climbing higher, we skimmed along the top of smooth white domes and nosed over the other side with much the same sensation of ploughing weightlessly down a mountain in fresh snow. It was like sledging in heaven. I don't think I have ever had such a powerful sense of moving in three dimensions as flying the edge of those wonderful clouds.

We were still in a beatific mood as we swept over the town of Jinja, where Lake Victoria empties into Rippon Falls, one of the sources of the Nile. Entebbe was another 50 miles or so further around the lake and I now started to prepare for the approach and landing. I was keen to see Entebbe Airport, having some memory of the Air France flight from Tel Aviv which was hijacked by the Palestine Liberation Organisation in 1976. The airliner was diverted to Entebbe and the passengers and crew taken hostage and held in the terminal building with the support of the President of Uganda, the notorious Idi Amin. After a week of tortuous and ultimately abortive negotiations, a dramatic night rescue was undertaken by a crack team of Israeli commandos. With the help of the Kenyan Government, the Israelis flew four C-130 Hercules transport aircraft into the airport without being detected by Entebbe air traffic control. The commandos stormed the terminal building and managed to save most of the hostages. As the Israelis beat a retreat with the hostages to their waiting aircraft, Ugandan soldiers shot at them from the control tower.

Entebbe Airport was right on the lake shore and I flew a wide arc and approached from the north to land on the southern runway pointing towards the lake. I was on a three-mile final to land when the air traffic controller suddenly told me to make a left-hand orbit to the west to give landing priority to an airliner on a long final behind me. This instruction was confusing because a left-hand turn was to the east and the controller appeared to have confused directions. In any event, I turned left as directed, sighted the airliner, and flew a wide left-hand circuit to reposition for landing.

While merrily flying this, I took in some of the sights of the city and spotted a rather splendid white palladian-style building with Doric columns. I veered around this for a better view and then continued downwind. The rest of the approach went without a hitch but, shortly after landing, I was again misdirected by the controller who confused left with right, east with west, and with these contradictory instructions, I was uncertain which way to turn off the runway. To the left was a large vacant apron area and the old disused terminal building where the Israeli raid had taken place. To the right was an even bigger apron and the modern new terminal building. The situation was resolved by the arrival of an airport vehicle with a 'follow me' sign, and this led us towards a parking area near the control tower. As we taxied in, I was surprised to receive a further radio call from the controller directing me to report to the tower. That didn't augur well.

I no sooner shut down the engine when another official vehicle swept up and several military police surrounded us. They escorted Ewald and I into a building at the base of the control tower and we were then taken up to meet the air traffic controllers. It was then explained to me that I had flown into a restricted area and over the official residence of the President of Uganda. This, of course, was the imposing white mansion I had admired and was the reason it was a restricted area. The controllers pointed out the airspace marked in red on one of their radar screens but it was interesting to note they also had a paper map which did not include the restricted area. We recognised it because it was the same map that we had and both were out of date. I explained that I had done exactly as directed and was of course flying the approach visually without reference to anything else, and I added

that their instructions had been confusing because of the direc-
tional errors. It emerged that the air traffic controller who had
given the instructions was a trainee, so there were errors on both
sides. But it didn't end there.

They took us to another room where the very formidable chief
continued to interrogate us about the flight. At one point he turned
abruptly, went to a drawer and pulled out a document which he
thrust at me without saying a word. It was marked 'Security' and
the front cover featured a picture of 9/11 with the airliner flying
into the World Trade Centre. I looked at this image for several
seconds and then finally I understood. Looking directly at our
menacing interrogator, I inquired if he had seen my aeroplane?
Not waiting for an answer, I said, 'It's a slow-flying vintage biplane
with wood and fabric wings. My flight is about a historic flight up
Africa by a pioneering female pilot. It is most emphatically not
an attempt at a 9/11-style attack on your president. My aeroplane
is not a security risk and it would look ridiculous if you tried to
make it one.'

It was all deeply unpleasant and quite unnerving. I had the vague
sense that he wanted something, perhaps money, but I didn't
have any and was not going to be intimidated into trying to bribe
him, because that too was a risk. At this point, our tormentor
announced he was impounding the Stearman and I felt a flare of
anger. I glared into that dark, implacable face and said that on no
account was the aeroplane to be touched. If he wanted to arrest
me, as the pilot, they could do that but he should be aware that this
would generate embarrassing publicity for Uganda. I was quite
sure they didn't want a full-blown diplomatic row on their hands
any more than we did. I couldn't help adding for good measure
that when Lady Heath had flown through Uganda in 1928 she
had given a glowing report of the country and it would be a great
shame if we couldn't do the same in 2013.

By this time another person had quietly entered the room

behind us – a woman who clearly held a position of authority. She caught the end of this exchange and I now looked at her silently appealing to her for help. After a few minutes they both withdrew to another room and when they returned they said we could go. I looked at the woman and gave her a grateful smile but she was impassive. We thanked them for their understanding and then beat a hasty retreat. Back outside on the apron I muttered under my breath to Ewald that I needed a very large drink.

It was a close shave and an unwanted reminder that we were at the mercy of officials if we did anything wrong or indeed anything they didn't like. They had detained us for nearly two hours and we now set about getting the Stearman sorted. I started up the engine and taxied away across the apron to a quiet corner with a tall, open-sided engineering hangar where Sam had arranged for the Stearman to be housed overnight. As we taxied up, he bowed with an exaggerated flourish, evidently pleased with himself for securing the cover and I gave him the thumbs up. That night there was a terrific thunderstorm with a thundering downpour that went on for many hours and I was even more grateful that the Stearman was dry and safe.

The next morning, we had an early drive into the capital, Kampala, to a local radio station where Annette had arranged for me to be on a popular morning show and Matt and Joao came with us to film the interview. The air was misty and humid from the rain in the night and it took the better part of an hour to reach our destination as we meandered through the outskirts of the city in the morning rush-hour. On the drive in, Matt filmed out of the window of the taxi and we caught a news report of troubles in South Sudan.

The two radio presenters who co-hosted the show were called Fat Boy and Seanice and you couldn't meet finer young people in the whole of Africa. They were a great double act – beautiful, bright and very funny. Seanice had amazing hair which was tightly plaited in narrow rows running from the central parting on her head and the plaits fell in a mass of gleaming black chords down her back. I sat in the sound-proofed room with a set of headphones clamped to my head, bantering with them and laughing at their sallies. During our conversation, I relayed what had happened at the airport the previous evening and apologised on air for the problem I had inadvertently caused. I also issued a personal invitation to the president to fly with me and cheekily suggested that he might enjoy a birds-eye view of his house from the open cockpit. Fat Boy adored the idea of our great romantic adventure up Africa and declared himself my 'soul mate'. Seanice immediately chipped in that it was entirely typical that he had made this earth-shattering discovery only to find that I was leaving the very next day.

Meeting these two was the highlight of our time in Entebbe. As we walked around the streets filming something of the city afterwards, there was a very strong military presence and a lot of guns on display. It felt hostile and we didn't hang around for long. Africa has some real horror stories of power gone berserk and Idi Amin embodied the very worst of it. He was known as the 'Butcher of Uganda' and up to half a million people were killed during his regime which was characterised by genocide, extra judicial killings and shocking human rights abuses. I came away thinking that Seanice should run for the presidency.

NOVEMBER 22, ENTEBBE TO JUBA

We were on our way to the airport – ahead of a long four-hour flight to Juba in South Sudan – when Sam announced there were going to be problems with the fuel availability in Egypt, where we were scheduled to arrive in a week's time. He advised there would be no fuel in Abu Simbel, no fuel for the Stearman in either Luxor and Mersa Matruh and no jet fuel for the Caravan in Cairo. I listened in stunned silence. Once we arrived at the airport, Gibbs came with Ewald and I to help with the Stearman while Sam went to file the flight plans in the tower.

I was incredibly stressed by all of this. We had a 300-mile flight ahead and were embarking on potentially the most dangerous part of the expedition. This troubled country, the newest in the world, had the longest running civil war in history with over 30 years of conflict between rival tribes and militia, and there were already reports that violence had erupted again.

I began to dread what was to come.

After taking off at 8.30am and heading north, we flew for many miles over dense jungle and part of the river known as the Victoria Nile and soon forgot our troubles as we became absorbed in the sights below. The river, quite narrow and fast flowing, twisted and turned through the dense undergrowth and broke into white rapids at various points. I flew down to about 200 ft to take a closer look and where the water slackened into deep pools, we could see pods of brownish pink hippos wallowing in the depths.

There wouldn't have been too many options for a forced landing if we had had an engine failure at this point and Ewald made one of his typically bleak jokes about our unlikely survival if that happened. But we both agreed how fantastically lucky we were to be doing this flight and, if the worst happened, there were worse ways to go. Three hours into the flight, the terrain and vegetation changed from tropical forest to open grassland, becoming increasingly more arid as the sun climbed higher, beating down relentlessly like a branding iron. We kept relatively cool with the rush of wind and the engine didn't miss a beat in the heat but, by the time we got to Juba, it was close to 50°C and simmering.

It was a big airport by African standards with one long runway and a vast apron area on which several turbo-prop aircraft were variously parked up or getting ready to depart. We tied the Stearman onto iron rings set in the tarmac, near to the Caravan, but didn't bother to refuel. We were going to have a rest the following day and Ewald wanted to get out early in the morning to sort the aeroplane out when it was a bit cooler. The airport was very close to the sprawling city and it wasn't far to our hotel compound, which was surrounded by guards and a high security wall. The hotel was used predominantly by United Nations and NGO personnel and was surprisingly comfortable, notwithstanding its unprepossessing entrance. Beyond the foyer was a wide covered veranda overlooking a garden where guests could relax with refreshments and our crew spent a lot of time here over the next two days. The poverty and devastation wrought by the civil war was never far away, however. On the other side of the barricade were piles of rotting garbage and dozens of flea-bitten dogs lying in the shade of crumbling, blasted buildings.

Over lunch, we discussed plans for the rest of our stay. Annette wanted to crack on with filming while I hoped to relax a bit and catch up on correspondence. The expedition was proving to be so all-consuming I hadn't managed to write a single email since leaving Cape Town, nor had I read a page of the books I had brought with me. I had a spacious, light-filled room and Ewald and I spent the afternoon flight planning until early evening, when we all went for drinks at another hotel on the river and sat in the shade of a big garden with several other westerners.

The film crew were up at dawn the next day and off to film at the airport. They had been given a specific time to arrive by the guide but arrived 15 minutes early at the security gate and parked up to wait. This proved to be an expensive mistake. Security guards approached their vehicle and as soon as they saw the cameras they detained the crew. Predictably they demanded money for their release and Annette woke me by hammering on my door not long after 7am. They had let her go to get the money so we now went through our collective resources to pay what was effectively a ransom. I had about $5,000 dollars in cash, our fuel kitty for the

Stearman, and I now handed her $3,000 which is what the corrupt security guards were demanding. She disappeared out the door again and an hour later the whole crew returned to the hotel and related their misadventure over breakfast.

The drama didn't end there.

Ewald and Gibbs went out to the airport after breakfast to refuel the aeroplanes and Sam went with them to collect the fuel he had pre-arranged with his agent. This drum was duly delivered and they hand-pumped the contents into the top wing of the Stearman. After they had emptied it, Ewald was unable to see the level of the fuel in the tank and just to make sure that it was full, wanted a second barrel to top it up. Sam duly obtained this from the agent and a further 25 litres was pumped into the Stearman, leaving the remaining 175 litres in the drum unused.

While all this was going on, a fuel truck had pulled up to refuel the Caravan parked alongside. The fuel man noticed Ewald with the barrels of fuel and asked why we had ordered our own fuel as they had Avgas for sale at the airport in drums at $800 a barrel. It emerged we were paying $2,500 per barrel for our fuel through the agent. I later called Steve Parkinson in Nairobi to discuss the situation. He confirmed Phoenix could have arranged the fuel in Juba at $600 per barrel, which was a sickening thought as it seemed we were paying over the odds.

As before, we put a brave face on it and pressed on.

Later that night, Annette came to join me for a cup of tea with some good news. She had contacted an old friend in Khartoum called Al Fatih, who was now a government minister for the Republic of Sudan. He kindly offered to host us in the city and arranged access to some rare sites for the filming when we arrived in a few days' time. Al Fatih was to prove a very good friend to all of us for entirely different reasons.

November 24, Juba to Malakal

With this pleasant prospect ahead in Khartoum, we were up early the next day for the flight to Malakal but, arriving at the airport, I was dismayed to see the Avgas had stained the Stearman's wings. In the intense heat, the fuel had expanded in the tanks and leaked, dripping down the top wing and onto the lower, leaving dark blue trails down the pristine paintwork. I could have cried. Matt told me I was obsessive about the aeroplane but I couldn't help it. It upset me to see it damaged.

As usual, flying was the perfect antidote to everything on the ground and by 8.30am we were airborne and turning north to follow the Nile. This part of the river is known as the 'White Nile', from the white clay sediment in the water. It looked more like gravy steaming gently in the early morning light and we followed its course for several miles until we sighted the 3,000 ft hill to the north of the town which hovered above the morning mist like a floating pyramid. Once clear of this obstacle, we started to climb steadily and picked up the instrument airway – a kind of aeronautical highway – and stayed between 3,500 and 4,000 ft on the altimeter to keep clear of any trouble with potential militias on the ground. Out to the left was the town of Bor, a thriving hub for the slave and ivory trade in the late 19th century. That was hard to imagine flying, as there wasn't a hint of ivory-bearing elephant on those ravaged plains and the slaves of earlier times had morphed into the victims of a different kind of abuse. Bor was right in the middle of Sudan's oil fields and much of the fighting had taken place in this area during the civil war as the different factions fought for control of the country's natural resources.

Keeping the river to our right we soon headed into the vast, verdant marshland known as the Sudd – the largest wetland of its kind in the world, fed by the Bahr al-Jabal part of the White Nile. Its Arabic name derives from the word 'sadd', meaning barrier or obstruction, and from Egyptian times the Sudd proved to be an impenetrable barrier to navigation along the Nile to the south and, equally, anyone trying to follow it north was similarly blocked. This region was regarded as one of the biggest hazards to the pioneers of the Cape to Cairo air route and it would have been a pilot's worst nightmare to ditch in this oozing primordial swamp, as it is riddled with crocodiles, snakes and malarial mosquitoes.

Our flight over this swamp was glorious but the beauty was deceptive. The most striking thing was the complete absence of any kind of animal life – most of it killed by the starving population or withdrawn into the relative safety of the rainforest to the south and the west. There were many birds, however, like the occasional lone eagle, many buzzards hunting in pairs and vultures with jaw-dropping wingspans. A few times I looked at one of these raptors, just a few yards above or off to the side, and found it spookily looking straight back.

It was another long hot flight of nearly 350 nautical miles and, after four hours in the air, we finally sighted the urban spread of Malakal with its distinctive grid of wide dirt roads. Situated on the eastern bank of the White Nile, it is the second largest city in South Sudan after Juba but looked more like a shanty town. It was a desperately poor place and had been ravaged by years of violence between the warring Dinka and Nuer tribes. The Dinka are exceptionally tall people – several of them have achieved global fame as super league basketball players – and, numerically, they are the predominant tribe. Both Nuer and Dinka are Nilotic in origin and ethnicity and both are semi-nomadic pastoralists who prize, indeed revere, cattle as the mainstay of their lives and culture. They are incredibly beautiful people, fine-featured with blue-black skin and sometimes bear striking facial scarification, inflicted as part of an elaborate initiation into adulthood. The Dinka have distinctive deep lines cut into their foreheads while the Nuer have intricate raised dotted patterns inflicted with thorns. Every time I looked at one of the locals I wondered which tribe they belonged to and wanted to ask why the conflict had been so brutal and seemingly irresolvable.

The airport was just beyond the city, with one long tarmac runway, oriented north-east and south-west, and we landed mid-afternoon during the hottest part of the day. It was like a furnace but the place roared with activity. Malakal is the centre of the United Nations peace-keeping forces in that country and there were several white UN aircraft parked around the apron, several large Russian Mi-8 transport helicopters and fixed wing aircraft with a lot of uniformed personnel. The helicopters caused a constant stir landing and taking off, sending up hot blasts of dusty air which whirled around us. Sudanese soldiers performed drills in a line at the far end of the apron and a Russian crew walked over from one of the helicopters to say hello. I was delighted to find that they knew Captain Sergey Bykov from our An-2 flight and made a mental note to write to him saying we had met his friends. It's a big world out there but aviation is a surprisingly small community within it.

We finally got away from the airport and the three taxis we found to ferry us to our hotel were unlike any vehicles I had encountered before. All manner of trinkets hung in front of the windscreen and thick sheepskin covered the seats, doors and ceiling of the small car. Climbing in, I had the bizarre sensation of being hand-inserted into a large muff. Perhaps this insulation kept the worst of the heat out in some way, but it wasn't obvious to foreigners.

We swerved out of the airport, the ornaments dancing and jiggling like little marionettes, onto the main road into the city, which was hard, dry dirt with potholes so big they could have been caused by mortar attacks. Every time we bottomed out in one of these craters I clenched my teeth and braced for the impact on my spine. Notwithstanding the padding, it was one of the most uncomfortable rides I have ever endured, but we groaned and laughed at the same time – the kind of ride you never forget.

We drew up at the hotel and, as we stepped out in front of a low white building with a narrow entrance and a single filthy window with a rag of curtain draped across, we all exchanged glances of deep scepticism. Inside were two old leather sofas but no air conditioning and we sat here for over an hour waiting to be given the keys to our rooms.

The accommodation was spread through a complex of single-storied buildings out the back. The blocks were set in a parched, unkempt garden with cracked, connecting concrete paths and in the middle was a token water feature – a round, dry as a bone swimming pool, deeply cracked, with tufts of grass poking through the crevasse.

The rooms were dark, malodorous caves with no air conditioning or running water. Mine had a little bathroom cubicle with a seatless lavatory, sink and a shower head in the corner, but, of course, nothing worked. A bucket of Nile water was provided to wash in or to sluice down the toilet. I tried to ignore several small cockroaches twitching in the filthy corners, but it was grim to say the least.

I had to get cleaned up for another satellite interview, which we filmed half an hour later, in the blistering sun. We then ventured out to explore the town, taking the same fur-lined taxis and this time I was able to take better stock of the inhabitants. The women were slender figures, swathed in cotton wraps which covered their heads and they struggled along with bags and baskets, some balanced on their heads. Their legs and arms seemed too emaciated to bear these oversized loads. Along those pitted roads, skinny little donkeys drew carts laden with plastic containers of Nile water and I was stricken to see one of them fall to its knees and whipped remorselessly by its driver. I screamed at the taxi driver to stop but he carried on, oblivious to the cruelty.

We stopped at another hotel, which was rather more salubri-ous than ours, and had a round of drinks sitting in the garden with a view of the river. Much like Juba, the hotel was largely occupied by United Nations personnel, but we kept to ourselves. That evening we did more filming by the river and I sat on the bank reading some quotations from Lady Heath's memoir. The view was sublime. Along the bank, a short distance from where we filmed, the locals were washing in the Nile, an evening ritual.

Our forward route was planned to El Obeid, the immigration entry point into the Republic of Sudan, which lay 150 miles to the north-west of Malakal, but we now questioned whether this was a good idea. At our hotel we had met a very nice Englishman, James Bevan, who had worked for the UN for the last two years, negotiating with some of the rebel groups. He strongly advised against proceeding to El Obeid and told us fighting had already broken out in the Nuba Mountains, which lay directly across our route. A village in the area had been torched and a UN helicopter shot down just two weeks before. He recommended we instead fly the Nile to Khartoum – the established safe corridor through the troubled border area – that should see us clear to the north.

Despite this warning, Sam insisted we should fly to El Obeid and refused to change the entry permits. In his opinion, based on his military experience, there was no risk of ground fire. I refused point blank to fly the Stearman to El Obeid and an argument ensued. Shortly after, fighting broke out at El Obeid airport and with that development, Sam finally changed his tune and put in the request for new entry permits for our transit to Khartoum.

The problem now confronting us was that Khartoum was over 400 miles to the north of Malakal and neither the Stearman nor the Caravan had the fuel range to fly this distance. We would therefore need to make a fuel stop. Gibbs had once landed at an airfield called Peloch, around 90 miles to the north-east of Malakal and he suggested this could be our refuelling point. It would mean landing without authorisation so we needed to simulate a technical issue that would justify this action so we could then refuel at the same time. We had been carrying extra fuel for the Stearman and Gibbs was certain he could get kerosene for the Caravan at Peloch.

We headed out early to the airport the next day on the basis that the new permissions were imminent. We hung around in the sweltering heat and filmed a bit but still no authorisation came through. At the end of the day, we went back to the hotel, thoroughly dispirited. That night Annette wanted to film us all flight planning, with a view to leaving the following morning, but when it became clear that we wouldn't be able to leave the next day either because the permits still hadn't come through, I blew up at Sam, packed up my maps in a foul mood and stormed off back to my room.

We finally got away from Malakal on day four, by which time the rest of the crew were thoroughly bored and frustrated. I was heartily glad to see the back of the place. The flaring tensions were not just ours. Lying awake at night in the stifling heat I had heard an odd popping sound which I thought was firecrackers but then realised was machine gun fire. Over breakfast the next day I asked the others if anybody had heard anything and Justin piped up to say that all he had heard was the couple in the room next door to him having sex. When Matt asked if he even knew what sex was, Justin indignantly threw a bread roll at him across the table, prompting the rest of us to join in the bun fight – a tension reliever if ever we needed one.

Barely three weeks after we got away, the rebels stormed the town again and Malakal was reduced to a blood bath. Thousands more were butchered in the civil war that never ends. I felt profoundly sorry for these people. We were lucky to escape it all.

November 26, Malakal to Khartoum

Ewald and I took off early, with Gibbs departing half an hour later for the staggered arrival into Peloch. The White Nile curved to the north-east of the city and we followed its course, keeping high and well out of range of any lurking militia. After an hour's flight, Peloch appeared in the distance and we radioed in requesting clearance to land with a technical issue, which by law they couldn't refuse. We taxied in off the runway and were immediately surrounded by men in military fatigues bearing machine guns. Ewald told them we had an ignition problem and immediately started to unpack the tools from the back locker of the Stearman and opened the engine cowlings, while they stood watching. He made a great show of removing several spark plugs and a few minutes later, right on cue, Gibbs landed and taxied over to park up next to us. With this distraction, I climbed onto the top wing while Ewald handed me the jerry cans to get it quickly refuelled.

Sam now went with some of the guards to the tower to explain our predicament and to elicit a drum of kerosene for the Caravan. He came back to collect our passports and then returned to the tower. Sometime after this, an aggressive soldier loaded us all onto two pick-up trucks and we were driven away from the airport. We had no idea where we were going and kept glancing at each other doubtfully. We didn't know if these men were government forces or an independent militia group, but they were evidently guarding the oil fields and the airport was the centre of their strategic operations. After a few minutes, we pulled up at a building and filed into an office to meet the local commander. Also dressed in military fatigues, this man spoke good English and was surprisingly pleasant, but he kept us there for an hour while he interrogated us about the flight. To our relief, they finally took us back to the airport and Sam again went to the tower in another attempt to expedite our departure. The controllers were apparently waiting for clearance from Khartoum but as the day wore on we started to get concerned that time was running out. We had managed to refuel both aircraft but still had more than four hours of flying to get to Khartoum and had to land before sunset. Another hour slipped by and the timing was now critical. The atmosphere was getting increasingly strained and Ewald had an angry exchange with two of the soldiers when he asked for our passports to be returned. They eventually obliged and after nearly four tortuous hours on the ground, they finally let us go.

It was a long, hot, exhausting flight to Khartoum. The arid scrub gave way to flat, featureless desert with whirling dust eddies and it was almost impossible to distinguish the occasional small town or village below from the sand which surrounded them. We flew over Kosti, where Lady Heath had landed, but there was no evidence of the runway which had been there in former times. The Stearman felt heavy and sluggish in the intense heat and it was proving difficult to gain height. I tried to ease up to 5,000 ft, the height we needed to be for our approach into the international airport. After several weary hours in the air, Khartoum finally appeared, spread out in the distance with the sun already below the horizon. We had only a few minutes to get on the ground before we lost the light altogether and now Ewald became concerned that we might get diverted because of the approach of an airliner which was still a few miles out. Such a diversion would have meant landing in the dark and, as I was already on a long final approach for the runway, I shoved the nose of the Stearman down and went to full throttle to keep our speed up to retain our number one position to land. Flying at 120 knots right up to the runway threshold, I landed on the front wheels and kept coasting down the centre-line with the tail up to expedite taxiing off at the next exit. I felt completely drained but light-headed with relief as we followed a guiding vehicle onto a big apron area before shutting down the engine. It had been one hell of a day.

We were met by Sam's agent, a pleasant westerner who helped

us push the Stearman into a small hangar. It was now nearly dark and as we entered the terminal building we were met by a small group of Sudanese officials in long white robes, evidently sent by Al Fatih to meet us. They escorted us through the building and, within an hour of landing, we were checked into the hotel, which must have been a record for the expedition. The hotel was modern and spacious with big fans rotating on the ceilings of our rooms and running water. Malakal was all but forgotten.

After a long, cool shower, we once again loaded into taxis and went for dinner at one of Khartoum's finest restaurants, a vast Aladdin's cave with tables set on two levels around a stage for a floor show. We ordered a banquet of Sudanese dishes but it was nearly two hours before the food arrived. By this time, I was slumped at the table, too tired to eat. It was nearly midnight before we got back to the hotel but the rest of the crew enjoyed it.

We were scheduled to film all the next day so, as usual, it was an early start and I was keen to see the city. Khartoum was founded by the Egyptians in 1821, which seemed surprisingly recent. There was a much older settlement 15 miles to the south, the ancient city of Soba, but we hadn't seen anything in the fading light of the previous evening. Ali Pasha, the ruler of Egypt, had incorporated Sudan into his realm and established Khartoum as a military outpost. It had grown rapidly into a regional centre of commerce and a hub for the slave trade and became the capital of Sudan. It lies in the confluence of the two main tributaries of the Nile – the White Nile, which we had been following from Juba, and the Blue Nile which flows west from Lake Tana in Ethiopia. From this confluence, the Nile widens and reaches its full majestic volume.

I had read about the Siege of Khartoum in 1884, which had been immortalised in the Hollywood film *Khartoum*, starring Charlton Heston in the lead role as British army officer General Charles Gordon. It is a story that resonates in modern times. A Muslim religious leader, Muhamed Ahmed, or the 'Mahdi' as he was known, had risen up and proclaimed a jihad against the Egyptian state in the early 1880s. The long exploitation of Sudan by Egypt led many Sudanese to rally to the Mahdi's black banner as he promised to expel the Egyptians and establish an Islamic fundamentalist caliphate. General Gordon, a famous British war hero, was called back to his post as Governor General of Sudan to counter the Islamist threat. At the outset of the conflict, the British government had cynically decided to abandon Sudan and Gordon was under orders to evacuate troops and civilians from the city. He disobeyed those orders, perceiving the conflict to be a kind of holy war with himself in the role of Christian saviour, and continued to hold out against the forces of the Mahdi during the year long siege. In early 1885, the Anglo-Egyptian defenders were finally overwhelmed and in the dramatic denouement, General Gordon was hacked down by the Mahdi's forces on the stairs of the governor's palace and beheaded. In a macabre triumph, his head was paraded around the city and the news of his killing caused outrage and an outpouring of public grief across Britain. The British took their revenge a few years later in the Battle of Omdurman, when General Horatio Kitchener, with a 20,000 strong army, annihilated the Mahdist forces and retook Khartoum. The Mahdi had died the year before but Kitchener now ordered the destruction of his tomb and in Winston Churchill's words 'carried off the Mahdi's head in a kerosene can as a trophy' – a grotesque eye for an eye.

I wanted to see where some of this epic conflict had played out, so we drove across one of the bridges to the western bank of the Nile to Omdurman to visit the new tomb of the Mahdi and the Khalifa House Museum where the Mahdi's successor had lived. The house was a low, square adobe building in the traditional Islamic style with a series of walled courtyards. There was an old maxim gun in the main courtyard and a stone cupola salvaged from the ruins of the original tomb. Inside were empty cool, dark rooms with beamed ceilings but one had a single leather library chair in one corner which had belonged to General Gordon and beside a glass box displayed the letter which the Mahdi had written to his adversary urging him to surrender. The letter, a single page, was couched in polite terms which barely concealed the aggression of the content. And the chair. Was this where Gordon had sat, calmly contemplating his own death? The fate of both men was sealed and they died within six months of each other.

The National Museum of Sudan was our next port of call and this was back in Khartoum, right in the apex of the confluence of the White and Blue Niles. We were met by museum staff at the entrance and were able to film some of the wonderful Nubian artefacts housed there.

Ewald and Gibbs came to meet us at the museum and then we all went down to the jetty where Annette's lovely friend, Al Fatih, arranged for us to cruise up the Nile on a big motor launch. A whole delegation of Sudanese officials came to meet us and we had a very convivial time, touring up the river in the late afternoon sun and talking with our hosts. Al Fatih extended a generous dinner invitation to the crew but I declined, opting instead for a quiet dinner at the hotel and an early night. Ewald also stayed back and we ended up getting the maps out as usual and planning for the next stage of the flight.

NOVEMBER 28, KHARTOUM TO DONGOLA

Annette knocked urgently at my door early the next morning, absolutely distraught. At Al Fatih's dinner the night before one of the highest ranking members of the Sudanese government had also attended and confronted her with the charge that we had entered the Republic of Sudan illegally. It transpired that the immigration forms that were filed at the airport entered the film crew as flight crew. Annette was appalled by what had been done on the crew's behalf and deeply embarrassed by the whole situation. One can only guess at the position that Al Fatih had been put in. This now caused an argument at the highest level and the Director of Civil Aviation wanted us arrested and put in prison. Al Fatih was somehow able to prevail and instead we were declared persona non grata and told to leave Khartoum immediately. It was a bitter, ignominious curtailment and we now hastily packed our bags and scrambled to the airport in a very subdued mood. We were told to proceed directly to Dongola nearly 280 miles to the north, where we would be under house arrest until our Egyptian permits came through.

The flight from Khartoum was going to be one of the highlights of the whole expedition. We were going to fly the Nile valley which sweeps in a broad curve to the east and north, filming the *Spirit of Artemis* against the spectacular backdrop of Nubian pyramids. There were over 200 pyramids in three groups and they had been built by the rulers of the ancient Kushite kingdoms. Their appearance is quite different to their Egyptian counterparts. They were constructed from granite and sandstone and are much smaller and steeper in profile.

But we were denied all of that. I can't imagine that I will ever have that kind of opportunity again and the loss to the film was incalculable.

We flew straight out over the Nubian Desert on a north-westerly course. Two-thirds of the way, we picked up the Nile again for the final stretch into Dongola. It was a remote and isolated place – a single runway in barren desert and there was a crosswind blowing as we approached to land on the northern vector. I rolled down the runway before finally turning off to the right towards the control tower. There was a little deputation to meet us and we all shook hands solemnly. I tried to lighten things by complimenting them on their runway which was a perfectly smooth asphalt strip. Evidently not many aircraft landed here, certainly nothing like a Stearman. They were very polite, hospitable people and several of them helped us push the aeroplane into a low covered area off to the side, where it remained grounded for the next two days.

We were taken to a small government lodge on the riverbank and each of us was allocated a little roundel hut. These were basic with tiny closet-like bathrooms and an intermittent power supply. The absence of air conditioning made sleeping difficult and the nights were spent lying in the suffocating darkness, dripping with perspiration, waiting for the dawn.

The governor of Dongola came to meet us and, by coincidence, his name was also Al Fatih, but no relation to Annette's friend in Khartoum. This Al Fatih was a very tall, dignified man dressed in the long traditional white robe and a large white turban adorned his head. He was very sympathetic and observed quietly that we had been badly let down. That was the only reference he made to our disgrace, as he seemed intent on looking after us, perhaps because Annette and I were women. The governor joined us again that evening and was curious to hear more about the flight. However, he shook his head at the thought of flying himself. As a man of the desert his camel was his ship. When he wanted to feel free and at one with nature, he rode deep into the desert and camped out under the stars. I responded that flying through the desert brought the same feeling of space and infinity.

Although we were officially under house arrest, Al Fatih gave permission for us to visit an archaeological site to the north of the town and kindly arranged for two cars to collect us first thing the next morning. We passed through several villages on our way and had the fleeting impression of toil and hard living in a pre-industrial age. There were no machines. People laboured in the wheat fields and threshing was done by hand on mats at the side of the road. Crouching figures rotated big circular trays as they sifted the grains from the chaff, like miners panning for gold. But the thing which really struck me was the blue doors, set into sun-bleached, adobe walls like jewels, which flashed a bright, cerulean blue as we drove past. These doors were always closed but it was tempting to imagine that they opened upon fountained courtyards and secret gardens that we were never privileged to see.

We arrived at the museum to find, not surprisingly, we were the only visitors. We entered a cool, white-washed stone building and in the foyer on a table was a large platter of dates, treacle-dark and fly-blown. I wasn't tempted, but it was typical of Sudanese hospitality. The artefacts were sparse but this minimalism seemed to enhance the significance of what was there. The centrepiece, bathed in white light, was two towering superhuman figures carved in dark granite. These were the black pharaohs of Nubia, the ancient Napatan kings who predated the Egyptian pharaohs and controlled Egypt for hundreds of years. We lingered for several minutes to marvel.

Beyond these, and in the open area outside, was another entirely unexpected sight – a huge crumbling Sphinx-like figure crouching on the hard dry earth, its paws extended and the face badly eroded by the elements. We could now see the entire perimeter of the site and this was marked by old, fortified walls with a tower and we walked up to take in the view of the open desert beyond. I couldn't resist extending my arms and closing my eyes, wishing I really could fly off like a bird.

On the way back to our lodging, we stopped for refreshments at a little open cafe serving coffee. Several old men sat in robes and turbans but barely acknowledged our presence. Women were noticeably absent. A strange thing happens in Muslim north Africa – the women seem to disappear. They are mere shadows, shrouded in dark fabric, obscure and vanishing through dark doorways. This is in startling contrast to sub-Saharan Africa where women festoon the streets in brilliantly coloured fabrics and elaborate turbans. They fill the marketplaces and run the fruit stands at the side of the road, the beating life of Africa.

Al Fatih invited us to lunch, which was a formal affair. We were told to arrive at 3pm and trestle tables had been set out for a buffet with more tables laid out with white cloths and napkins. With uncharacteristic reserve, the crew hesitated on the threshold and Matt urged me to start first. Trays of food were brought in and as I approached the main table I gasped with horror when I saw the main course. There, on a steaming bed of rice, was the freshly boiled foetus of a lamb. I stood rooted to the spot and Gibbs, who was standing right behind me, whispered dramatically, 'The Silence of the Lamb …'

We all packed up laughing at what turned out to be the best line of the whole expedition. I resolutely took up a plate and the boys followed suit. They did their best with the banquet but it was beyond me to eat this, even though I knew our host was extending a great courtesy and this had been done in our honour.

That night, we drove into the desert to see the stars and cooked up a feast of beans over a small campfire, another arranged scene for the film. Ewald and I sat on the ground with our bowls and bread feeling ridiculous, while Matt and Joao filmed around the edge of us. God knows what our Sudanese escorts were thinking: stupid bloody tourists, I suspect.

But the heavens were incomparable in that pure desert air and there was no moon to dilute the brilliant spray of diamonds across the vaulting darkness. I saw several shooting stars and found myself wishing, but for what? I didn't even know anymore. Of course, I wanted us all to get back home safely, but beyond that was a void as vast as the night. When we climbed back into the car, we discovered several scorpions had joined us. Our guide, who had gathered the wood for our campfire, had evidently picked up one or two of these little stingers in his clothing and he yelled for the driver to stop as he leapt out and shook himself off.

We got back to our lodgings at about 10 pm and got ready for bed, anticipating yet another day of hanging around. At 8.30am the next morning, however, Sam advised that permission had come through. We were on the move again.

DECEMBER 1, DONGOLA TO ASWAN

In a mood of distraction, I really had no great expectation of the flight ahead. Once we got off the ground, however, the grandeur overtook everything else. The 330-mile journey from Dongala to Aswan, in Egypt, was mind blowing.

Our first objective was to try to capture the sphynx we had seen the day before on the GoPro cameras. I was going to do a low pass over the site so we tracked the Nile from Dongola and within a few short miles it was easy to see the ruins lit up in the morning sun. I told Ewald to keep his eyes peeled for cell towers, which were always a potential hazard with such low flying, and then positioned for the pass. We roared down and swept low over the ramparts of the old fort and curled past the crouching figure in a topside pass and then pulled up over the palm trees on the far side. It was more fun than I'd had in days and I whooped with joy. The slender white spires of the many mosques rose above the trees like delicately carved ivory towers as we continued down the swathe of green along the side of the Nile.

Lady Heath avoided the desert where she could and flew at high altitude over the river to keep her engine cool. In her memoir she wrote about 'her lovely Nile' – her green corridor to Cairo and it made navigating a breeze. To while away the time, she read a novel and ate chocolates, glancing down periodically to make sure she was on course during the nine-hour flight from Wadi Halfa. When Cairo appeared in the distance, she declared it to be the most beautiful thing she had ever seen and managed to take a few photographs of the pyramids and the Sphinx.

We followed the river for a short time but I couldn't resist the greater allure of the open desert and steered off into that vast, glowing empty seabed. The Caravan came to join us for a few minutes for some air-to-air filming and Matt captured a lovely sequence of the Stearman against this immensity.

Further ahead, we picked up the Nile and now we were looking for more ancient ruins and small pyramids somewhere ahead which we hoped to pick up on the GoPro cameras, a futile if amusing exercise. It was impossible to detect the antiquities from more recent buildings because they were all made from mud. They looked as if they had been fashioned straight out of the ground, like clay pots. We gave up looking and enjoyed the sights along the river, including the Third Cataract, just to the north of Kerma. After that, I peeled away to the east and back into the lunar landscape of the Sahara.

We were now in the heart of the Nubian Desert and it became more rugged and mountainous with rocky canyons and dry riverbeds. As far as the eye could see were perfect pyramids, naturally formed by geological and atmospheric forces, and on a scale that dwarfed the other more famous man-made ones. It was a staggering spectacle. This geometry seemed to be an intrinsic part of the desert. Were the ancient Nubians and the Egyptians mirroring nature when they built those distinctive pointed necropolises for their dead kings? Having witnessed this phenomenon from the air, I had little doubt.

Ewald and I were in a state of awe for most of the flight and he was making notes for Justin about particularly dramatic sights en route recorded by the GoPros. In the north of Sudan, Lake Nasser came into view, a vast elongated reservoir, one of the largest man-made stretches of water in the world, formed when the Egyptians built the Aswan Dam across the Nile from 1958 to 1970. The part of the lake which extends into Sudan is called Lake Nubia. Once we crossed the border into Egypt we were told by the air traffic controllers to climb to 8,000 ft. We soared up above puffs of fine weather cumulus with the lake below us a deep azure blue against the pale sand of the desert. It had a convoluted shoreline of coves and bays but we were too high to see any detail. There was no fuel at Abu Simbel, as Sam had previously told us, so we didn't stop there but carried on to Aswan. Thus, we also missed the Nubian statues which had been relocated when the area was flooded.

After a four-hour-plus flight, we landed at Aswan. The famous dam and the sand dunes, high as mountains made for spectacular views. Feluccas with full breasted sails tacked across the wide expanse of the river and invested the scene with a timeless beauty.

We stayed at a modern hotel on the west bank and behind us the dunes formed a high ridge rimmed with gold which plunged in dark purple shadows straight into the Nile. The crew congregated on the roof-top terrace of the hotel for refreshments and we were thrilled to find a large swimming pool. The heat was still intense and Joao was so hot he just stepped sideways and dropped into the water, fully clothed. Justin followed suit and the pair of them bobbed around while everybody else laughed and went to change into their bathing costumes. I threw myself down on a sun lounger in the shade, incapable of speech or anything else for that matter. I was still punch-drunk from the flight and just lay there back in the moment, back in the desert. It was always an anticlimax being back on the ground.

That evening, when things had cooled down, we caught a ferry across the river and walked a short distance along the bustling waterfront to the souk. The Egyptians were plying their souvenirs and imploring us to buy something. I felt desperately sorry for them. They'd had a terrible time since the Arab Spring of 2010, the aftermath of which brought the virtual shutdown of the Egyptian tourist industry. One vendor, eager for a sale, draped a silk scarf in soft saffron yellow around my shoulders as a gift. It was remarkable how some of the most indigent people on Earth are also the most generous. We bought a few things, scarves, scarabs and small bronze statues of Isis and Anubis before tearing ourselves away.

We remained in Aswan the next day and, as it was Ewald's birthday, decided to have a celebratory dinner at the hotel that night. This started off pleasantly enough with a few cocktails and toasts, but the tensions running below the surface were never far away. The debate now was about the route ahead and whether we should go to Libya as provisionally planned. The security situation was getting worse but Sam insisted it would be perfectly safe to transit through. His good friend, Hadi, had a reliable network and by their reckoning our risk would be minimal given that we just had to get to and from the airports. The rest of us disagreed and it was a clear 7-1 vote against going. That led to a heated argument with the crew and some were unwilling or uncomfortable to go to Libya.

DECEMBER 3, ASWAN TO LUXOR

It was a short flight of just over 100 miles the next morning to Luxor and when we arrived we were met by a swarm of Egyptians and some local press, including one very suave character, dressed in a white linen suit, who looked as if he had stepped straight out of the 1920s. He was a fixer by the name of Fuad and he came with us everywhere for the next two days.

We stayed at the grand old Winter Palace Hotel right on the river with a sweeping view across to the west bank. The thrilling view from the balcony of my room on the top floor was one I had seen so often before but only in old Imperial Airways posters. Now, with half closed eyes, I could see again the great silver flying boats of the 1920s and 30s landing out there on the water. The wealthy passengers would have disembarked onto tenders and been whisked up to the jetty in front of the Winter Palace Hotel. From there they would have been ushered by white uniformed waiters onto the paved terrace and up the sweeping double staircase into the lobby. I didn't think very much had changed. The place was redolent of old-world glamour with tall, gently swaying palms and balustraded formal gardens. There were vaulted reception rooms with acres of Axminster carpets and large gilt-framed oil paintings hung on every wall. Next to a large potted palm was a particularly fine portrait of Lord Byron, theatrically dressed in oriental robes with a dramatic swirl of fabric around his dark head, which perfectly framed the handsome features. Perhaps more than any other figure in history, Byron is the embodiment of the restless romantic in search of risk and adventure – the ultimate outsider. I was pretty sure Byron had never been to Egypt but our paths would cross again in Greece.

The Temple of Luxor, the Valley of the Kings, the Valley of the Queens – these wonderful sights were all there but I didn't get to see any of them. The next day we went filming at Karnak, which required a degree of discretion, as cameras are treated with suspicion in Egypt. Matt, Joao, Ewald, Gibbs and I had a lovely morning meandering through the huge, fluted columns and statues of this extraordinary temple. That is, I meandered and they filmed with a small camera which resembled a conventional one but could film as well. I was dwarfed by the columns which looked disproportionately large and unreal, as if the whole thing was a movie set. That evening we did more filming in the grand old bar at the hotel. We laid our maps on the bar and discussed the pros and cons of flying through Libya versus heading straight across the Mediterranean to Crete. This was all entirely contrived for the film, as we had already made the decision in Aswan, but now we talked about the historical perspective of Lady Heath's flight. Her route took her across north Africa across Libya to Tunisia and then across the sea to Catania. It was the shortest crossing over the Mediterranean and Mary chose this way for good reason – she was terrified of flying over water. As a girl, she had nearly drowned swimming in the sea off the Irish coast and wasn't taking any chances in her aeroplane.

Our problem was of a different nature altogether. In 2013,

Libya was in the throes of a civil war after the deposing of Colonel Gaddafi during the insurgency of the Arab Spring. The conflict among the rival factions had flared up again and, even as we had been flying up Africa, there were reports of fighting around Tripoli and Benghazi and several westerners had been kidnapped. Interestingly, Lady Heath had been shot at while flying across Libya in 1928 but she was blissfully unaware that she was a target at the time. It was only the discovery of a bullet hole in the wing of the Avian when she landed at Tunis that revealed the true peril. This was a cautionary tale. However much I longed to fly Mary's route, I felt it insane to expose the crew to the risk.

But I sought further advice. Several months before, the Assistant Chief of the Air Staff, Air Vice Marshal Edward Stringer, had offered to help with the expedition and had very kindly appointed an adviser from the Ministry of Defence to talk us through the security issues. I had met with this officer at Shuttleworth with Sam in the September before our departure. While in Sudan, I had asked Sam whether he had been in contact with this advisor to get an updated report on Libya. He hadn't. When I phoned Edward Stringer from Luxor his advice was unequivocal. On no account should we proceed to Libya and he recommended we get out of Egypt as soon as possible.

While the Egyptian press was reporting with pride that the 'oldest aeroplane' in the world was flying up Egypt, they made our lives hell in the air. Since entering Egyptian airspace we were under strict military air traffic control and tracked on radar. The air traffic controllers reported directly to the authoritarian military regime and no deviation was tolerated regardless of the weather conditions. They wanted us flying the instrument airways at altitudes that were difficult, if not impossible, in a vintage aeroplane and there seemed to be a terrible kind of paranoia about their insistence. We realised this was fear. The air traffic controllers were terrified of the military and the consequences of doing something wrong and this, in turn, made our experience of flying through Egypt deeply unpleasant and stressful. The best of the flying was finished as far as I was concerned.

Before we were able to get away from Luxor we were mobbed by people and press. Various officials milled around the Stearman posing for photographs and others clamoured to sit in the cockpit. I was up on the wing refuelling the Stearman and when the tank overfilled, sending a small spillage of fuel onto the tarmac, it prompted a scream of abuse from an airport official. Feeling incredibly hassled by all of them and just wanting to get away, I urged Justin to hurry up with the cameras. Thankfully, nothing was damaged and we finally started up and taxied away but, as I waited for take-off clearance, I suddenly realised I'd left my flying jacket in the rear locker of the Stearman. It was too late to stop and retrieve it.

December 5, Luxor to Cairo

For the 300 miles to Cairo, we had headwinds all the way. Straight after take-off, I had to keep climbing to the specified altitude and the groundspeed fell away to 50mph with the high nose attitude of the Stearman and the increasing headwind. The controller kept shrieking at me over the radio that I was too slow, as if he feared I was going to stall. He would have seen me on his radar screen but didn't appreciate the difference between the true airspeed of the aircraft and the speed at which it travelled over the ground, which can change dramatically according to the wind. I finally levelled out at 8,000 ft but it continued to be slow progress with a 25-knot headwind. After flying for 40 minutes at that altitude, I requested a lower level where the wind wasn't so strong but the controller wasn't having any of it insisting we stay at 8,000 ft or turn back. It was miserable.

Flying this slowly raised the prospect of running out of fuel before we reached our destination and we kept a close eye on the situation. To make matters worse, I got colder and colder without my flying jacket. The ambient temperature was about 10°C but there was an added wind chill factor with the open cockpit. I hunched down in my seat with my teeth chattering and thought longingly of a cup of hot tea. It was a painfully slow flight and there was nothing to see from that high altitude. Nearly five hours later, we finally landed at the strangely named October 6 Airport on the outskirts of Cairo. By now I was rigid from the cold and I couldn't feel my feet. I dragged myself out of the cockpit and tottered down the wing and Ewald caught me as I fell off. Now safely on the ground it was possible to laugh at the situation.

The date of the airport's name underscores the pre-eminence of the military and commemorates the start of the Arab-Israeli War in 1973. It is also Egypt's Armed Forces Day. The airport is 20 miles to the south-west of Cairo and about 11 miles from the Sphinx and the Great Pyramids at Giza. It lies in open desert and alongside the runway and scattered around were the sundry wrecks of crashed aeroplanes. After landing, we were ushered into the little aero club where our Egyptian handlers were based and plied with hot drinks and biscuits. General Aviation Support Egypt (GASE) had been set up by a British expatriate and aviation enthusiast, Eddie Gould, and his Egyptian partner, Ahmed Hassan, to promote and support general aviation in Egypt. With a team of dedicated volunteers, they provided a full support service to visiting aircraft transiting through Egypt, so we were in very good hands and they couldn't do enough for us. Eddie was a delightful character, full of stories as one might expect from a native Liverpudlian living abroad. He had married an Egyptian woman and lived in Cairo for more than 20 years so he was well attuned to the vagaries of Egyptian politics and was circumspect about the military dictatorship. To my great relief, the volunteers pushed the Stearman into a private facility belonging to General

Badran, a retired military commander. At least security was not going to be a problem.

The night drive into Cairo took nearly two hours in gridlocked traffic. It was late by the time we pulled up at our hotel and we were met by several security guards and told to wait. It was exhausting but we finally got checked in 40 minutes later. The hotel was a high-rise tower on the bank of the Nile and for the first time I started to get some sense of the city. I had a fantastic view of the river from my room on one of the top floors and it shone like a great ribbon of light through the darkness. It was spectacularly lit up on each bank with bridges arcing across like rainbows and sundry boats darting and flickering across the surface, in a glow of reflected neon.

It was the next day before it dawned on me that we had completed the famous, time-honoured Cape to Cairo route and I felt a wave of sadness that Africa was behind us now. It also made me realise how superficial and inconsequential are these human milestones. One leaves a city and arrives in another 8,000 miles away, but the sense of achievement at arriving is almost immediately overtaken by the desire to leave again.

Annette had arranged a surprise meeting with an interesting man called Marius Cipolla, the grandson of Emil Millin, one of the drivers on the Chrysler Cape to London expedition. Emil had met Lady Heath in Johannesburg and the two expeditions, her flight and the driving team in their Chrysler car, had teamed up in a wings and wheels jamboree up Africa to augment publicity. I was amazed that Annette had managed to find Marius and it was rather wonderful that he lived in Africa. I was very keen to hear the family story. We drove through the suburbs to his house and approached up a short flight of stairs.

Marius was waiting to greet us at the top, smiling broadly and with his arms open in welcome. He was a large man with an extraordinarily beautiful face with huge, serious green eyes. A writer by profession, he spoke of his grandfather with poignance, as if he too would rather have lived in that earlier era. On his kitchen table he had laid out all sorts of interesting bits of memorabilia to show us: Emil's diary, letters, and various photographs from the Chrysler expedition and he spoke at length about the romance and beauty of these old adventures. I was intrigued to hear that Marius believed that his grandfather and Lady Heath had had a brief affair during their time in Southern Africa. Marius was uncertain whether they had ever met up again after parting company in Abercorn.

After we left Marius we continued to the airport to join Ewald and Gibbs, who had spent the day working on the Stearman. It had been a great hit with the locals. A small crowd of student pilots and enthusiasts had turned up to take pictures and Ewald had done a brilliant PR job letting them sit, one by one, in the rear cockpit. After he completed the maintenance programme, he also adjusted the tensioning on the tail wheel cables to reduce the shimmy on the wheel during taxying. Ewald wanted to do some high-speed taxi runs on the runway to check this and he took Allah, the engineer and hangar caretaker, along with him for the ride. Allah was beaming after the ground ride. I smiled to think what his reaction might have been had he got airborne, but, sadly, we didn't have time to take him flying.

DECEMBER 7, CAIRO TO MERSA MATRUH

We woke to a blanket of smog cloaking the river and the city but, by the time we left the hotel at 8.20am and completed the 45-minute drive to the airport, it had dissipated to a fine mist. It was completely surreal to see a glimpse of the pyramids through the apartment blocks as we drove through the urban sprawl that is Giza and tried to imagine waking up to that view every morning.

The film crew were packing up their equipment and Ewald

and I were reviewing our flight plan to Mersa Matruh when we suddenly became aware of an altercation in the hangar with raised angry voices. Sam and Eddie were arguing about fuel. Apparently there was none at Mersa Matruh so we would have to divert to Alamein and spend the night while fuel was delivered. I felt at the heart of this quarrel was inadequate forward preparation and lack of communication. Had Eddie been advised of our requirements in advance he could have got everything set up.

Despite the last-minute arrangements and negotiations about fuel, we got away just after 9am. I was cheered to find myself speaking to a female air traffic controller as we taxied out, something of a rarity in this part of the world. But now we were up against the same old issue of flight altitude. The controller wanted us to climb to 8,000 ft overhead the field and this took nearly 40 minutes of flying round and round in a big ascending holding pattern before we could set heading and get on our way.

We finally headed north-west and I could see Alexandria out to the east. It was desert below but very soon the Mediterranean came into view, a vast blue line rising above the horizon. The coast marked the true geographic end of Africa and we turned left along the shoreline, tracking west.

We were heading for Alamein but, halfway through the flight, Gibbs radioed through from the Caravan and told us to continue to Mersa Matruh. Apparently they had been able to confirm there was fuel available and this was very welcome news. We reverted to our original plan and carried on. It was something to fly over the top of Alamein, site of the famous battle in the Second World War in 1942 where Montgomery prevailed over Rommel with his German Panzers. It had been a tremendous victory and a much-needed morale boost for the Allied forces. Churchill wrote after the war: 'Before Alamein we never had a victory. After Alamein, we never had a defeat.'

Mersa Matruh was a military airport which is not always

terribly conducive to civilian operations. We had already experienced the constraints with the military-controlled air traffic control and now we were going to get a taste of it on the ground. It was a big airport with two crossed runways, each 3,000 metres in length. There were some huge hangars off to the side but we taxied over to what appeared to be a civilian terminal. Several soldiers came to meet us but they weren't exactly friendly, their manner was curt and most of them didn't make eye contact, no doubt because I was a woman. A fuel truck duly appeared and I climbed onto the top wing to take the proffered hose. The nozzle was too big for the Stearman's fuel tanks and, as it was a pressurised delivery, it was hellishly difficult to control the flow. Some of the Avgas flooded down the wing onto the tarmac. I grimaced and half expected the Egyptians to shout at me as they had done in Luxor, but the soldiers didn't react. Despite the huge facilities around us, the Egyptians said there was no hangarage available, so we anchored it to the apron and pulled the covers on. It struck me as being very inhospitable.

We were then taken in a minibus to the terminal and processed through with our bags and equipment. We were all in high spirits and longing to see the Mediterranean. Thankfully, a beachfront hotel was just a mile or two from the airport and we yelled at the taxi driver to stop and piled out. We crowded into the reception, overloaded with bags and the sea was beckoning through the glass doors at the opposite end. I dropped my luggage and went straight out the door, running down the beach, laughing with joy. I ran straight into the foaming back-wash of a retreating wave and caught the sea water in my hands. The rest of the crew followed me down and, brilliantly, Annette arranged for the hotel staff to bring us out a couple of bottles of champagne in ice buckets to celebrate the moment. Corks were exploding into the air amidst great jubilation and glasses raised to each other, to the Mediterranean, to Africa, and just being there. It was a euphoric moment and I already felt drunk without taking a drop of alcohol.

That was our happy hour on the beach. Further up and set in the sand were two small fairground horses, one black and one white, racing towards the surf. They were for children but Annette and I couldn't resist going for a ride. We tripped over clutching our champagne glasses and climbed into the saddle. There we sat for the next half an hour talking and laughing with our steeds beneath us in one endless, eternal gallop.

This wasn't the hotel where we stayed the night. Sam had arranged another place and we collected our bags and went in a hotel minibus to a ghastly marble palace nearly an hour's drive away, which was devoid of anything, including other guests. No doubt, this would have been pleasant accommodation for a tour group but for a crew in transit like us it was pointless and inconvenient being this far away from the airport. We should have stayed where we were and enjoyed the evening but the mood had gone sadly flat by the time we arrived. And we had the same drive again first thing tomorrow morning ahead of our Mediterranean crossing.

By then, however, we had a more serious problem on our hands. A deep weather depression had been building in the eastern Mediterranean and, looking at the forecast, we had a very narrow window of opportunity to get to Crete before it overtook us. We had to get out the next day or risk getting stuck for several days while the storm passed. Even as we drove to the airport, the sky had an ominous hue and the wind was already picking up. We didn't have a second to lose. We moved smartly through the airport and rapidly went through our preparations. Ewald and I strapped in and taxied briskly out to the holding point for the engine run up. As I increased the power to check the magnetos, there were a couple of loud bangs as the engine detonated. I nearly jumped out of my skin at these explosions which sounded like gunshots. This had never happened before and I swore violently at the truly awful timing. How was it possible to have a technical problem at this extraordinarily critical moment? I tried again with the ignition, flicking the switch first onto the left magneto and then onto the right, with the same explosive response. I had no choice but to cancel our clearance and taxi back to the ramp. The rest of the crew came to meet us as I shut down the engine and got out. Ewald practically vaulted out of his seat and was down the wing and into the rear locker getting the tool kit out. In a matter of minutes, he had the engine cowls bolted open and was removing the magnetos to take a closer look. I was in an agony of apprehension, hovering over him and casting doubtful looks at the sky.

We were there on the ramp for the next six hours kneeling on the tarmac while Ewald tried to fix it. Joao joined us and the Egyptian guards hovered around but generally left us to our own devices. Nobody was allowed to go anywhere unescorted, not even to the lavatories in the terminal building. Annette and I were taken into the terminal with an armed guard for a relief stop. There was a little cafe inside the building and we managed to get some hot tea to take out for Ewald and Joao. While we were waiting for the drinks to be prepared, I happened to spot some rolled carpets in a corner of the terminal and thinking these might be for sale, walked up to take a closer look. They turned out to be prayer mats and I chuckled at my mistake and the lost shopping opportunity. Several times a day these mats were rolled out in the terminal for the airport staff to pray and everything else would grind to a halt while this ritual took place.

We returned to our vigil in the minibus while Ewald toiled on trying to resolve the problem. He installed a new double magneto which we carried as a spare but, frustratingly, this didn't work either. He now painstakingly rechecked the rest of the ignition system and found that once again, the problem seemed to be in the new magneto which he had just installed. It was perplexing.

After a long and frustrating day, by late afternoon we decided to throw in the towel and find a hotel for the night. There was no question of returning to the marble palace, so we went back to the first hotel where we had champagne on the beach and, thankfully, they were able to accommodate us. We immediately took over the small lounge just off the reception area and Ewald sat down with the two magnetos and disassembled both on the coffee table. As the night wore on, there was still no solution.

In the meantime, Matt, Joao and Sam went out into the town in search of food and returned with the news they had found a garage in the backstreets which specialised in motorbike repairs and, crucially, magnetos. Ewald packed up and the boys returned to the garage together. After much deliberation the Egyptian mechanics declared all four of the electrical coils to be unservice-able and suggested welding in new ones. Ewald knew this wasn't the case and he stopped them before they inadvertently caused even more damage. This had all taken hours and it was after midnight before they returned to the hotel.

Ewald and Joao left again for the airport first thing. Together they started from scratch, working systematically to diagnose the problem. Both magnetos were now completely disassembled and Ewald proceeded to build a new one, made up of the good parts from each unit. After making the internal adjustments, this hybrid magneto was installed back into the Stearman. They were able to start the engine but it was still running badly on one magneto. After several more starts, with tuning adjustments each time, they got it running smoothly and within test limits.

It was now early afternoon but too late for us to file the flight plan with the Egyptian military. The weather was already closing in. The rest of us went to join them and sat in a minibus close by. Matt surreptitiously set up one of the cameras in the Caravan and started filming discretely through the open door while I stood in front explaining what had happened. It was now blowing a gale and my hair was whipped up into tangled rat tails as I brushed it out of my eyes, glancing nervously around to see if there were any guards watching our covert activity.

We clearly weren't going to get away that day and the challenge was how to protect the Stearman from the approaching storm. We implored the Egyptians for hangarage but were once again rebuffed. Casting around, Ewald now had the idea of using two industrial steel baggage trolleys parked up nearby. It was all hands to the pumps as we dragged these over to the Stearman and positioned them off the end of each wing and anchored everything with ropes. We also secured the tail and chocked the wheels. One of the more helpful Egyptians, warming to the theme, suggested he could park one of the airport buses in front of the Stearman as a windbreak.

Having done our best, we returned to the hotel. Late that afternoon we filmed another interview on the beach near the fairground horses. It was darkly overcast and the sea was already in a high swell with a gusting onshore wind. I was distracted and anxious and it had already started to rain as we wrapped up. The huge storm system was forecast to hit that night with gale force winds. They were even forecasting snow in Cairo. It struck with a vengeance a couple of hours later.

It was the worst to hit the eastern Mediterranean in 20 years and one of the worst nights of my life. Rain fell in slashing sheets and the wind roared like a hurricane, making a sobbing sound as it battered the building in the darkness. The awful racket of breaking glass, doors slamming, and unknown objects crashing into things as they were picked up by the wind and hurled down again in the onslaught. I lay in my room fully dressed on the bed listening to this terrible din, rigid with fear and incapable of sleep. I was in a rictus of anxiety over the Stearman, believing it would be destroyed and there wasn't a single thing we could do about it. This hell lasted through the night and felt as if it would never end. I finally got up in the darkness and sat rocking by the window.

At the first hint of dawn, I slipped down the corridor and tapped quietly on Ewald's door. He was already up and he too hadn't slept a wink. Gibbs then emerged from his room and the three of us went downstairs and arranged for a taxi back to the airport. I can hardly describe the dread as we drove through those desolate, flooded streets.

As we pulled up to the airport gate, however, I could see the Stearman still tied up and sheltering behind the airport bus. Somehow, it had survived the night. The airport wasn't yet open and the gate was locked so we parked up and I stood there gripping the vertical bars of the railing like a prisoner in a cell, nearly crying with relief. The Egyptians, busy with their morning prayers, wouldn't let us enter. They were still rolling their prayer mats up as we hurried through the terminal building half an hour later.

The Stearman had survived but was dripping wet and we removed the covers to try to dry these out in the wind. It was still blowing a gale and some of the guards came to see how the aeroplane had fared. Annette and the rest of the crew arrived but we still had no hope of getting away. I was desperate about the Stearman and we appealed again to the Egyptians for hangarage. I think it was beginning to dawn on them just how awful the situation was: a fabric covered aircraft with wooden wings and an open cockpit out in this punishing weather. They now changed their tune and said that hangarage was available for $500-a-night, an eye-watering sum of money and really taking advantage, but there was no choice. We gratefully accepted and started to untie the Stearman from its unlikely moorings on the baggage wagons.

I slept that night, exhausted but relieved to know that the plane was tucked up safe and sound. The battering winds continued for the next two days. I went filming with Matt and Joao a little way down the coast where we walked out onto a stretch of white sand with a promontory of rock islands. I could hardly stand up in the wind and kept my sunglasses on like goggles because I was getting sand blasted and soaked by the onslaught. The surf crashed on the beach with 15 ft waves and further out we could see white caps rolling in and breaking over the heaving green of the sea. The sky was low and swollen but several shafts of white light pierced the cloud and illuminated the waves in the distance which gave a strange theatrical vividness to the whole scene.

In ancient Egypt, Mersah Matruh was used by the pharaohs as a summer retreat. Cleopatra came here and bathed in the natural rock pool which had formed off the beach and still bears her name. I half expected Matt to ask me to go for a swim in her pool – for the film of course – but we didn't last long in those elements. After 20 minutes, I ran back to the car with the wind carrying me along while Matt lingered on the rocks for one long take of the crashing waves. When we got back to the hotel, we were warned jihadists had arrived in town from neighbouring Libya and Iraq and we would need to be extra vigilant. I laughed out loud at the ludicrousness of the situation. This was all we needed on top of everything else, a pack of murdering Islamist fanatics at the seaside resort where we were stuck. That night we went 10-pin bowling and ordered in pizza for dinner.

December 14, Mersa Matruh to Heraklion

Two more days passed before the wind finally dropped sufficiently for us to attempt the flight across the Mediterranean. We had lost a whole week in Mersa Matruh, it was now mid-December and the cumulative delays through Sudan and Egypt meant we had run out of time. The plan was to fly to Crete and from there most of the crew would disperse. Gibbs needed to get the Caravan back to Nairobi, Ewald needed to get back to Austria and Matt and Joao both had other work deadlines before Christmas.

The Cape Town to Goodwood expedition was not over,

however. There were still over 2,000 miles to fly and I was faced with the daunting prospect of getting the Stearman back across Europe on my own in the middle of winter.

Sam offered to help and told Annette he was willing to join me in the Stearman. She warned him his offer would be unwelcome but he brought this up with me over breakfast. Over my toast and marmalade, I ruminated over my response.

Sometime, before the start of the expedition, Sam had asked if he could fly a leg with me and I had readily agreed. Now, he was the last person I wanted in the Stearman.

Finally, I shook my head and said, 'No, Sam. There's nothing you can do to help me.'

Now we just had to get out of Egypt.

We returned to the airport to do another engine run and everything was ready for an early departure the next day. The day dawned, still windy and overcast, but the weather forecast was for improving conditions. I was now so desperate to leave I would have swum the Mediterranean.

I called through to the control tower for a start clearance and the Stearman fired up at the first turn of the propeller. I felt a rush of gratitude towards Ewald for all his tireless efforts.

The military air traffic controller now instructed me to climb to a staggering 16,000 ft with a long detour to the south-east before turning north to pick up the instrument airway to Crete. I should have expected something like this, but I was stupefied. It was an impossible, killing command for an open cockpit biplane without instruments. There was a solid cloud base at 2,000 ft with embedded thunderstorms and I couldn't fly through it, either legally or practically. The Stearman was incapable of reaching such an altitude, which was more applicable to a commercial aircraft with pressurised cabins, heating, anti-ice equipment and oxygen. And we certainly didn't have the fuel for the diversion south especially with 250 miles of water to cross in uncertain winds. I knew then that if I said I couldn't do it, the controllers wouldn't let us take off.

Without missing a beat, I acknowledged the clearance and repeated it back to the controller. With that I taxied onto the runway, kicked the Stearman straight to line up with the centreline and went smoothly to full power. The engine surged to maximum revolutions and the aeroplane accelerated down that long runway, which pointed exactly due north and directly towards the Mediterranean.

We climbed straight ahead at maximum rate right up to the cloud base and then I levelled off, flying just below it to shield the Stearman from the air traffic controllers. We were now over the water and I made one final radio call advising the controllers of our estimated time for leaving Egyptian airspace. Then we conveniently 'lost' radio contact. I also switched off the transponder, so they couldn't track us on radar and, once we were a few miles more out to sea, dropped down to precisely 160 ft over the water which was our own interpretation of 'Flight Level 160'.

Ewald and I laughed heartily at that and now we had several glorious hours over the waves, all on our own except for the occasional ship. With one cargo vessel, we winged past level with the bridge and, as the sailors waved at us, we rocked our wings in response and flew on. The weather improved and finally, after four hours in the air, the snow-covered mountains of Crete appeared, shining on the horizon. It was a marvellous sight.

Crete to Goodwood

December 15, Heraklion to Split

'YASSOS. Kalimera.' The deep, seductive voices of the Greek air traffic controllers were like balm after their Egyptian counterparts and their words of welcome felt like olive branches.

After a fantastic flight over the Mediterranean, the last part was a scenic tour of Crete. We tracked along the coast and did a low-level circumnavigation of the eastern part of the island before coming into land at Heraklion on the northern side. After the dead flatness of miles of sea and sand over the last weeks, the mountains appeared huge and dramatic, Himalayan, even, with their snowy peaks and craggy rock faces. Crete was the mythical land of the Minotaur and the dark labyrinth and the home of that legendary man of wings who had flown too close to the sun, Icarus.

The air traffic controllers in Mersa Matruh knew we had given them the slip and took their revenge on the Caravan when it took off an hour after us. Poor Gibbs was diverted a hundred miles along the east coast and, although he did as he was told, it meant by the time he landed at Crete he was dangerously low on fuel. It was outrageous that the Egyptians would compromise the safety of a flight in this way and I swore I would never again risk my aeroplane in that country.

The Caravan landed around 20 minutes after we did and, after the crew poured out onto the apron, we converged under the wings, hugging and talking excitedly.

As this was our last night together, we were in a mood to

celebrate but it turned out to be a muted affair at the hotel. The staff gave us the use of a small function room to sort out and repack our equipment and this is where we had a round of drinks and a few canapes with our baggage heaped around us in untidy piles. It never ceased to amaze me just how much kit we had hauled up Africa and now the crew had to get it all back to London on commercial airliners as excess baggage. I was going to carry as little as possible, just a few warm clothes, several litres of engine oil, a hair dryer and the usual bulging toilet bag of Estee Lauder and Clarins – vital kit for a female aviator.

It was emotional saying goodbye to everyone the next day. We waved Matt, Joao and Justin off in a taxi from the hotel, and then Annette and I made our way to the airport with Ewald, Gibbs and Sam. Gibbs was the first to take off in the Caravan and we stood waving as he climbed steeply away and headed south for Africa. Annette and I had hatched the plan overnight for her to come with me in the Stearman and we decided to take one of the big professional cameras so that we could carry on with filming. We wrapped up warmly for the long flight ahead, fastened our 'Mae West' life vests as most of the flight was going to be over water again, and climbed in. We were airborne at 10.30am and Ewald was there to wave us off. It felt slightly strange leaving him behind but I hoped that we would be reunited back at the base in Hungary in a few days.

My plan was to track the northern coast of Crete to the farthest point west and then head across the Sea of Crete to the Peloponnese Peninsula. We would need to refuel somewhere in Greece and overnight before pressing on up the coast to Croatia. There was still more than 2,000 miles to cover to get back to England, a fifth of the distance of the whole trip. With decent weather and a following wind, I anticipated this would take between seven and ten days and with any luck we would be home in time for Christmas.

We had a beautiful flight along the Cretan coast for the next hour with the sheer rise of mountains on our left, before we struck out across the water and it wasn't long before we crossed the southernmost Ionian islands, and beyond that were the mountains of the Peloponnese.

I hadn't appreciated how mountainous Greece was until that flight. We had a 10 to 15 knot headwind for most of the way and flying several miles inland in the lee of these mountains I suddenly became aware of downdrafts – and just to underscore the peril, the engine gave a rare cough. My heart lurched in panic.

Thinking this could be the onset of icing in the carburettor, I immediately applied carb heat and and full power, monitoring the engine revolutions. I was also scanning the ground 2,000 ft below for possible places to land in the event of this developing into a more serious problem. Thankfully, however, there was no repetition and the Stearman purred on. I reassured Annette, turned 45° and headed back out towards the coast away from the mountains.

Open cockpit flying is not terribly conducive to conversation because of the roaring engine and wind noise but Annette and I chatted away the whole time. I loved her quick wit and gutsy approach to life. It wasn't everybody who would get into a single-engine aeroplane and fly countless miles over the sea, but Annette was always up for an adventure and there was a distinct *Thelma and Louise* feel about the whole thing and we couldn't help but laugh at the lunacy of it all.

We flew to the east of Kalamata, the city famed for black olives, and could clearly make out the big articulated cranes at the container port which was the largest on the Peloponnese. After nearly 300 miles I started to think about where we could land for the night. I tried both Andravida, a military air base, and Araxos airport but there was no Avgas. I wasn't unduly perturbed and flew on across the Gulf of Patras to the mainland.

Ahead of us was a small town by a lagoon and a couple of miles beyond what appeared to be a small, disused airfield with a short, asphalt runway and hangar. A collection of old jets parked at the end of the runway suggested it was a home-grown museum.

I thought we might find some friendly aviation enthusiasts who could put us up for the night. Going down for a closer look, I saw half a dozen people flying remote-controlled model aircraft, which they soon landed for my approach. I taxied up to the front of the hangar and the group came forward to meet us. I think they were surprised when two women clambered out of the cockpit. They were very friendly but their English was almost non-existent. One of them drove off and reappeared 10 minutes later with Georgio, a retired air force pilot who instantly appointed himself our guardian angel. His English was decent and he opened the hanger and helped us push the Stearman inside. There was no Avgas so I would have to fill the Stearman with petrol from a local garage the next day. Georgio promised to help us with the refuelling in the morning, so with our problems solved, he took us on a tour of the local sights.

The town was called Missolonghi and I suddenly realised this was where Lord Byron had lost his life fighting in the Greek War of Independence against the Turks. George Byron, that great, restless figure of the English romantic movement, had died a heroic death, ensuring his life would be immortal. We drove past the big house where he had lived and visited the cenotaph which the Greeks erected in his honour. They buried Lord Byron's heart here and this is where it remains.

Georgio had noted the Stearman's name and told us that on the northern outskirts of the town was a Temple of Artemis. We asked to see it but it was little more than a few crumbling columns and slabs of stone, the remnants of a classical cupola, however we could feel her spirit and she was with us all the way.

Georgio found us a hotel for the night and left us there, promising to come again in the morning with several jerry cans for the petrol. Touched by his kindness, we invited him to have dinner with us, but he politely declined. Perhaps dining with two women didn't quite accord with his notions of propriety. And so, at the end of a marvellous day, we sat in the little conservatory with a bottle of wine enjoying a gorgeous sunset over the marsh.

After a civilised breakfast the next morning, Georgio appeared as promised at 9am and drove us to the fuel station. Annette started filming while I filled the half dozen cans, laughing helplessly and feeling rather self-conscious amid the morning commuters, but Georgio carried on directing the operation as if he did this sort of thing every day of his life.

At the airfield, after a brief look at the old jets, we had the arduous job of getting the fuel into the aeroplane. With each can carrying 20 litres of fuel, it was heavy work and I did myself some damage struggling with the weight. Months later, while being treated for back pain, a chiropractor advised that my whole pelvis had rotated slightly from intense torsional strain, probably from that refuelling.

Annette continued to film but now another camera crew arrived. Word had gotten around and a local television station wanted an interview. Their lack of English was a problem but Georgio once again stepped in as interpreter. Annette and I expressed our great pleasure and gratitude landing at Missolonghi and finding Georgio. We exchanged cards, gave him a big hug in farewell and, with a final wave, roared into the air again.

We headed north-west for about 130 miles to Corfu, reaching there two hours later. The international airport, situated on an elevated terrace to the south of the town, had been built in the 1930s and was used by German and Italian forces during the Second World War but there were just a couple of small tourist airliners when we landed early in the afternoon. The service was first rate and several people came to meet us in high-visibility jackets before we had even got out of the Stearman.

Our plan was to fly on to Dubrovnik, in Croatia, a further 200 miles up the coast, but, when I checked the weather at the tower, a 25-knot gusting crosswind at our destination would make it impossible to land and there were no alternatives to divert to. We therefore decided to stay the night in Corfu. The airport ground crew helped us push the Stearman to the sheltered side of the apron and tethered it firmly to iron rings in the asphalt.

We caught a taxi into the town and found a hotel on the waterfront with an excellent Thalasso spa, where two weary aviators spent the rest of the afternoon. Over cocktails later, looking out on a bay smooth as a mill pond, we doubted anyone would believe we had been delayed due to the weather. Annette set up the camera and we filmed a Christmas message together for the rest of the crew. Giggling throughout, we said we were, naturally, terribly sorry they couldn't be with us but – panning around our luxurious location and the sunlit bay beyond – we were just about coping without them. With that, we blew them kisses and ordered two more pink cocktails.

We got away as planned the following morning and, after taking off towards the south, turned back to the north following the distinctive promontory of land with views of the old town and its medieval fort, which the Venetians had built when they ruled the island. Beyond the town, lemon and olive groves gave way to oak forests, all of it bathed in clear, radiant light. We slipped over the top of the mountains to the north, sailing just a hundred or so feet above the rocky peaks which were just below the right wing, and soon found ourselves over the sea again.

After three hours, we crossed into Croatian waters and a short distance ahead was the old, fortified city of Dubrovnik. The crosswinds were still blowing so I decided to fly on to Split, which had a runway pointing almost directly into the wind. It was another 100 miles north and we groaned at the prospect of another two hours in the air as we both needed a relief stop – an occupational hazard on long flights such as this. One must strike a fine balance between drinking water to keep hydrated and managing one's bladder. The pioneers devised various ingenious methods of relieving themselves with bottles, tubes, nappies and, in one case, a strategically placed trap door. We didn't have that luxury in the Stearman. We just had to hold on and endure the agony.

At least it was a scenic flight. The islands along the coast of Croatia were a glorious sight and each one had a lighthouse, and in some cases two or three. The water was a deep, clear marine blue and the mainland off our starboard wing a sheer, barren, shelf of yellow rock. It was surprisingly desert-like.

After five hours in the air, we welcomed the sight of Split on the horizon. No sooner had we landed when we both made an undignified dash for the lavatory.

We loved Split so much we stayed for two nights to have a break and see something of the historic town. Annette found a modern, boutique hotel set within an old medieval building right in the centre and we strolled around the narrow streets and alleyways, exploring old churches and fortifications and stopping for coffee along the bustling waterfront.

We filmed a final interview that night, although I would continue with my own video diaries. With little more than a week to Christmas, I suggested to Annette that she fly back to London while I pressed on alone to Hungary. Although we were having a marvellous time, I didn't want to expose her to any more unnerving flights and I wasn't sure what lay ahead. The weather was only going to get worse as we went further north and already the forecast was beginning to change.

Annette was keen to get home and grateful, I think, for the reprieve, so the next day we said goodbye, both of us slightly tearful at the parting.

I prepared my flight plan at the little operations room at the airport and had a full briefing on the weather. There was a big depression over Italy and a blanket of freezing fog inland over Zagreb, but it was still good on the coast so I decided to keep flying north up the Croatian coast and then try to get over the mountain range to the east for the leg into Hungary.

December 19, Split to Rijeka

One consolation was that, with Annette's baggage and camera equipment out of the Stearman, I could close the rear door with ease for the first time in the expedition. I got airborne shortly after midday and the aeroplane felt gloriously light and raring to go like a thoroughbred on the morning gallop.

I enjoyed a beautiful flight up the coast and the air traffic controller routed me offshore to various reporting points via the many islands which run in long thin strands parallel with the mainland for the entire length of Croatia. The first couple of hours were relaxing with smooth conditions and a 10-knot tailwind but it got steadily more overcast as I flew north.

The sky seemed strangely empty and I didn't see a single aircraft or hear anybody over the radio for the entire flight. Perhaps, as it was winter, lighter aircraft were staying on the ground. I never get lonely flying alone but sharing the sights with someone else somehow makes the experience more vivid and the shared memory afterwards a double bonus.

I wished somebody had been with me to see the haunting quality of the light. The sea was inky black like obsidian, and the bare rock islands rose steeply out of the water in jagged points, glowing yellow like old teeth. I had never seen anything like this before.

Even stranger was the seemingly impenetrable wall of darkness just a few miles away to my right. The land was completely obscured by a shadow that resembled a black veil. It didn't seem to be cloud but I wasn't exactly sure what I was looking at and what caused that murky visibility. It looked decidedly ominous, so I opted to land at Rijeka, 40 miles ahead, and check out the weather reports.

With 20 miles to Rijeka, my global positioning system (GPS) suddenly started playing up, flashing the message 'No Satellite Positions'. I tried resetting it but the screen went blank. This had occasionally happened in Africa so I wasn't unduly concerned. I still had the route on my backup iPad and a map to hand for exactly this reason. I knew that Rijeka was straight ahead and right on the tip of the big island to my left, so I flew on as the sky seemed to contract around me.

Ten miles out I sighted the runway, perfectly in line with my heading. The wind was calm so, after receiving clearance for a straight-in approach, I completed a perfect wheeler landing.

Rijeka airport was quiet, with all light drained from the sky. It took a few minutes after I had taxied to the control tower before I saw stirrings of activity. A fuel truck appeared and a couple of airport men pulled up in another vehicle. With their help I refuelled and they led me to a flight briefing office. Surveying the weather report, I saw there was low cloud across Croatia and most of the way to Hungary. Maribor, one of the airports in Slovenia just to the north of my route, was reporting clear but they had a 26-knot crosswind on the runway, so that made it unsuitable as an alternate place to land. The main problem, however, was the dark cloud bank over the mountains I had seen flying in.

After discussing the weather situation for over an hour, it was now past 2pm and with 160 nautical miles to Hungary and a flight time of potentially over two hours, I was in danger of running out of daylight. With Ewald and the Hungarians waiting for me at Fertőszentmiklós, it was tempting to try and press on but over-eagerness to get home in marginal conditions had been the death of many pilots far better than myself. And so, erring on the side of caution, I decided to flag it away for the day.

Back at the airport the next morning, I hadn't appreciated how much of a cul-de-sac Rijeka is, lying at the head of a bay, the land curling around to the north where it borders with Italy. It was cold and damp with fog and I couldn't even see the end of the runway. The windsock hung limp and everything seemed to be in suspended animation. I spent the entire day in the control tower hoping the cloud would lift. Once again, the air traffic controllers were wonderfully kind, brewing up cups of tea and sharing biscuits. They cheerfully told me this weather was typical and could last for days, not what I wanted to hear. By 3pm, tired and dispirited, I threw in the towel and looked for a new hotel.

The next day, I repeated the ritual of going to the airport but, if anything, the weather was worse. It had rained in the night and although I tightened the straps on the covers, I never slept well when the Stearman was parked out in the elements. I spent another day in the control tower. It was now Friday, December 20, and I was dismayed to learn that airports were starting to close for Christmas. The longer I was forced to stay on the ground the more I could feel my energy draining away.

By Monday, December 23, I didn't even bother going out to the airport, instead hiking up to the castle. There were no people but all around were medieval statues and carvings set in the stone. Gryphons stood on the parapets, their wings spread, and other heraldic creatures were carved into the sheer walls or crouched in shelved alcoves. A few ravens struck black and harsh against the smothering whiteness.

The town was bustling with Christmas festivities and people gathered in the streets at beer bars under awnings and winter parasols. Strains of carols emanated from doorways and a large, decorated tree dominated the main square. Every day I saw the same man performing in the street with what I thought was a dog but then realised was a small goat. This enchanting little animal cavorted around the cobbles on its back legs like a circus pony and then launched into a series of spectacular vertical take-offs, like a spring lamb.

I spent Christmas Day in Rijeka, enjoying a splendid breakfast of bacon and eggs, before going back to bed with a book and a six-pack of Toblerone.

On Boxing Day, with the airport closed, I stayed in town and a very nice girl from the aero club dropped by with her pilot boyfriend to say hello. They had good news – the forecast was improving. I hardly dared to think so.

The next day brought another visitor. When I went down for breakfast, who should be waiting in the foyer but Ewald. It was like the cavalry had arrived. In his usual understated way, he just grinned and said, 'Happy Christmas.'

I had never been so happy to see a friend in my life and all the frustrations of the week disappeared in a second. I launched into his arms, laughing ecstatically and demanding to know what had taken him so long. Poor Ewald. He had got back from Chicago the night before and, with little more than three hours of jet-lagged sleep, had taken an early flight from Vienna to Zagreb and then had a two-hour taxi ride to Rijeka. It said much about his dedication. We sat down to breakfast and he had several cups of strong black coffee before we headed out to the airport, just like old times.

DECEMBER 28, RIJEKA TO FERTŐSZENTMIKLÓS

It was a brighter morning and the cloud had lifted to about 1,500 ft with patches of pale blue sky glinting through. Ewald gave everything on the Stearman a quick check over, given it had stood outside for a week, and an hour later, when the cloud lifted enough for us to view the mountains, we were good to go.

We headed down the coast for a couple of miles, climbing all the time and then doubled back towards the north in a tacking pattern to gain height. We picked our way through the mountains, the tops still partially obscured by strands of cloud, but beyond was clear air and out to the south-east a blanket of pure white fog obscuring the ground. Two hours later we landed at home base in Hungary and suddenly I was back in a familiar world.

The Hungarian engineers were opening the hangar doors even as we taxied towards them and I practically drove the Stearman straight into the hangar. The relief at arriving was immense. I sat in the cockpit for a full minute feeling the tension drain away. I finally hauled myself out of the seat and stepped down on to the wing as the engineers clustered around in welcome. We had a little celebration with champagne and palinka. I had one shot of the Hungarian fruit brandy, gasped at the shock of it, and then reached for a glass of champagne.

This was only a pit stop, however. There was a lot to be done and we now set about removing the covers, the tools and spare parts, the emergency equipment, first aid kit, life vests, and laying everything out on canvas sheets on the hangar floor. The engineers were going to do a full 100-hour maintenance check, with several of them working late into the night, so we would be ready to go first thing in the morning. I had lost so much time in Rijeka there was now huge pressure to get back to England and I wanted to arrive before the New Year.

Ewald had a few days off from his airline schedule and proposed to come with me. This was an absolute godsend because the route across Europe looked uncertain with many airports closed. It was now the evening of December 28 and with nearly a thousand miles to cover in three days it would be touch and go.

December 29, Fertőszentmiklós to Schwäbisch Hall

I didn't get much sleep that night as I was just too keyed up. It was a pre-dawn start and after a hasty breakfast we launched straight into the final preparations. The engineers had done an amazing job on the Stearman, even cleaning it so the aeroplane looked dark and gleaming for the last dash across Europe. We still needed to refuel and repack, but this time with minimal kit. We were now back in expedition mode and moved swiftly through the check list.

I went through the pre-flight checks while Ewald set the GoPros, which he had recharged overnight. I had already filed the international flight plan with Budapest control so by 9.30am we were ready to go, waved off by the entire Hungarian crew.

Twenty minutes later we were crossing the Hungarian border into Austria to the west of Lake Neusiedl and entering Vienna airspace. Ahead of us, 30 miles away, was the Snow Mountain, a monolith of around 8,000 ft, sometimes visible from the airfield on a clear day. It looked dark and forbidding and as we got closer we flew through light flurries of snow. I kept the Stearman in a steady climb to clear the ridge to the right of the peak and we roared over at 6,000 ft. It was freezing cold and the added windchill of the open cockpit put the temperature several degrees below zero. Even with multiple layers of thermal underwear, woollen tights, layers of jumpers and a sheepskin jacket, it was hard to keep warm. I clenched my hands and feet repeatedly to keep the circulation going.

The foothills of the northern Alps in Austria were the highest terrain we had to get over and we cruised steadily overhead with a light but turbulent headwind, keeping just below the dark cloud base. In such conditions it was hardly a scenic flight and I was literally counting the miles off as we flew, which made for slow progress. We headed for Schwäbisch Hall, in southern Germany 300 nautical miles away. Our route west took us north of Linz and Munich and through the north-eastern part of Baden-Württemberg. It brightened up and I felt a surge of optimism, as the sun cast a perfect shadow of the Stearman on the stratus cloud below with a halo of light around it.

Giant wind turbines are a hazard to aviation and I was constantly on the lookout for these rotating monsters. We winged past several as they poked up through the cloud, their huge propellor blades slicing the air in slow motion. We got steadily colder as we pressed on over those many miles of dark wintery terrain and by the time we reached Schwäbisch Hall four and a half hours later we were frozen to the bone. With watering eyes and a streaming nose, I couldn't have flown another mile.

With brilliant German efficiency, the ground staff at Schwäbisch Hall appeared in a vehicle within seconds of us arriving. I was swept off to the loo in the terminal building and practically had to strip to relieve myself. I then stood for several minutes with my hands under a hot tap. I went back outside as Ewald and the Germans were finishing the re-fuelling and jumped back into the Stearman to taxi it around to the block of hangars behind the terminal. We tucked the Stearman into a superb modern hangar with gleaming floors and central heating and I knew that I would rest easy that night.

We stayed in the town at a lovely old hotel called the Golden Lion, a huge timber framed building facing the medieval square. There was a towering Christmas tree in the centre and everywhere was festooned in fairy lights with lanterns glowing in windows which made it look like a magical scene from a Hans Christian Andersen story. Soon we found ourselves sipping hot Glühwein in front of a roaring fire and looking forward to dinner.

So far so good, but the forecast did not look great.

DECEMBER 30, SCHWÄBISCH HALL TO MERVILLE

As dawn broke, I peeked out under the high gable at a heavily overcast sky with rain spattering the window and went back to bed for another hour.

We made our way to the airport and sat down with a cup of tea and the weather reports. It didn't look quite as bad as I had first thought but there was a lot of low cloud and intermittent showers forecast all the way along our route into France. Once again, we would have to pick our way through and have a clear exit strategy if we needed to divert and land somewhere. Having waited for the cloud to lift a bit, we finally got away mid-morning. We were now

The launch of the England to Australia expedition from Farnborough, October 2015 (Inset image copyright: The Times/News Licensing)

My flight in homage to Amy Johnson, the first woman to fly solo from England to Australia in 1930

Me with Judy Chilvers, Amy Johnson's niece, at Farnborough for the big send-off, October 2015 (Copyright: John Goodman)

Above, the start of the expedition, flying over the Kent coast before heading out across the English Channel on the way to Hungary

Left, me with HRH Prince Michael of Kent at Farnborough, October 2015 (Copyright: John Goodman)

Ewald Gritsch and his team of Hungarian engineers at Rare Bird Aviation. Back row, from left, Ewald, Lazlo, Yanni, Bennie, Janosh, Peter. Front row, from left, Gaby, Peter ('Strani') and Robert

Above, a parachute jump with Skydive Jordan at the Dead Sea, October 2015

Right, flying in formation down the coast at Tel Aviv, Israel, with my military escort, an F-15 pilot in another Boeing Stearman, October 2015

With Princess Reema Bint Bandar Al Saud (second from left) at Al Thumama Airport, Riyadh, Saudi Arabia, October 2015

Right, approaching Dubai on the Gulf of Arabia, November 2015

Below, coming into land at Abu Dhabi with a wonderful view of the Sheikh Zayed Grand Mosque

Above, a welcome break to tour Petra in Jordan with the crew, from left, Ewald, Matt, me and Markus

Left, outside the Jordan Airline Training and Simulation Academy in Amman with the statue of a famous 9th century birdman, Abbas Ibn Firnas

Flying over the temples at Bagan in Myanmar, December 2015

Left, flying through the beautiful Arakan Mountains in western Myanmar shortly after crossing from Bangladesh, December 2015 and, above, with Boeing at Seletar Airport in Singapore where a local girls' school came to see us

With a group of female military pilots from the Indian Air Force at Hindan Air Force Base in New Delhi, India

An early morning flight over Uluru, January 2016 (Copyright: Caroline O'Donnell)

Flying into Charles Kingsford Smith Airport, Sydney, on the last leg of the expedition, January 2016

A terrifying crash in Arizona following an engine failure after take-off from Winslow, May 2016

Flying near Mount Rainer in Seattle, May 2016

Below, winging past the Golden Gate Bridge in San Francisco on the first expedition in America, May 2016

Above, back to Los Angeles with the Stearman fully restored for the second attempt at the US Transcontinental, June 2017

Above, reaching New York for an epic final flight up New York Harbour and around the Statue of Liberty, July 2017 and, right, a lovely welcome reception at the American Airpower Museum, Republic Airport, Long Island. With Jackie Clyman (left) and Julia Lauria-Blom, curator of the WASP and the Ninety-Nines, Inc., International Organisation of Women Pilots exhibits aiming for Le Touquet on the French coast, 340 nautical miles away. Ahead of us lay the northern part of the Black Forest and after crossing this dark expanse of hills and fir trees we made steady progress.

The French coast was now tantalisingly close but I could hardly bring myself to think about it. Lots could happen in the space of 24 hours and I was taking things hour by hour. Sure enough, as soon as we crossed into France, the weather deteriorated again and the cloud descended, bringing drizzle. It was still flyable, however, and we pressed on into the Ardennes in central northern France, tracking the border with Belgium.

We had flown for nearly 200 miles when suddenly the engine missed and then surged and faltered. My heart stopped with it. Thinking it was icing, I instinctively applied carburettor heat and power and shoved the fuel mixture to the full rich position.

'What the hell was that?' I yelled through to Ewald on the intercom.

'I'm not sure, but the engine may be about to fail altogether.'

Having just flown up Africa the possibility of crashing in a field in France seemed slightly farcical.

The engine seemed to stabilise but I watched the rpm gauge like a hawk for any fluctuations. I was thoroughly spooked and just wanted to land at the earliest opportunity. As luck would have it, the little rural airport of Charleville was just four miles ahead and this is where we now tracked with a degree of trepidation.

We knew the airport well, having landed there twice before on previous transits, but nobody responded to our radio calls. The airfield soon came into view but as I circled overhead I saw with dismay large, baled rolls of hay dotted along most of the runway.

'Bloody hell!' I shouted.

It was so typical of the French to be farming in the middle of winter and obstructing a perfectly good runway at this precise moment. There was just enough length to land carefully at one end of the runway and that's what we did. We then taxied onto the apron where we proceeded to run up the engine for several minutes. It didn't miss a beat. Whatever had caused the surge had clearly passed through and it now appeared to be operating normally.

What a nightmare though. I was thoroughly bemused as we climbed out and suddenly felt cold and tired. The little airport was deserted. The aero club and office were closed so we wandered along the row of small hangars and found a car parked up beside one of them. We tentatively stepped inside, calling out to see if anyone was there. After a while, a figure materialised out of the gloom, smiling and welcoming, but he didn't speak a word of English. After several 'bonjours', I rubbed my hands together to indicate cold and he ushered me towards a small log burner in one corner.

What followed was like a comedy sketch. I tried to convey that we had just flown from Africa and were trying to get back to England, but he looked at us uncomprehendingly. I dug out a piece of paper from my pocket and drew a rough map of Africa and Europe and suddenly he understood. His face lit up in amazement and he exhaled a long and very Gallic 'Nonnnnn!'

'Champagne, champagne!' he exclaimed, waving his arms about in excitement, as if conducting an orchestra. There was no tea but, this being a French hangar, there was champagne in the fridge and our new friend, Marcel, now cracked open a bottle and poured us a glass, toasting our flight and the festive season with great ceremony. It was almost worth having an engine failure for that moment and I found myself chuckling at the sheer lunacy of all of it.

There may have been champagne at Charleville, but there was no fuel. Forty minutes later, we took off again. We still had enough fuel in the tanks to get to the coast, about 130 miles away, so we braced ourselves for this last bit and pressed on through the murk. I now flew with the carburettor heat on the whole time, just in case of more engine icing. It was hard going and, ominously, getting darker by the minute. We were flying into a front and I kept thinking that in the worst case we could turn back, but suddenly we were engulfed by it and in a matter of minutes we were flying on the deck.

Le Touquet was just 30 miles away but it was too bad to continue. Some 12 miles away back to our right was the closest airfield, so with Ewald navigating I turned the Stearman through 120° and flew towards this. We inched our way through the heavy rain, the sky a mass of darkness.

Below us we could see one or two cars on the roads, their head-lights making shafts of horizontal light. After what felt like an hour, but in truth was just 10 minutes, the airfield finally came into view. I turned straight onto a short right base leg and keeping the speed up came into land on the wet runway in a gusting wind.

It was one of those flights when, after you land, you swear you'll never fly again. I hated it but Ewald always took things in his stride. He loved the adventure and was incredibly unflappable in stressful situations. It had taken our combined efforts to get out of this one and we knew it. We parked the Stearman up on the apron and went up to the tower. There was just one female controller and she was like the lighthouse keeper in a storm, very polite and pleasant, but nonchalantly French. She told us there were no facilities at Merville, for that was where we had landed; nor was there hangarage or fuel. We apparently needed a card for the French fuel company, Total, to access the pumps, which naturally we didn't possess. Normally, a control tower would have one of these cards and cash paid for the uplift but apparently not here in Merville. We persisted, and finally she was persuaded to pick up a phone to see if she could find somebody who could help us.

While this was going on, I glanced down at the Stearman below and was horrified to see it moving slowly backwards, blown by the wind. I shrieked in panic and flew out the door with Ewald close behind. We charged down the stairs onto the apron, catching the wings just before the tail collided with the hangar. We laughed ruefully at the situation but it wasn't easy managing the aeroplane in these conditions with nothing in the way of ground support. I certainly couldn't have managed on my own. We now pushed the Stearman across the apron to a grass area and managed to tether it to the ground with our steel pegs and tie ropes.

With our fuel situation still unresolved, we made plans to spend the night. There was a small local hotel within walking distance of the airfield and we now took our overnight things and tramped there in the rain. I would never have believed that such places exist but this hotel had funny little prefabricated units, like plastic caravans. It was like sleeping in a shower unit with a narrow bed and a small lavatory off to the side. We joked that all the worst places we had ever stayed at began with the letter 'M' and agreed this was awful but not as bad as Malakal or Mersa Matruh.

There was a takeaway cafe in the town so we walked a further mile or so to get some food, which did little to enhance our experience of Merville. Our most pressing concern was getting fuel and, with a telephone number provided by the air traffic controller, we now managed to speak to a local pilot. He agreed to come and meet us at the airport the next morning and let us use his fuel card.

I spent a dreadful night, tossing and turning in that oppressive plastic capsule, fretting about the Stearman, the weather and the fuel.

It was excitement too, keeping me awake. I had been away for nearly two and a half months on what had been a phenomenal journey and this was the last leg.

Daybreak finally brought a ghostly pale line of light along the eastern horizon.

We were heading north-west and it was now December 31. This was our last chance to get back before the end of 2013.

DECEMBER 31, MERVILLE TO GOODWOOD

We had only 140 miles to run to Goodwood. There were intermittent rain showers all the way to England but the reported cloud base at 700 ft was good enough to get across the Channel, if it was accurate. We didn't want to risk getting stuck at Le Touquet so our plan was to fly straight on over the water without another stop.

As we headed along the plain towards the coast, there were several wind turbines which we dodged around. The farmland below was dark, wet and featureless but I hardly noticed any of it. My gaze was fixed firmly ahead through the wings and the rigging and I watched the rain droplets spreading into long rivulets of water as the wind blew it down the wing.

Suddenly, we were crossing the French coast and over the English Channel mired in cloud and rain. It is only 30 miles across this stretch of water but, in conditions like this, it can seem much greater. The sea was an implacable grey and the horizon a dark blur, but the main thing was that we could see it. We would have turned back without that all important view.

England looked even darker with great brooding rain clouds but once we were tracking the south coast and heading west it felt like a safe passage to Goodwood.

Two and a half hours after leaving Merville and finally there was just 10 miles to run. It was a deep thrill making that radio call to the control tower: 'The Spirit of Artemis is 10 miles to the east and inbound to land.'

I couldn't see the airfield until we were almost upon it. I just wanted to get on the ground as quickly as possible but seeing the little throng of people below we couldn't possibly land without a final flourish.

I came in for one low pass then pulled up and into the downwind position for the final approach. Even in that subdued light, through a curtain of rain, the grass looked greener than anything I had seen in a long time – the deep, eternal, reassuring greenness of England.

As the wheels touched down on the grass runway, a spray of mud splattered up onto the wings of the Stearman, but it didn't matter. We were finally home.

It was amazing to me that anybody came out in that foul weather to meet us. The first person I saw was Carol and it was a choking embrace under an umbrella knocked sideways. Annette was also there, with Caroline from Artemis, and then my cousin Melissa and her husband Damien pressed forward and then there was Rob Wildeboar, the airfield manager and the team from Goodwood.

It was completely overwhelming.

I turned around and hugged wonderful, brilliant Ewald. It wasn't possible to hug the Stearman but I pressed my face to the cowling just behind the engine and it was still warm from the flight, like a living thing. Once again, the champagne was cracked but I was already drunk from the euphoria of the moment. Suddenly, I felt like the lightest person in the world.

That night we saw in the New Year from Annette's apartment in Battersea overlooking the Thames. Caroline was also there, so it was just the four of us leaning over the balcony as on the deck of a ship watching the fireworks explode over the city in showers of light. It was a fantastic end to the year and I felt something like the most perfect peace and joy suffuse my being. What a hell of a year, but we had come through all of it, this flight from the end of the Earth.

I raised my glass in the darkness and Ewald, Caroline and Annette also raised theirs and together we drank to Africa and the incomparable *Spirit of Artemis*.

Trouble Brewing

OVER the next few weeks, we continued to film the final pieces of Lady Heath's story which took us back to Goodwood and to the National Aerospace Library at Farnborough.

Artemis Investments hosted a celebratory dinner for the crew at their offices in St James's and Annette screened a 10-minute trailer of the film which was thrilling to watch. John and Dick presented me with a beautiful silver model of the *Spirit of Artemis*, a possession to treasure, along with the original, of course.

There were other accolades. The Air League honoured my Africa flight with a framed address which they presented to me at St James's Palace and in March 2014 the Light Aircraft Association announced that they were awarding me the Bill Woodham Trophy, to be presented later in the year. I was the first woman to be so honoured, and the citation read: 'To Tracey Curtis-Taylor for her flight from Cape Town to Cairo in a Boeing Stearman – a feat of navigation, aviation, tenacity and endurance.'

It was a privilege to be recognised in this way.

I attended the Dakota Dinner at the House of Commons with the Chief of the Air Staff, Boeing personnel and various prominent aviation people. Drinks were served on a balcony overlooking the Thames, providing a breathtaking view of the star act – a lovely old Dakota which soared into view over the towers of Westminster in a peachy sunset. I spoke at the dinner and was presented with another model of a Stearman in cherry-wood, inscribed in silver. It took pride of place on the bookcase in my study alongside a model of the *Spirit of St Louis*. In my mind, one can never have too many Stearmans.

Since my return to England, I'd been searching for a place to live. I was staying with Anthea and Ian in Newmarket but began flat hunting in London. Although everywhere I looked appeared to be small, dark, dingy and overpriced, I felt I needed to be at the centre of things for work and London offered a fresh start. It wasn't long before I found a flat in a new apartment block in the south-west of the city and made an offer on it the same day, which was accepted. I moved there in the spring and relocated the Ryan from Shuttleworth to Goodwood, which was more convenient at just under an hour's drive away.

Before then I hadn't flown for several weeks. While British winter and the pressures of life once more had closed in, the Stearman had remained hangared, its wings still bearing the mud from that final landing of the expedition.

We held a debrief on the Africa expedition at the end of January.

I left Annette and Helen to resolve things with Sam since they had agreed his terms but made the point that I didn't feel we could provide him with any reference or endorsement.

I tried to put it all behind me, however, as I had a busy summer of activities ahead.

I took part in the Goodwood Festival of Speed in June, landing the Stearman on a small grass strip so it could be towed by tractor closer to the sprint course which was the main drive leading up the hill towards Goodwood House. We were on static display so I stood there talking to the crowds, enjoying the carnival atmosphere.

TAG Aviation of Farnborough had a pitch close by with their corporate hospitality tent and they invited me to join them for lunch. I sat next to the chief executive, Graham Williamson, and we enjoyed an amusing and convivial afternoon chatting about corporate aviation and life in general, the start of a great friendship.

The public events continued thick and fast through July and August, as I flew the Stearman to the Royal International Air Tattoo at RAF Fairford, in Gloucestershire, which ran back-to-back with the Farnborough International Air Show, so I flew directly from one to the other, taking one of the young air cadets along with me for the ride.

I met up again with the Boeing team, Chris Chadwick who was now head of Global Defence, and Geoff Kohler who was his second in command and had previous association with the UK in his capacity as base commander at RAF Mildenhall, when he served with the US Air Force.

Along with several other members of the Boeing team, we all met at the Royal Air Force Club in Piccadilly one warm summer evening after the Farnborough Air Show. The Americans were very relaxed in blazers with open shirts but they didn't get past the reception, because of the club's strict dress code which required ties. Luckily, the concierge brought a selection on a tray and there was a dressing session in the foyer with much laughter about the questionable sartorial choice. When we finally sat down to a round of gin and tonics, Chris asked me what my next adventure would be in the Stearman.

When I said I was thinking of flying to India, he immediately replied, 'Why not go on to Australia?'

Why not indeed?

So, right there and then, light-headed with gin, I made the decision to fly to Australia, and it was intoxicating to know that Boeing was once more going to be with me all the way.

As the explorer WH Murray, who took part in the Scottish Himalayan Expedition of 1951, commented about all acts of initiative, 'There is one elemental truth ... that the moment one definitely commits oneself, then providence moves all. All sorts of things occur to help one that would never otherwise have occurred.'

I heartily concurred with this wisdom. It was amazing how quickly things came together once the decision was made.

I started to think that an Australia flight would be the perfect tribute to Amy Johnson, whose story, of all the pioneering aviators, resonated with me most. I consider her 1930 flight to Australia in a flimsy Gypsy Moth to be one of the finest solo achievements in history.

The more I thought about my tribute the more I was determined that she would also be the inspiration for an outreach programme focused on women in aviation that would extend along the entire route.

That was all for the future, however.

That summer led to yet more intriguing connections on several levels and saw my introduction to the Royal Navy, for which I attended a formal dinner in London with Prince Michael of Kent. That led, the following year, to me being made an Honorary Lieutenant Commander of the Royal Naval Reserves, a tremendous honour especially given the naval tradition in my family.

Prince Michael was keen to come flying in the Stearman and a few weeks later we met at Goodwood and had the most delightful flight out along the south coast and over the Solent to the Isle of Wight. We flew over Osborne House, the Italianate Renaissance palazzo on the northern tip of the island which Queen Victoria and her husband Prince Albert had built as a summer house. It was where Victoria retreated in deep grief after Albert's death in 1861, when he was just 42, and it was here she died in 1901. As Queen Victoria was Prince Michael's great-great-grandmother, this flight felt very special. The prince had never seen the house from the air and we circled overhead the belvedere towers, marvelling at the elaborate geometry of the Italian gardens and chatting about the history.

Towards the end of the summer, I joined a gaggle of biplanes flying over the English Channel to commemorate the Battle of the Somme flight in France with flying friends, Paul Beavor and Cate Pye, who joined me on the flight over. They then swapped around and Paul flew back with me. Although we had a lovely time dropping in at various airfields and a buffet lunch had been laid out at Amiens, it was a windy couple of days and the increasing gusts meant we raced back to England to avoid the approaching weather front.

In our haste to beat the weather and, struggling with a poor internet connection, I was unable to confirm if our immigration had been processed prior to re-entry. Shortly after we landed, I was surprised to be met at Goodwood by two very nice officers from UK Border Control. They laughed when they saw the Stearman as it was clear this wasn't an illicit drug smuggling operation. I apologised for wasting their time but, as they turned to leave, one of them confided that I had been 'dobbed in' deliberately by one of the Goodwood air traffic controllers. It seemed petty, but I shrugged it off. The Goodwood team were very helpful, I liked them very much and always dropped in to see the controllers in the tower before going flying.

Towards the end of 2014, Annette completed the Africa film, now called *The Aviatrix: The Lady Who Flew Africa*.

I had seen some of the rushes of the flying but otherwise had no part in the editing and did not see the finished film until it was screened at the premiere in London that October. I was pleased to see how well told Mary Heath's story was in the film. Annette had skilfully juxtaposed our footage with old black and white archive film from the 1920s. The *Spirit of Artemis* looked spectacularly beautiful against the immensity of Africa and the flying sequences were set to a stirring original soundtrack. It won best film at The Explorers Museum Film Festival – a remarkable testament to Annette and her crew and all the work put in to make the film such a triumph.

Four Letter Word

I WOKE early on the morning of September 20, 2014, to impenetrable fog. It was definitely not flying weather. I couldn't even see the other side of the road.

'Bloody hell!' I swore under my breath.

I was due at the launch of a fundraising campaign for a bronze statue to be erected of Amy Johnson, close to where she was last seen alive at Herne Bay, in Kent.

The original plan was for me to do a flypast at the event in the *Spirit of Artemis*, as the presence of a green biplane overhead had special significance. Amy's Gypsy Moth *Jason* had also been green but with silver wings, and it was planned as a splendid tribute.

I felt privileged to be taking part but my hopes that this was just a London fog were dashed when I rang the control tower at Goodwood, who confirmed the whole of the south coast was engulfed all the way to Kent and it wasn't expected to clear.

On the spur of the moment, I decided to drive to Herne Bay instead and now scrambled to get ready, uncertain what to wear. I needed to look like someone's idea of an old-fashioned aviator, so I pulled on a pair of jodhpurs and riding boots, threw on my leather flying jacket and draped the requisite white scarf around my neck.

Few adventurers were more deserving of a statue than Amy. When she left Croydon Airport in south London on May 5, 1930, to begin her epic journey Down Under, she had less than a hundred hours in her logbook. She had only learnt to fly the year before and her longest flight had been 200 miles up the east coast of England from London to Hull.

Given her lack of experience, her plan was staggeringly ambitious. Amy not only wanted to be the first woman to fly to Australia, she also wanted to break the solo record of 15 days, set two years earlier by Australian flying ace Bert Hinkler. The flight was an extremely perilous undertaking, even for a seasoned pilot. Amy was proposing to fly halfway around the world crossing mountain ranges, vast expanses of unmapped desert, jungles, remote volcanic islands and shark-infested seas.

I found it extraordinary to reflect on what Amy had experienced. She was a 26-year-old slip of a girl flying on her own, without a radio, using basic dead reckoning for navigation, with little in the way of weather forecasts. In addition, she had no idea what she was in for. She was flying legs of up to a thousand miles, sitting in her open cockpit for as many as 10 or 11 hours at a time, exposed to the extremes of cold and heat, shearing winds and turbulence, blinding monsoon rains, burning sun, relentless engine noise and vibration, debilitating stiffness and cramp from sitting in a confined position. Relieving herself would have been an added challenge and I am not sure how she met it as the sources are silent. To this physical aspect, add the psychological challenge of dealing with fear, stress and extreme isolation. With barely three hours of sleep a night, Amy was living on adrenaline and nervous energy.

By the time she reached Australia she was on the edge of physical and mental collapse. The whole world was gripped by her epic journey and, after 19 gruelling days, she finally landed in Darwin. Hundreds of thousands of people turned out to meet her as she flew across Australia and overnight she became a global celebrity.

'Show me a hero and I'll write you a tragedy,' wrote F Scott Fitzgerald, and that seems especially apposite in Amy's case. Lauded by the rich and famous, for 11 manic years she lived the high life and continued to break records and make headlines with her long-distance flights. From the beginning she was overwhelmed by the fame and the relentless media attention that came with it. She came to resent the intrusions into her private life and, in time, became completely disillusioned by what she perceived as the empty trappings of celebrity. She felt she had been turned into a 'commodity' and her naivety ruthlessly exploited.

Despite a brief marriage to fellow aviator, Jim Mollison, personal happiness ultimately eluded Amy and she was to struggle with nervous depression for the rest of her life. Her flying feats were considered 'stunts' and she never succeeded in working as a commercial pilot in the face of implacable hostility and obstruction from the male establishment.

Then the war came and, in 1941, while flying for the Air Transport Auxiliary, Amy lost her life aged just 37 when, in appalling weather and running low on fuel, she was forced to ditch her aeroplane in the Thames Estuary, in sight of the Kent coast at Herne Bay, the proposed site for the new statue.

All this was on my mind as I hurried to get down there on time but I was already running late by the time I parked up in Herne Bay. I half ran to the pier, where a small crowd of residents and end-of-season holiday makers were gathering around a newly erected display board dedicated to Amy's life and achievements.

The mayor was there in his ceremonial chains and with him were members of Amy's family, a diorama featuring an old car which had belonged to her, and several people dressed in the style of the 1940s, including a lady singing Vera Lynn songs to add a bit of atmosphere to the event.

It was cold and damp with a pall of low cloud as I threaded my way through the crowd and introduced myself to the mayor. He immediately launched into his opening welcome speech and invited me to say a few words to the crowd.

The singer had just sung 'Wonderful Amy', so I continued with that theme, speaking for just over five minutes about Amy, her achievements in the male-dominated world of flying, her spirit, bravery and the tragedy of her premature death on a day of hauntingly similar weather.

Speaking off the cuff, I shouldn't have mentioned the forthcoming Australia flight. It was still only in the early planning stage and I didn't want to pre-empt anything. Perhaps it was in trying to draw a somewhat presumptuous parallel between Amy's flights and mine over Africa that I let slip the word 'solo'. I shouldn't have even referenced it. That was a mistake.

We piloted our respective planes, but Amy never carried a passenger, as I had done for many legs of the flight. Nor, of course, did she have a film crew and support team in attendance, as I did.

My Herne Bay speech had been filmed and – immediately kicking myself over my error - I asked for the footage to be edited to remove reference both to my Australia plans and flying 'solo'.

Later, as I was to discover, one request was excised, but not the other.

I gave it no more thought, never imagining that one four-letter word would come back to haunt me in such a devastating fashion.

Keeping Vigil

IN the early days of planning for Australia, I spent a wonderful day with Amy Johnson's two nieces in Norfolk. I had first met them at the Herne Bay fundraising event and, after they kindly invited me to visit, I travelled to meet them a few months later. It was very moving to hear about the family and to read some of Amy's hand-written letters and look at the fan mail she had received – one of them addressed simply to 'Amy, the most bountiful bird in the sky'.

Sadly, Susan and Judy never knew their famous aunt, but Judy looked a lot like Amy in pictures, with the same Nordic bone structure and attractive, wide-set grey eyes. Their mother, Mollie, was one of Amy's younger sisters and Amy was with her the night before she died. In ferrying an aircraft from Scotland for the Air Transport Auxiliary, Amy had stopped off at Blackpool to see her sister for the night. Mollie was already a mother then to Susan, who was two, and was pregnant with Judy. The sisters had exchanged Christmas presents, with Mollie giving Amy a beautiful mirror in a ceramic frame of painted flowers, which the aviator tucked away into her kit bag. Amazingly, Susan and Judy still had this mirror, which had been perfectly preserved. Amy and Mollie said their goodbyes and Amy left the next morning to deliver the Oxford Airspeed to Kidlington in Oxfordshire. The weather was appalling with snow and sleet forecast and nobody else in the ATA was flying that day. Amy made the fateful decision to press on.

Her aircraft was known to have a compass problem and that may have explained why Amy ended up over 150 miles off track over the Kent coast. More likely, however, in a desperate bid to escape the weather, she elected to fly east, where she was more familiar. She was trying to find somewhere she could descend safely through the heavy cloud before running out of fuel and daylight and the safest place to do that was over the sea. Amy had a morbid fear of jumping out of an aeroplane with a parachute and on a previous occasion, when she had become lost in bad weather, she had also made for the coast with the intention of ditching the aircraft in the water. On that occasion she had been lucky and managed to land on the beach.

On that January day in 1941, over the outer reaches of the Thames Estuary, sailors from a convoy of merchant ships saw the aircraft come through the cloud in a controlled descent before it hit the water. The eyewitness accounts of this event are contradictory and one or two of the sailors believed they saw a parachute and the accepted view is that she jumped. I have a different theory. Seeing that unbroken mirror convinced me that Amy did not in fact parachute out. She ditched the aircraft on the water, hence the perfectly executed descent, and then managed to get out before the aircraft sank, jumping into the heaving swell with her bags in the hope of being rescued by the convoy. The tragedy was the sailors came so close to rescuing her – an arm's length away – and they heard her say, 'Please hurry.'

Then, before their eyes, she was sucked under the stern of the ship and, one surmises, through the churning propeller blades. It was a horrifying end.

Meeting Amy's relatives made me even more determined to pay my own tribute to her heroics – and planning for the trip began in earnest in February when Artemis Investments generously agreed to continue their sponsorship.

Tim Kelly, who had handled some of the communications for the Africa expedition, was now appointed as the PR manager for the flight to Australia. Tim was first rate at what he did and with his easy intelligence and dazzling good looks, it felt like we had a great team. We now approached the 'Britain is Great' campaign, which promotes British initiatives both at home and overseas, and were invited to Downing Street for a meeting to discuss how we could connect with foreign delegations to support the outreach programme.

With Boeing and the 'Britain is Great' campaign, it was an intense time preparing the flight schedule and building an outreach programme around women in aviation across the entire route to Australia.

My aircraft insurance broker, Simon Howell and his loyal and very capable assistant, Coran Barford, also stepped up to the plate with their customary brilliance. I had met Simon years before while I was at the Fighter Collection. He had brokered most of the insurance for the aircraft at Duxford and Shuttleworth and had pitched in to help with the pilot and aircraft documentation in the run up to the air shows, often working late into the night. A pilot in his own right who flew a T-28 Trojan, he understood the risk like few others and had a deep empathy for the pitfalls of aviation. He was now working for KM Dastur and it was through this agency that we secured fantastic insurance coverage with GIC Re of India, the biggest reinsurer in the world. They gave us world-class protection and, with this partnership in place, I wanted to make India the centrepiece of the flight. Geographically, it was about halfway to Australia and we planned on spending two weeks with several important stops across the country.

In March 2015, with things starting to fall into place, *The Aviatrix – The Lady Who Flew Africa* was screened by the BBC to glowing reviews.

Just when I was thinking the timing couldn't have been better, I received devastating news.

Julie called from New Zealand.

Dad had suffered a massive stroke, was in hospital and was not expected to survive.

I dropped everything and arrived in Nelson, on the South Island, 48 hours later. I was braced for what I would find but the physical damage was dreadful to behold. Dad looked gaunt and ill, but his face lit up when he saw me.

Despite the years and distance that had stretched between us, we closed hands, never to be parted again. Although he couldn't speak very well, we managed to communicate well enough and his eyes were darkly eloquent and full of fear.

Julie had returned to Auckland for a few days to get her young son, John, sorted out so I had arrived after she had left. I set up camp in Dad's room and remained there with him for the next two weeks. Julie then joined us a few days later and together we kept vigil until the very last moment. It was somehow consoling to reflect on the extent to which Dad had lived life on his own terms, refusing to be pressured into conforming and I always felt a particular affinity for his irreverent, anti-establishment side.

But of all the principles which guide the universe, it is the law of unintended consequences which seems to me the most powerful. It was the terrible consequences of my father's actions which had caused so much unresolved anguish and physical separation in our family. It was this that prevented my mother, my twin sister and my brother from coming to his death bed. And now it was all gone, all those years of separation, I was overwhelmed by the sadness of it all.

Yet, in those last terrible, dying days, I felt only the most profound tenderness for my father and, ultimately, a sense of forgiveness. Afterwards, Julie and I went for a long walk, arm-in-arm, along the beach at Rabbit Island and the next day we went back to Dad's old homestead at Brandy Creek to clear out his few belongings.

There was no funeral but, a few weeks later, I received some of Dad's ashes and we had a little gathering at Tarn Hows in the Lake

District, with his two remaining sisters, Mary and Moo, my adored aunts, and my cousins, Jonty and Jill.

When the time came to return to England, I felt relieved at coming home. I just wanted to look forward and once again I immersed myself in the preparations for Australia.

Under Attack

IN early June, Prince Michael of Kent invited me to Shuttleworth with him to attend the annual fly-in of the Light Aircraft Association.

We were met by Sir John Allison, in his capacity as President of the LAA – the first contact we'd had since our fallout in 2013. Next to him was the Chairman of the LAA, Brian Davies, the first time I had met him. The day seemed to pass convivially, but a little while later, at an LAA board meeting, Brian was reported to have said, 'Who does this woman think she is coming here with royalty?'

I wondered who might have influenced that remarkable prejudice – and it wouldn't be long before I had an idea.

I was also approached by BBC producer Chris Jackson, who was making a short documentary about Constance Leathart, another female pilot who had flown for the Air Transport Auxiliary, and he wanted me to present it. I was filmed flying the Stearman around Goodwood and also at the Northumberland aero club, the oldest in the country and where Constance had been a founding member. While there, I spent a couple of nights with my brother Russell, who lived in nearby Tynemouth, and it gave us a chance to talk about Dad and the events of the last few months.

Back in London, I was invited to be guest speaker at the RAF Club for a very enjoyable lunch with No 1 Squadron, with Sir Peter Squires presiding. Squadron Leader Mike Sutton and DJ Greenhowe, squadron 'Auntie', gave me the squadron badge to wear on the forthcoming flight and presented me with a signed print of a Typhoon. They have remained good friends who I see every summer at the Royal International Air Tattoo. Another memorable event at the RAF Club was the launch of *Spitfire People*, the book on the human story behind the legendary fighter, written by my friend Paul Beaver.

Once again, however, when it appeared life was moving forwards, dark clouds appeared on the horizon.

On 9 January 2015, I received an email from Sam Rutherford to notify me he had objected to the LAA's award of the Woodhams Trophy on the grounds I had claimed to be flying solo. This was strange. Not only had the Woodhams award not been made to me for a solo flight, but Rutherford knew very well that mine had been a supported flight with a crew. Indeed, he himself had asked to fly with me on one of the legs. I did not respond, and heard nothing further for five months, when I received a further email from him making further complaints.

Three days later Artemis Investments were contacted by one Mike Flynn, claiming to be a journalist and accusing them of being party to my 'fraudulence' in claiming to fly solo. Since Artemis had been receiving repeated requests from Sam Rutherford for a reference it seemed plausible that this was not a coincidence, but – with hindsight perhaps unwisely – I agreed with Artemis that we would ignore them.

I pressed on with a busy public programme and spoke at various events, including Ranulph Fiennes's Transglobe Expedition fundraiser at the Royal Geographical Society.

In the middle of August, I returned to Herne Bay to fly in the Amy Johnson Air Show, which this time was blessed with glorious weather. Then I was back at Goodwood to meet the affable newsreader Mark Austen who, despite having a fear of flying, joined me for a short flight and some low passes over the airfield for a piece for the ITN news a couple of nights later.

Meanwhile, preparations for the Australia expedition were coming along and we now had a departure date from England – October 1. The location once again would be Goodwood.

As the date approached, the media interest became more intense and I flew with various journalists to give them first-hand experience of open cockpit flying.

We struck a deal with the *Mail on Sunday* for exclusive coverage of the flight and I arranged for senior editor John Wellington to come flying with me in August at Goodwood. It was the most perfect summer morning but everyone there was in the thick of preparations for the Revival in September and the whole aircraft operating area was effectively a building site. I strapped John into the front seat of the Stearman and talked him through the emergency procedures and then climbed into the rear cockpit for the start up.

A large articulated truck was manoeuvring nearby on the apron so I taxied around and onto the grass area beyond. I now steered the Stearman very slowly in a straight line over metal sheets lining the ground and between prefabricated buildings and fences on either side. I had used the same path on the previous two days but this morning a helicopter had landed on the grass right in the middle of the 'corridor' onto the grass runway.

I managed to hit the helicopter head on. The Stearman shuddered at the impact and shards of metal and Perspex exploded into the air, piercing the aeroplane's fabric wings like a shower of arrows.

I shut down the engine and leapt out of the cockpit aghast. The Stearman's propellor had sliced some 18 inches into the canopy of the Robinson 22 helicopter. Amazingly, there was no contact between the shell of the helicopter and the aeroplane's front end. The first strike with one of the helicopter's rotor blades had carved a one-inch chunk out of my propeller but, beyond a couple of small tears in the left wing, the Stearman was unscathed.

Mercifully, there was nobody in the helicopter and it didn't bear thinking about what might have happened if there was. I immediately called Simon Howell, my insurance broker.

This all happened barely 20 feet from the control tower, where there were three air traffic controllers at the time. Not one of them had been looking my way, despite the fact I was taxying through a minefield of obstacles and they had allowed the helicopter to land in the clear corridor just half an hour before. I had also noted two other people to the right, standing by another parked helicopter, but neither of them signalled a warning as they watched me taxi straight into the Robinson.

Only if you've sat in the cockpit of a vintage taildragger would you understand that there is zero forward visibility over the engine. It is normal to 'weave' the aeroplane to see in front but I was unable to do that because of the obstacles, so I was virtually taxiing blind.

The press coverage the next day was predictably awful. One tabloid report dripped with sexist sarcasm – this woman who styles herself 'Bird in a Biplane' and purports to be about to fly to Australia can't even manoeuvre on the ground without crashing into a stationary object.

I took it on the cheek. It was my fault. It was a damaged propeller, one badly savaged helicopter and wounded pride, but at least nobody was injured. The Stearman was unserviceable, however, just six weeks before our departure date and I had no idea if the engine had been shocked by the impact.

The whole incident took on a very different perspective though, when, just four days later, a Hawker Hunter jet killed 11 people at the Shoreham Air Show just down the road. I was there and I witnessed it. The pilot was a highly experienced ex-RAF fast jet pilot with a lot of air show experience. I was surprised to see him pull up vertically from what appeared to be a slow positioning pass over the airfield. The trajectory of the Hunter was slightly skewed and it looked very low, and as he pulled over the top suddenly it became terribly clear that the plane was stalled and falling to the ground.

Standing there with several other pilots, we all froze in disbelief as we watched the descent. It disappeared behind trees but then we heard two distinct impacts as the Hunter hit twice, like a skimming stone, and fire-balled down the A27 highway. The people in its path didn't stand a chance. They included Richard Smith, the 26-year-old son of a friend from Shuttleworth, who had nothing to do with the show and was just cycling down the road when the Hunter struck from somewhere behind.

The pilot, Andy Hill, was especially lucky in this case – he survived. We didn't learn this until a few hours later and we could scarcely believe it. In one of the most freakish escapes, barely a second before it hit the ground, the cockpit had cracked open like an egg and he ejected at the last moment.

The inferno which followed when the Hunter hit the ground was nothing short of apocalyptic. A tower of black smoke rose several hundred feet and at some distance away on the hill behind was the gothic cathedral towers of Lancing College chapel which gave the scene the appearance of a baroque horror movie. The public was prevented from leaving the airfield for many hours because the main access road had been blocked by the crash.

I didn't get home until 3am the next morning and felt so sick in my soul that I never wanted to go to another air show ever again.

Two days later, Ewald arrived to inspect the damage to the Stearman. To my great relief, the cam shaft had not moved so the engine was undamaged, but we needed a new propeller. One arrived from America the following month, which Ewald returned to install. By this time the Goodwood Revival had taken place and the site was in an even worse state than it was before, with acres of mud and garbage, deconstructed buildings, grandstands and stacks of railings everywhere. The hangar doors were blocked by containers and rubbish skips and it was only with the help of the Goodwood engineers and the entire ground crew that we were able to extract the Stearman and wheel it carefully through the detritus.

It was now clear that our plan to hold the big departure at Goodwood Aero Club was not going to work. Approaching desperation, I called Graham Williamson at Farnborough and asked if he could help. I needed to get the Stearman out of Goodwood as soon as possible and I needed a venue for the public launch of the Australia flight barely two weeks away. 'Bring the old bird over,' he said. 'We'd be delighted to have you.'

Seldom have I encountered such fantastic and generous hospitality as we received at TAG Farnborough. I flew over shortly after and was met by several ground handlers who pushed the Stearman into a vast, modern, pristine hangar with automated doors and gleaming floors. A team of people descended on the aeroplane with sponges, cloths and sundry polishes and spray cans to clean it up. It was like the best aeroplane spa in the world. With the TAG events manager, we worked on the details of the departure event and a farewell dinner for family and friends the night before at the Aviator Hotel, which sits on the airfield with a glorious view right down the runway. The curved roofs of the architecturally designed hangars formed a great undulating wave down the western side which makes the airfield so distinctive from the air. Looking at modern Farnborough today it is hard to believe that this is where the first flight in England took place in 1908.

And so, by the skin of our teeth, we were ready for the grand departure on October 1. It was a gathering of family and friends, sponsors and supporters and those last 24 hours before our departure were a convergence of everybody I loved most. Everything came together for this moment of magic.

During the customary formalities, Prince Michael, Dick Turpin from Artemis and Tim Wheeler from Boeing gave lovely speeches to wish us well and Godspeed on the long journey ahead.

Tim Kelly did a brilliant job co-ordinating the media and the interviews, which had started at 6.30am continuing throughout the morning. At 12.30pm, I finally tore myself away and climbed into the Stearman. Ewald pulled the propellor through and I started up the engine and gave the crowd a final wave. I took off and flew a tight circuit around the field for one final pass in farewell.

Then I headed for the south coast, ecstatic to be in the air, unspeakably relieved that everything had gone so well, and just so grateful to TAG Farnborough for everything they had done.

Skimming along in the dazzling sunshine in a kind of trance, I dodged a large buzzard near Hastings, which I took to be a good omen. The birds were with us. Before long I headed out over the English Channel, once more bound for France.

If Farnborough was the big public send-off, the real preparation for the expedition took place in Hungary, where we arrived two days later.

Our expedition this time was going to be: 12 weeks, 23 countries, 62 stops, 13,600 miles, with a departure date from Hungary of October 9.

Our approach was going to be different to Africa, however. We had half the number of crew and we would spend much less time filming. I employed one accomplished cameraman, Matt Wainwright, and he was our only film crew. In his mid-thirties, Matt was very English, with a witty sense of humour and with all the affinity for modern technology of the younger generation. The support aircraft, a Pilatus Porter PC-6 - a single-engine, high wing utility aircraft designed by the Swiss in the 1950s – would be flown by our Swiss friend, Markus Loeschenkohl, a seasoned pilot and engineer. Ewald was going to fly with me. We did our own flight planning and used the same company, White Rose, to arrange the flight permissions for most of the countries we were going through with one or two notable exceptions where Boeing stepped in to help. We planned to use the PC-6 to carry barrels of Avgas for the Stearman and the supply of oil for the whole trip, with the aim of being entirely self-sufficient in all aspects of aircraft maintenance, as there would be little in the way of back-up on the way.

Markus arrived at the base over the weekend and Matt flew into Vienna from London on the Tuesday night with an eye-watering amount of equipment. We hardly had space in the car for it, let alone in the aircraft. We spent the next week sorting the kit. The Hungarian engineers made a small jump seat in the back of the PC-6 and installed a safety harness for Matt for the filming with the side door open. Although he had never done anything like this before, he embraced the challenge with youthful enthusiasm.

Working long days, we were ready as planned on Friday, October 9 and got away by 10am, just an hour later than scheduled.

However, we were only in the air for half an hour before we were forced to land because of low cloud. After waiting for an hour for the cloud to lift, we got airborne again, but were now advised by air traffic control that Serbia had closed its northern border for military exercises and we were diverted back to Győr. By 2pm that afternoon we were still on the ground in Hungary, further back than we had been from our original starting point at Fertőszentmiklós.

It was hardly a great start to the expedition.

Was this a sign of things to come?

Hungary to Pakistan

OCTOBER 9, GYŐR TO BUCHAREST

WITH slightly better weather to the south, we finally took off again and Markus tucked the PC-6 behind my right wing as we flew over a low line of hills and crossed the Danube. After two and half hours in the air we landed at Arad in western Romania in the early evening and settled in for the night.

Ahead were the Carpathian Mountains and the weather wasn't looking good. First reported in the Egyptian astronomer Ptolemy's *Geographia*, the discontinuous range across eastern Europe rises to the highest point of nearly 9,000 ft in Slovakia. The ancient name of *Carpates* comes from the Albanian for 'rock' and this stone wall encircles the whole of the Transylvanian plateau of central Romania. The densely forested mountains are the home of Europe's greatest population of brown bears, wolves, lynx and chamois goat-antelopes.

Flying straight towards the mountains, we climbed steadily up to 9,000 ft with the engine purring steadily in the smooth, cold air. At the highest point were several dramatic snow-covered peaks and ridges and we sailed over the top of these with aquiline ease, thrilled by the view. To the south-east, however, and directly on our track lay a sea of white cloud. It looked beautiful and benign but would have been a death trap flying over this without breaks or holes to descend through. Forced to find another route through, we turned back and descended several thousand feet down the lower slopes. We made our way down a valley on the western side, flying due south, but it got darker and darker as the cloud got lower. We crossed several low ridges with some unpleasant downdrafts and the Stearman was buffeted around in the turbulence. A lake then appeared, forking east-west, and things seemed to improve for a few miles but the visibility reduced again and we flew low over a vast black, open-cast mine with monstrous, crane-like machines raking the surface of the earth. It could have been a vision of the underworld from Dante's Hell and as we descended, it got worse still.

The rain started and as the visibility reduced further it felt like we were flying in a dark tunnel. I became seriously worried, but Ewald assured me we could land in one of the long thin fields that striped the valley floor below, if necessary. This seemed vaguely reassuring, but landing was one thing and taking off again was another. We kept going, knowing that a few miles farther the valley opened out onto the plain and ahead of us was the airport of Craiova. We inched our way towards this safe haven with the intention of landing but when we got within five miles the conditions improved sufficiently for us to think we should press on. We turned due east, directly on track to Bucharest, approaching Baneasa International Airport 40 minutes later. What we thought was going to be a three-and-a-half-hour flight had turned into a five-hour epic. When we landed just after 2pm it was a huge relief to be on the ground. In a howling gale, we quickly refuelled from the mobile bowser, half thinking it might be possible to fly on, but the severe weather front was advancing rapidly behind us and our chance of out-running it was remote. Plus, it was all getting late. We were both chilled to the bone and exhausted, so decided to call it a day. A few photographers were waiting behind the wire fence and I went to speak to them. Inside the terminal were a couple of journalists waiting to interview me so I quickly got through this and then went back outside with Ewald to get the Stearman sorted out. There was no hangarage available so we pushed the Stearman onto a rough, sloping shoulder of grass and tethered it firmly to the ground.

We had no option but to sit out the heavy rain and gale force winds for the next two days – a deeply frustrating start to the expedition.

October 13, Bucharest

We planned to leave by 10.30am but were held up filing the flight plan and paying fees. When we finally got to the Stearman, it was a terrible mess, covered in a filthy, black grime which was a combination of jet blast and pollution. Due to the grass slope, fuel had drained from the tank, leaving a blue stain down the left wing, which was now saturated. As we pulled the metal pegs out of the mud and heaved the Stearman out onto the hard surface, I told Matt to start filming – as it was a perfect example of the unglamorous side of the expedition. Ewald thought we might have lost up to an hour of fuel so we had to get the truck back for a top-up, which ate up more precious time. We then had to set the GoPros and were wet and cold before we even climbed into the cockpit.

We finally got airborne at 11.30am and for the first half an hour cruised along at 1,500 ft but were forced to descend as the cloud base sank lower and once again found ourselves flying on the deck. Ahead of us was a strange, amorphous whiteness and I felt an involuntary spasm of fear. It almost looked like the horizontal surface of water, but it was an optical illusion. It was a massive fog bank over the Danube and I hastily turned back. We continued to skirt around the edge of the fog, to see if there was a breakthrough to the south or east. We flew around a whole area of flat marshland at barely a hundred feet, trying to avoid a large military zone to the west but, after an hour and a half of this, feeling cold and dispirited, we finally landed back on at Baneasa. Markus had managed to get through to Constantia on the Black Sea, so while the boys overnighted there, Ewald and I stayed once again in Bucharest.

The Romanians were very sympathetic and did their level best to make sure we enjoyed our enforced stay. This time they managed to organise some hangarage, which instantly cheered me up, and kindly arranged a sight-seeing tour for us that afternoon with the luxury of a private car and a driver called Valentine. I had to buy some supplies as my overnight bag was in the PC-6, a stupid oversight I made a mental note not to repeat.

OCTOBER 14, BUCHAREST TO ISTANBUL

The weather was much brighter the next day and, with the Stearman clean, dry and ready to go, we posed for a few pictures with our hosts and then climbed in. We were given the same instrument departure out of Baneasa and took off into a light haze but with altogether better conditions.

Finally, we made it over the border into Bulgaria – one of the great surprises of the trip. The landscape was utterly beautiful – a wilderness of forest with rocky escarpments rising to 2-3,000 ft out of the trees. Laid out in a diaphanous light, it reminded me of Africa in part, but also of Tuscany – a whole world away from the atmospheric horrors of the previous days.

We routed via Burgas on the Black Sea and turned east to follow the shoreline flying at a thousand feet. Below were several large resorts and beaches but as we continued the development petered away and it grew much wilder and more rugged with deeply scalloped bays, and trees growing right to the waterline.

We landed in Turkey at Çorlu, on the outskirts of Istanbul, to process through immigration and were reunited with the crew. Markus and Matt came bounding up to us on the apron but I cut the greetings short and scolded them for launching ahead of us. Getting separated had cost us the opportunity for air-to-air filming over Bulgaria and the Black Sea. It wasn't my way to order people around and I didn't like trying to manage a team, even a small one, but I expected the crew to be a bit more considerate. It put a dampener on the reunion but the point was made.

An ExecuJet representative called Levent met us and drove us to the terminal to do the processing and advised that the fuel needed to be paid for in cash as they didn't take credit cards. After shelling out €650 that cleared out our reserve. We still had a stash of US dollars but were keen to keep hold of these in the event of a real emergency. We then flew on to a small, privately owned airstrip called Hezarfen, our base for the next few days. This was named after Hezârfen Ahmed Çelebi, a 17th century Ottoman birdman who, with a pair of eagle's wings, launched off the Galata Tower and flew across the Golden Horn in what might have been the first sustained, unpowered flight after Icarus attempted to fly from Crete with his waxed wings.

We used the short flight down the coast to Hezarfen to trial air-to-air filming. The airfield was a lovely, paved strip up a hill with a reservoir at the bottom. It was quite short and, with the pronounced slope, aircraft had to land uphill and take-off downhill.

A little crowd was waiting to meet us, amongst them Tim Kelly, my PR man, and Ayça from ExecuJet, both of whom had been waiting for the past four days for us to arrive. We posed for a few photos with the Stearman, which the locals offered to clean, but when I saw the buckets and heavy scrubbing brushes they were proposing to use on the gleaming paintwork, I politely declined their offer.

We had a two-hour drive into the city and didn't get there until 8pm. Tim briefed me and explained the improvised plan given that we were now four days late. We had to cancel the arrangements to spend time in Anatolia with Pegasus Airline to make up for some of the lost days. Our most pressing problem, however, was the hotel reservation. I wasn't sure our booking could be extended and Tim also had to leave the next morning so I would be on my own for the press day which had been rescheduled for Friday. When I finally got to my room, I was exhausted but my priority was writing a thank you letter to our host in Istanbul,

Mustapha Koc. He had been wonderfully supportive and it was his hotel we were staying in. I fielded calls from journalists until late and didn't get to bed until after midnight.

Tim and I sat down in the cafe the next morning and recorded a couple of interviews for him to transcribe and to finalise the media programme for the following day. I was able to reconfirm the hotel accommodation and now started to relax a bit. We were keen to see something of Istanbul, old Constantinople, and that afternoon the four of us loaded into a taxi and with our guide, Ozgar, set off to visit the Blue Mosque and the Hagia Sofia Grand Mosque. My hope had been to fly down the narrow Bosporus natural strait for the film with these beautiful and heavenly mosques in the background but, much like the pyramids in Cairo, we weren't allowed anywhere near them in the air.

I wanted an elevated view of the city and Ozgar obliged by finding a hotel with a roof garden with a breath-taking 360° outlook. Even in the high wind, it was a sublime moment to stand up there amongst the tiled roofs for what must be one of the best views in the world.

October 16, Istanbul

Friday's big press day kicked off with a 6.50am interview with BBC Radio 5 Live. We then drove out to the airfield for back-to-back interviews with local media from 10am to 3pm. Equal opportunities for women was a very big subject in Turkey and one of the main topics we discussed. Turkey had the distinction of having the first female fighter pilot in the world, Sabiha Gökçen, the adopted daughter of the country's first president, Mustafa Kemal Atatürk, who flew with the Turkish air force during World War Two. Ataturk gave her the surname 'Gokcen', meaning 'belonging or relating to the sky'. Sabiha wasn't an aviator at this point but six months later developed a passion for flying and went on to participate in 32 separate military operations. The

Turks honoured her by naming Istanbul's second airport after her.

We stopped for a lunch of bean stew at the little aero club and later a group of students came to see the Stearman and marvelled at the basic cockpit. Most of their flying training had been on simulators and they flew with instruments with little or no experience of VFR (visual) flying. One of them remarked that he couldn't imagine how it was possible to fly this way, illustrating that what we were doing was already a dying art.

October 17, Istanbul to Rhodes

When Amy Johnson flew to Australia her strategy for breaking the record was to put a ruler on a map and draw a straight line for the shortest possible route. From Istanbul, this took her through the 15,000 ft Taurus Mountains on Turkey's border with Syria, where she had her first near-death experience. Flying along a narrow valley she rounded a corner and inadvertently flew into a cloud bank. Momentarily disorientated by the white-out, she dived the Gypsy Moth out of the cloud and nearly flew into a rock face as she surfaced into clear air. Thoroughly shaken, Amy flew on across the Syrian plain and stopped in Aleppo for the night. The next day she was off again, crossing the desert into Iraq, and flew into a huge sandstorm. In a vortex of swirling sand and downdrafts, she came hurtling earthwards from several thousand feet and touched ground at 120 miles-per-hour. It was a barely controlled landing over rough ground and broke part of the Gypsy Moth's undercarriage. When the aircraft rolled to a halt, Amy leapt out and managed to secure it by loading her bags onto the wings to weigh them down and with her entire body weight she lay across the tail. Three hours later, she took off again.

Today's war zones compelled us to divert south from Istanbul to the Greek island of Rhodes – a four-and-a-half-hour flight covering around 360 miles.

On Saturday, we were back to Hezarfen first thing, where once again Markus set about repacking the PC-6 now using heavy nets attached to the cabin frame to secure the bags. Ewald went to file the flight plan but there was a problem with Ankara air traffic control. We wanted to stop at Sabiha Gökçen Airport but we weren't allowed and the controllers, unsure of what to do with a vintage aeroplane, finally cleared us to leave as a ferry flight, routing us back to Çorlu to clear customs and immigration. We finally got away late morning and, flying down the coast, managed to do some air-to-air filming, this time with Matt in his harness with the door slid open.

We started off in gloomy conditions, as we tracked the coast, but it soon brightened and we now headed inland, flying due south right down western Turkey. The most memorable part of this flight was flying down a dramatic ravine in the mountains with vertical rock faces and emerging out of this over a 1,500 ft drop to the coastal plain. Ahead of us lay a huge naval base and we skirted to the south of this before heading out over the Aegean Sea. The PC-6 pulled alongside for some more air-to-air filming.

In the distance were the rugged mountains of Rhodes. Markus landed ahead of us and was met by an irate Greek woman who managed aircraft movements on the apron and wasn't expecting us. We left Markus to calm her down and tied down and covered the Stearman for the night. Our hotel was close to the airport but, although it featured a deck with open views of the sea, it was a fleeting pleasure, as I was in bed by 8pm.

OCTOBER 18, RHODES TO CYPRUS

From Rhodes we wanted to fly to Cyprus but were held up all morning waiting for our clearance to Akrotiri, the RAF base on British Overseas Territory on the island. The controllers refused to authorise this flight plan and insisted that we redirect our flight to land at Paphos, in the Greek part of the island. We had no option but to agree and finally got airborne at 1pm. I had phoned ahead to Akrotiri to warn we were going to be late but our man on the ground there, Bryn Williams, told us to ignore the air traffic instructions and proceed directly to Akrotiri. We had to remain 10 miles off the Turkish coast as we flew to the east and over what was now the northern Mediterranean. Given the choice, we would have stayed within gliding distance of the shore, but such were the sensitive geopolitics of the region we remained over the water.

When we came within range of Cyprus we established contact with the air traffic controller at Paphos. Markus was also on the frequency and we repeated the joining instructions but at the very last moment we confirmed that we would not be landing at Paphos but would continue to Akrotiri, as per our authorisation from the British. I left Ewald to handle the communications with Markus and couldn't help but smile at his cool, calm insistence as the Greek controller got more and more irate. Markus, having confirmed he was on left base for Paphos, simply turned his radio off and didn't bother to speak to them again. We flew a wide arc around Paphos, several miles out to sea, and tracked east along the south coast of the island. We now contacted the controllers at Akrotiri and were given radar vectors for the long approach to land. The visibility by this time was very hazy with little in the way of a horizon and the radio contact was intermittent, but we landed half an hour later and were met on the apron by Bryn, amongst others. They laughed about our run-in with the controllers and assured us it was a regular occurrence with foreign registered aircraft (the Stearman was still American registered). They called the controllers at Nicosia the next day to smooth things over.

The RAF quartered us in the officers' mess and made our two-day stopover great fun from start to finish. We drank brandy sours in the bar that night and I had a lively conversation with Jackie, the psychotherapist from Scotland who was there to help the forces. The next day we visited the primary school on the base for its assembly and, dressed in jodhpurs and boots with my flying goggles, I gave a talk for them about the flight. The four-year-olds were enchanting with questions that were more like statements about their own lives. One little boy told me his grandfather's dog had been called Artemis and another told me that his great-grandfather was older than the Stearman. They were especially fascinated to hear the macabre details of Amy's final crash and wanted to know how she went to the loo in her cockpit.

From there we went to see 84 Squadron's sea rescue operations and, while being shown around a Huey helicopter, I climbed into the sling they use to winch people off distressed ships. We drove around in the afternoon and spent an hour or two at an open bar on the beach and did some filming at an old stone quarry. That evening, from a deck by the control tower, we watched 93 Tornado Squadron taking off for night operations and, later, I did a talk over drinks in the mess for the company.

OCTOBER 20, CYPRUS TO JORDAN

Arriving at the Met office the next morning for our departure briefing, there was a bit of drama. A small boat carrying migrants from Syria had washed up on one of beaches belonging to the base and there was some confusion about what to do with them. This was effectively a British beach and the political implications a sensitive issue. Later, while waiting to take off, a U2 spy plane landed on the runway ahead of us and shed part of its wing in the long ground roll. Vehicles roared out onto the tarmac to find the bits and we waited while they did this, amused by the unusual predicament. The U2s had been based on Cyprus for many years and were the worst-kept secret for miles around given their unmistakable, black dart-like appearance. The squadron motto was '45 Years of Service and still not here'.

We took off shortly after and roared out over the beach into a glorious morning. I looked down to see if I could see any more migrant boats but the rocky bays were devoid of people.

We had been warned of a weather front blowing into Cyprus later that day but were well ahead of this as we swept across the north-eastern Mediterranean to Israel. Flying at 2,500 ft towards the sun, we were in extremely sensitive airspace, within 150 miles of the warzone in Syria. When we reached 200 miles from the Israeli coast we had to establish contact with its controllers and went through a series of pre-agreed, coded security identifiers as we got closer. The Israelis do not allow anyone to fly in their airspace without rigorous security checks and, in this case, Boeing helped to facilitate a special clearance for us with the military.

As we approached the coast we kept a lookout for our official escort – another Boeing Stearman. We circled around for a bit before spotting our escort above us in his bright blue and yellow aeroplane and quickly joined up in formation. The pilot, Avnor, had his girlfriend in the front seat and they both waved at us smiling and laughing. Avnor turned out to be that rare thing, a man capable of incredible multi-tasking. He flew around me, above then below, and pulled up in close formation. Then he backed off slightly with his head down as he did the radio communications in Hebrew, changing frequencies through eight different control zones on the way. During parts of the flight, he also held up his mobile phone and filmed, unseeing, with his head still down while he did the radio. I was highly amused by it all.

We flew in formation down the long stretch of beach at about 50 ft and, as we advanced, various people who had helped us with this incredible access came over the radio to say hello. It was the most wonderful welcome and to my lasting regret we were not able to land in Israel to thank them properly for their help. At least we had the aerial tour of our lives. Avnor led us over Tel Aviv at low level, over the Temple of Jerusalem at about 200 ft and then we headed over the rock desert mountains to the east. As we roared over the sheer edge, I was completely gobsmacked by the sight before us – a primordial landscape of a rift valley between the two tectonic plates of Africa and Arabia. The 5,000 ft vertical rock faces on either side glowed a rich warm gold in the afternoon sun and the valley plunged thousands of feet below to a depth of 1,300 ft below sea level. On its floor was the Dead Sea, a saline lake fed by the River Jordan which flashed like sapphire in the golden sand. We flew along the western cliff face and then dropped down to the water and I followed behind Avnor as he flew to about 15 feet over the surface, just skimming along like a seabird.

With this breathtaking finale, he finally peeled away, saying he was nearly at the end of his fuel reserve. We thanked him profusely over the radio and I couldn't resist asking, 'Avnor, what are you?'

The voice over the radio laughed. I suspected he was an ace and it turned out he was a pilot with the Israeli Air Force and flew F-15s for a living. It was a fine touch of the Israelis to give us a military escort perfectly disguised in a Boeing Stearman.

We climbed slowly back up to 6,000 ft towards the eastern rise and suddenly there was Amman, the capital city of Jordan, lightly veiled in cloud. We landed at Marka Airport behind the PC-6 and received a royal welcome. Their Royal Highnesses Prince Hamzah and Princess Basmah, both pilots and avid skydivers, were there to meet us with their two little daughters. They were very charming, encouraged us to visit the Jordan Skydiving Club, and, with great generosity, also offered to arrange for us to visit Petra. This had been on my wish list for a very long time and we gratefully accepted their kind offer. I also wanted to see King Hussein's Car Museum.

There was a crowd of Jordanians to help us with the aircraft and everybody lined the wings to push them into the huge hangar near the control tower. They were endlessly helpful and desperately keen for us to see their country. We made plans for the next day and, soon after, repaired to our hotel for a late lunch. We ended up staying in Jordan for a week and enjoyed every single minute of it.

The next day we were taken to the Jordan Skydiving Club. I somehow got talked into doing a jump and once again found myself over the Dead Sea, this time sitting on the cabin floor of a Cessna 206, peering over the open side and looking straight down at the ground from 10,000 ft. I had done a parachute jump in New Zealand years before and I had the same feeling of, 'What the hell am I doing here?' It was surreal climbing out of the cabin and clinging to the wing strut in the buffeting airflow. Once in the air in freefall, however, it makes perfect sense. I spread my arms and tried to imagine that I was really flying and not falling. Below was a radiant gold haze and I fell through space to a perfect landing, thanks to the instructor strapped behind me.

One phenomenal place seen better from the ground than air is Petra, that 'rose red city, half as old as time'.

It was a two-day trip and a royal limousine duly arrived to take us there. It was beyond anything I had imagined. Approached through a narrow, winding corridor of high rock, it opened to those extraordinary colonnaded facades carved straight into the towering sandstone rock face. There were a few heavily garlanded grumpy looking camels sitting around waiting for tourists but we weren't tempted. Our guide looked suspiciously like Johnny Depp in *Pirates of the Caribbean* with his eyes lined in black kohl but he insisted the American actor was impersonating him.

Following our return to Amman we picked up our visas from the Saudi Arabian Embassy and finally got ready to leave the next day. There was a suggestion King Abdullah might be at the airport to see us off but in the end he was caught up with other business.

As we made final preparations to leave Marka Airport, a strange cloud of fog literally rolled down the runway, completely obscuring it for several minutes, but, quickly as it arrived, it rolled away again like milkweed in the wind.

BIRD

OCTOBER 27, JORDAN TO RIYADH

We said goodbye over the radio to our lovely friends in the control tower and took off through the apartment blocks surrounding the airport before heading out over the city into the desert beyond. Over the previous few days there had been a lot of rain, which was another reason why we stayed for so long. Now, as we flew over the flat stony desert, it was possible to see braided threads of water over the surface. This unseasonably heavy precipitation caused poor visibility for most of the way. We were effectively flying in a fine mist and the only real features below were occasional irrigated circles of green crops which broke the monotony of the sand.

It was desert all the way to Al-Jouf, our first stop and immigration entry point into Saudi Arabia. Once again, Boeing facilitated our entry into the kingdom. Mike Kurth, who ran Boeing's Saudi operation, was there to meet us when we landed three and a half hours later. I had first met Mike with his vivacious wife, Debbie, in London in 2010 when I was with Robert and notwithstanding our split, they became great friends of mine. Originally from Wisconsin, Mike had served 24 years with the US Marine Corp, retiring as a colonel with more than 5,000 hours in more than 30 types of aircraft, mainly attack helicopters. He commanded a light attack helicopter squadron during Desert Storm in the Gulf War in 1990-91 and was awarded the Navy Cross. Following his military career, Mike had joined Boeing and worked for nearly 20 years for the company ending up as a senior vice president. I was very lucky to have him as a mentor and he has continued to help and advise me through all the expeditions.

With Mike to help us in Al-Jouf were two of his very able Boeing team – Khalaf Alkhatami, who liaised with air traffic control and managed the bureaucracy along our route, and Bader Al Bedair, who assisted with everything else. I was immediately handed an abaya and wrapped this around my flying suit to cover up, as Saudis expect of women. This made it hard to climb up onto the top wing to refuel and it was going to be a positive hazard pulling the propeller through with this voluminous fabric flapping around me in the wind. Processing through immigration, I was corralled into a separate processing section for women and searched by a female officer. When she saw my flying suit underneath the robe, she broke into a smile and impulsively took my hand, shaking it vigorously. She clearly approved and I returned the compliment regarding her own uniform.

We didn't linger on the ground, just long enough to process and refuel and then we were on our way again to Ha'il in the north-west. It was more sand and rock but this is the terrain I most love to fly. The desert has a pure, elemental, mineral beauty and we were now flying into the heart of Arabia. We saw lots of camels dotted around and the occasional settlement but the real surprise was the weather. I had somehow expected dry conditions with good visibility but as we got closer to Ha'il it was clear we were approaching a thunderstorm. The sky darkened, turning an eerie violet and we followed a highway, flying just a few hundred feet above. We threaded between two low pyramids of dark rock, which rose straight out of the sand. With lightning now flashing in the distance, we were relieved to finally land at Ha'il. We taxied onto a vast almost empty apron area but were concerned by how late the crew were in the PC-6. We secured the Stearman just before the rain came. We tried in vain to contact Markus and Matt but it transpired they had been diverted back to Al-Jouf. Mike was again there to meet us and we took a taxi to a local hotel. Due to torrential rain for the last few days, there was a lot of standing water in the streets – a novel problem in the Arabian Desert.

We finally reunited with the crew when they landed at Ha'il the next morning. They had been quad-biking in the desert so were none the worse for their detour.

We got ready for our next flight to Riyadh, 380 miles to the south-east, routing via Al-Qassim, an old desert watering hole turned metropolis. Strong winds were forecast in Riyadh but we enjoyed a fantastic journey, flying low and roaring up and down the sand dunes with wingovers over the top. We might have been one of the first biplanes to fly the Arabian Peninsula since Sopwith Camels in the First World War. The landscape was uninterrupted golden sand and we spotted several brilliant white camels scattered in the lee, without a blade of grass to pick at.

We landed at Al Thumamah, a private airfield used predominantly by the Saudi royal family. We stayed at a very nice hotel in the centre of Riyadh and the breakfast buffets were something to behold – a banquet of Middle Eastern and western cuisine – the best of the expedition by far. In a wing reserved for women, I had a superb view of the city. Although a nice novelty to be separated from the boys, it was strange going everywhere swathed in a long black robe, as if one was in deep mourning.

The following day, Friday, was our media day at Al Thumamah. The highlight of the day, indeed of our whole stay in Riyadh, was meeting Princess Reema bint Bandar Al Saud, one of the most prominent women in Saudi Arabia today. In a country with one of the highest rates of breast cancer in the world, she set up her own foundation to promote women's health and wellness. Her charity was called 10KSA after 10,000 women congregated in a football arena in support of better health.

The princess came to meet us at Al Thumamah with a small entourage and I invited her to come flying with me. She gracefully accepted and slipped discretely out of her abaya before climbing up the wing into the front cockpit.

We then took off and, after climbing just a few hundred feet, flew along the dramatic escarpment known as 'the Edge of the World', and I could see why. We then roared off down an open valley, flying along a dry riverbed at just 50 ft, something I don't think she had ever done before. When we landed 40 minutes later the princess was elated. She made me an ambassador of her charity and I carried her Wings of Hope logo on the *Spirit of Artemis* for the rest of the flight.

OCTOBER 31, RIYADH TO DUBAI

We left Riyadh having been hugely impressed with Saudi hospitality and everybody we met. I would have loved to spend more time in the city – there was a vast modern university for women near our hotel I wanted to visit and several museums – but we had to press on.

We had a two-hour flight to Al-Ahsa in the south-west of the country for our final fuel stop before crossing the border into the United Arab Emirates. It was a relief not to wear my abaya for the refuelling.

We now had another four and a half hours in the air to reach the Persian Gulf. With it being Halloween, we should probably have not been surprised that Abu Dhabi proved to be more of a trick than a treat.

A beautiful white mosque with four minarets glowed in the sunset to our left as we approached Al Bateen Airport. We were bone-weary from the long flight, but the airport staff were almost completely indifferent to our arrival. There were no facilities but although no assistance or service was offered it was disconcerting to find ourselves under close surveillance the whole time. In the terminal we met the same cool response and were held up for over an hour and a half processing our paperwork before we finally got to the hotel.

The following day I had another busy schedule, visiting a local girls' college before giving a presentation to a group of university students at the Boeing offices in the city.

It was then back to the airport for a photo call with Bernie Dunn, the head of Boeing's Middle East operation. We needed a special permit to do this and we hung around for nearly two hours before getting access to the Stearman for the two-minute photo session. We weren't allowed to spend any time with the aircraft either for basic technical checks.

As a result, I decided we'd leave early and fly on to Dubai, where ExecuJet would look after the aeroplanes properly.

After all the desert flying, the 120 miles along the Gulf – a sheet of shimmering pale blue light which mirrored the sky – were surreal. The skyline of Dubai appeared like a mirage, quivering and insubstantial in the heat haze, becoming more distinct as we got closer. As we skirted around the edge of the city we could clearly make out the Palm Islands development fanning out into the Gulf. We landed at Dubai International Airport and taxied straight to the ExecuJet facility, where we had a great welcome. Ewald immediately started work as the Stearman was due its 25-hour maintenance check, while I cracked on with the oil change. We finished late that night and the following morning he flew back to Europe for 10 days while I concentrated on the outreach programme and the Dubai Air Show.

From my hotel room I had a jaw-dropping view of the Burj Khalifa – the sky-piercing, glass laser of a building that was, in my opinion, the only true wonder of Dubai, as it dwarfed everything else in scale and beauty. It is the highest structure in the world and I was told that somewhere on one of those 163 floors, at some vertiginous height, was an Irish pub. Sadly, we never got to visit it.

For the air show official opening on the Sunday, November 8, the crew came with me but Markus forgot his passport and after a lengthy hassle trying to process our documentation, he gave up and returned to the hotel, while Matt and I joined the show and managed to do some filming and interviews around the Stearman.

Charlie Miller, Boeing's communications director, gave me a tour of the Dreamliner and I sat in the cockpit and inspected the state-of-art cabin. Various friends and VIPs dropped by to say hello – including Shuttleworth pilot Frank Chapman – and His Royal

Highness Prince Sultan bin Salman Al Saud of Saudi Arabia also came by to see the Stearman with his entourage. A former fighter pilot and astronaut, Prince Sultan was the chairman of the Saudi Space Commission and it was he who had sponsored our stay at Al Thumamah Airport in Riyadh. I was enthralled to meet him. In the late 1970s, when he was a student at the University of Denver, the prince took a flight in a Stearman and this was the beginning of his love affair with aviation. I invited him to fly a leg with me in the *Spirit of Artemis* and we talked about meeting up again in America to do this. Ghouse Akbar, our friend from Pakistan, also arrived with Captain Khan to discuss the logistics of the flight with Prince Nikolaos of Greece and Denmark which was now due to take place in a few days' time.

At the air show we also met up again with Mike Kurth and Bader Al Bedair. Bader wore the traditional white robe with headdress and his dark eyes, framed by his Buddy Holly-style spectacles, shone with delight at our reunion. He was very solicitous towards me, would cue me with names before I was introduced and endearingly held my hand at odd moments as if I was a child.

The following day, Tim Kelly and Caroline O'Donnell from Artemis arrived and Tim came with me to the International Association of Women in Aviation (IAWA) event, where I was one of the keynote speakers. There were hundreds of women from all over the world in attendance and the atmosphere was buzzing with energy. I was amazed, having never witnessed this degree of enthusiasm at flying gatherings for women in the UK.

That evening, I attended a big reception, with a heaving crowd of women passionate about aviation and hell-bent on having a good time.

Ewald had arrived back from Europe and I caught up with him the following morning. We had a rare day of leisure and the whole gang of us, including Tim, went shopping at the famous Dubai Mall.

November 13, Dubai to Muscat

Friday the 13th saw us fly direct to Muscat in Oman and with John Kloppenberg's help we were able to get away in good time. We headed inland, cutting across the 'horn' of Arabia, and crossing the rugged Al-Hajar Mountains before we picked up the coast again on the Gulf of Oman.

We were held up for seven hours at Muscat Airport, not this time due to bureaucracy but by Markus and Matt inadvertently checking through immigration when they landed ahead of us. It took us all afternoon to get them re-entered back into the airport only to repeat the whole process again after we had refuelled, secured the aeroplanes and collected our kit. By the time we got sorted we were all tired and irritable and our hotel, the Golden Tulip, a grubby little place with an unpleasant smell, a short drive from the airport, hardly improved the mood. Matt and I did some filming the next morning before we enjoyed an al fresco lunch at the Al Bustan Palace, with its spectacular backdrop of shark-tooth mountains. Caroline joined us that evening and when she invited me to stay with her for the night in her very chic, boutique hotel with a private beach I didn't hesitate, leaving the boys to rough it at the Golden Tulip.

The following morning, on Sunday, I gave a talk to an assembly of school children at the British Embassy. Later, at night, we were all back at the embassy for a presentation about a British expedition to cross the Empty Quarter on camels. It was a pleasure to listen to someone else talking for a change and it was enthralling to listen to their trials and tribulations. The camels turned out to be one of their biggest challenges. They were unfit and querulous and had struggled during the long and arduous trek, the soft living of modern life having taken the edge off their ability to survive in the desert.

NOVEMBER 16, MUSCAT TO GWADAR

The following morning dawned bright and clear for the next leg to Pakistan. Ahead was the Gulf of Oman, nearly 250 miles over water, and we all donned life jackets and joked about ditching in what was one of the busiest waterways in the world. Fortunately, we didn't have to.

Pakistan is where we would pick up Amy's route again. She had flown from Baghdad, stopped at Bandar Abbas in Persia and then to Drigh Road Airport in Karachi. Our landfall in Pakistan was a place called Jiwani, recommended by my old friend Christopher, who had visited many times when he was based in Aden with the RAF in the 1950s. It is also where the Queen used to visit privately and liked so much she had a small residence there. As we flew over, I could see the runway, which appeared disused and, not far away, a splendid house, which just might have been a royal retreat.

We continued along the coast to the port city of Gwadar. Except for the very occasional fishing village it seemed a deserted landscape. The blinding pallor of the beach and the limestone rock formations on our port side were an astonishing sight and the greatest surprise to us. Castellated towers of white chalk, chiselled by the wind, ran parallel to the shore and we flew along the edge of this marvelling at the weird, wind-made forms.

On close approach to land at Gwadar, I was momentarily distracted by the sight of a C-130 Hercules parked on the apron and the big throng of people waiting to meet us, causing me to make the worst landing of the entire expedition. There was a light crosswind and I caught a bit of sinking air just before crossing the threshold and managed to bounce badly. The controller, slightly hesitant, asked if I was okay. I laughed in embarrassment and said, 'Yes, I am. But what a *shit* of a landing! I do hope they captured that on camera.'

Ewald laughed helplessly in the front seat. Later, over dinner,

I apologised for scaring him and he just looked at me and said, 'Hey, we walked away, didn't we?'

From the crowd of photographers waiting to meet us it was apparent the Pakistani Air Force had flown the entire press corps from Karachi for our arrival. It was overwhelming. There was a female military pilot called Sara, there as part of the delegation and I shook her hand warmly. Women could be fighter pilots in Pakistan and it was a special pleasure to meet one of them.

The questions came thick and fast and I stood for nearly an hour talking with them all before we got packed up to go to the hotel. While we were securing the Stearman, dust eddies blew up on the apron like mini tornados. I glanced at the windsock and it was careering all over the place. It was deceptive, because there was no wind to speak of, and I wondered then if I had caught some capricious movement of air with my landing.

Our drive to the hotel was completely surreal – in the back of a closed Jeep, with two machine gun-wielding guards hanging off the crossbar. Behind and in front were more vehicles, all with flashing lights and sirens wailing the entire way as we drove at high speed to the city. I kept exchanging looks of amazement with the boys. We were obviously very grateful for the protection but it certainly made us wonder what hazards were lurking out there to justify this degree of security.

Our hotel had a prominent position on cliffs overlooking the Arabian Sea, with a sweeping view of the harbour. Captain Khan was our host for the night and over dinner we discussed the plans for the next day – when I'd be taking a prince flying.

Pakistan to Indonesia

AFTER making the most tentative of plans back at Farnborough to take Prince Nikolaos of Greece and Denmark flying, providing he was able to meet us in Gwadar, I scarcely believed it would happen. But, lo and behold, here we were and Captain Khan ran through the arrangements for our flight. Prince Nikolaos would meet us at the airport and I had to follow a prescribed route in accordance with various military restrictions. The air force would provide a helicopter escort, flown by the captain, into Jinnah International Airport and so we agreed on a rendezvous point on the map.

We were at the airport early ahead of Prince Nikolaos's arrival. With the prospect of royalty on board I felt added pressure but he was so charming we were soon chatting away like old friends. He had done quite a bit of flying and as a keen photographer was hoping to get some good shots on the way.

We tracked out to the coast, along the same limestone formations we had seen the previous day, then loosely along the shore before cutting inland into the Kirthar mountains, which forms the boundary between the Lower Indus Plain to the east and southern Balochistan in the west. In her memoir, Amy had described her terror at flying over this 'hideous' yet dramatic landscape of jagged black rock 'all carved with pinnacle-like hills forming ranges with serrated summits'.

Certainly, as Amy would have feared, we faced certain death should the engine fail us now.

However, I was completely mesmerised by the terrifying beauty of these mountains; the intricate folding and slip of the rock faces spoke of metamorphic forces on an unimaginable scale.

Prince Nikolaos looked out over the side taking pictures. We caught up with the PC-6 and fell into formation along the edge of a sharp edge of granite that formed a spectacular wedge inclined into the sky.

We arrived at the rendezvous point but there was no sign of Captain Khan in his helicopter. It had become very hazy, partly due to smog spilling out from the city. We circled around but when our escort still failed to appear after 15 minutes we pressed on to the airport. Amy described flying through dozens of huge buzzards and vultures as she flew over the city and, spookily, we experienced the same large raptors wheeling and diving overhead. I told the prince to keep his eyes peeled as I swerved to avoid them. The last thing we needed now was a bird strike.

Jinnah International Airport, formerly the old Drigh Road Airfield, is where Amy landed in 1930. Our reception on arriving in front of the terminal was completely overwhelming. A big crowd, including the commander of the Pakistan Air Force, the British Ambassador, Ghouse Akbar, several other dignitaries and a swarm of photographers, was there to meet us. Heavily armed soldiers guarded the apron and, as we proceeded up the stairs, attendants scattered rose petals over us as if it was a wedding.

We attended a big reception that evening and stood with the Stearman while people posed for photographs with us. We slipped away at about 10pm to Ghouse's home for supper with a gathering of their friends. Among them was a relative of Jawaharlal Nehru, India's first Prime Minister after independence in 1947, and I spent a very interesting hour talking with him about that turbulent time. When we got back to the air force base, Matt suggested we film another interview so it wasn't until nearly 3am when we finally finished.

I only had a few hours' sleep because I had an 8am start at the

Dawood Foundation School, a not-for-profit family educational organisation, where Prince Nikolaos was joining me again. Mr Dawood, the businessman and philanthropist who runs the school and who I had met at Farnborough, was there to welcome us. Also joining us was Samina Baig, the first Pakistani woman to climb Everest and the Seven Summits, and the two of us with the prince were ushered on board an open float decorated with paper flowers and bunting. Escorting us were two decorated camels, each carrying a girl in traditional dress.

As we rode in a procession up the school drive, girls lined the route, waving and laughing, and gathered in the assembly was the rest of the school – thousands of cheering girls, dancing and singing. Aged between four and 17, they had green biplanes attached to their hair bands and several little ones were dressed as airline pilots and many had Louis Blériot handlebar moustaches. I clapped in delight at the humour and spectacle of it.

We were ushered onto a stage and after the formal welcome from Mr Dawood we were all invited to speak. Prince Nikolaos gave a very eloquent speech and told them that each one of them was very special and he wanted them to have freedom and choice in their lives and to live bravely.

It was one of the most profoundly moving experiences of my life to see those girls, not least because I knew many if not all would never actually get to fly. For girls, an education in Pakistan was no small thing. As I got up to speak, a group of little girls came forward, presenting me with a model of the *Spirit of Artemis* on a board and several cards and poems. They were full of joy and gratitude and they all wanted to be pilots, just like me.

One card read: 'She folded all of her fears into a paper aeroplane and flew away forever.'

I nearly cried because it meant they understood – that flight was a metaphor for something far greater. And they understood Amy.

BIRD

November 18, Karachi to Jaipur

When Amy flew across the subcontinent in 1930, Pakistan was still western India and all of it part of the British Empire which extended east through Bengal, Burma, Siam, Malaya and Singapore. She joked that wherever she landed within 10 minutes an Englishman in a pith helmet appeared.

From Karachi, Amy planned to fly nearly 900 miles to Allahabad in central India. However, realising she didn't have enough fuel, she doubled back to Jhansi but, unable to locate the airfield, brought the Gypsy Moth down in military barracks.

One soldier described her landing: 'The plane was down. Down on the regimental parade ground and charging at high speed towards the barracks. It twisted its way round trees, barely missed an iron telegraph post, scattered a group of men waiting to mount guard, smashed into the name board outside the regimental offices, and then came to rest wedged between two of the barrack buildings. There was a race to reach it. From the cockpit climbed a figure – it was a girl – young, almost a child, fair, wearing only a shirt, an ill-fitting pair of khaki shorts, socks and shoes, and a flying helmet. The skin on her face, arms and legs was burnt and blistered by the sun, and tears were not far from her tired eyes. "I am two days ahead of Bert Hinkler's time so far," she said, "and now I'm afraid everything is ruined."'

There was little chance of any of this in 2015. As we flew out of Karachi, Ewald with me in the Stearman, we headed 400 miles to Ahmedabad in the Gujarat Province of India, across the white Thar Desert. Also known as the Great Indian Desert, it covers 200,000 square kilometres and forms a natural barrier between Pakistan and India. The miles of desert, coupled with my lack of sleep and exhaustion from the previous days' activities, made it seem like an endless flight. We droned on, buffeted by a light headwind for nearly five hours.

Eventually, Ahmedabad came into view and the small regional

airport, with its palm trees and a flush of greenery, was a veritable oasis to two weary aviators. We were relieved to find the locals relaxed and helpful on our arrival, providing hangarage for the two-day stopover.

I was so tired I fell asleep in the terminal while waiting to process immigration. I perked up sufficiently, however, for a meeting with Geoff Wain from the British High Commission at our hotel. Our first taste of India was a spicy, vegetarian Gujarati feast – the perfect introduction to our new surroundings.

Gujarat province is where Mahatma Gandhi was born in 1869 and in the capital Ahmedabad there was much evidence of this early association. Gandhi established an ashram spiritual retreat for yoga and meditations bearing his name in 1917 and this quickly became a hotbed of nationalist activism. Walking around the ashram's modest buildings – dark little shacks with earthen floors – it was hard to believe this was where the long battle for independence from British rule had started. We also visited Gandhinagar, a city to the north of Ahmedabad, where a museum on the banks of the Sabarmati River celebrated Gandhi's life.

That evening I gave a talk for students at the British High Commission as part of the 'Britain is Great' campaign. At the outset of the expedition, I wanted to make India the centrepiece, not only because of the historic relationship with my homeland but also because it is a fabulous country with a burgeoning aviation industry. India might have a chequered history where women's rights are concerned but 12 per cent of commercial pilots employed by one of the country's airlines Indigo are women – well above the five per cent or less figure which exists in most other countries.

We planned to spend 10 days visiting Jaipur, New Delhi, Agra, Varanasi and Kolkata, formerly Calcutta. So, instead of tracking directly east as Amy had done, we now diverted north to Jaipur, the capital of Rajasthan and legendary 'Pink City' founded by the Maharaja Sawai Jai Singh in 1727. It was he who also built the famous floating palace in the middle of the lake, which resembles a yellow lotus flower. Joining us there were Simon Howell and Colin Reen from KM Dastur and we spent a wonderful afternoon with them exploring the Amber Fort in the nearby town of Amer which overlooked Maota Lake. The sheer opulence of these palaces conveyed the prodigious wealth and status of the maharajas who were effectively princes of their own provinces.

NOVEMBER 23, JAIPUR TO NEW DELHI

We tried some air-to-air filming over the Amer Fort but due to poor visibility and some ropey formation flying we failed miserably and I pulled away, thoroughly exasperated, for the capital.

Rajasthan comprised arid terrain with low, rugged hills and lines of natural rock formations resembling stone walls. The visibility worsened as we advanced towards New Delhi and didn't improve for the rest of our flights through India.

We landed at Hindon Air Force Base early afternoon and were met by the base commander and a group of female military pilots. Posing for photos with the girls – all fabulously *Top Gun* in their military uniforms and Ray-Bans – I was fascinated to discover they were nearly all air force children, whose fathers were pilots.

At a girls' secondary school early the following day I spoke again at the morning assembly in front of 300 pupils, who bombarded me with questions about flying and life choices. They struck me as far more intelligent, articulate and thoughtful than I was at their age. Although I feared I couldn't dispense any great pearls of wisdom, I did try to emphasise that they strive to build something for themselves in their lives, over and above any family considerations.

The afternoon saw us back at base for more media interviews and I participated in a formation flight with their historic Tiger Moth. The crew accompanied us in the PC-6 and, although conditions were quite bumpy from the thermals, Matt managed to film the flight. After landing, an officer asked if I had seen the blue buck on the runway just before touching down. Apparently the nilgai, a moose-like animal, had ambled across the tarmac and then disappeared into undergrowth. I missed it, sadly, but was intrigued to learn that leopards ranged the precinct at night, sometimes preying on local dogs.

NOVEMBER 26, NEW DELHI TO AGRA

After two days at Hindon, we took off in a thick, soupy haze of smog and wood fire smoke, past various high-rise buildings looming out of the murk. At certain times of the year, the smog is too dense for visual flying but we just made it. For much of the way we had less than two kilometres of visibility and kept a good lookout the entire time. It made flying unpleasant and the smelly, acrid, dirty air made our throats sore and our eyes stream even through our goggles. It was only a short flight to Agra and that evening we made straight for the Taj Mahal as it was going to be closed the next day, Friday.

Even though I had seen a thousand pictures, gazing at such sublime and ethereal beauty with my own tired eyes took my breath away. It is surely the most beautiful building in the world, perhaps ever built – and very fitting that it was a monument to love. The Mughal emperor Shah Jahan dedicated it to his favourite wife, Mumtaz Mahal, who had died giving birth to their 14th child. The enduring monument to their love and mausoleum houses their tombs within the main inner chamber of the dome. Although it appears pure white from a distance, on closer inspection, the marble walls are covered in a fine tracery of Islamic calligraphy and exquisite vine-like patterns with floral motifs inlaid with stones – lapis lazuli, turquoise, carnelian, jasper, malachite. The whole thing is like an exquisite jewel.

We were up early the next day to explore the red sandstone fort of Agra, the main residence of the Mughal emperors until the mid-17th century. It is not so much a fort as a walled city. We dropped into a pietra dura workshop, where coloured marbles and semi-precious stones are cut and inlaid into a base stone, the same technique that was used with the Taj Mahal, and in a moment of insanity, I bought a black marble dining table with a beautiful pattern of cream flowers entwined in a trellis of vines. Obviously, it was just the sort of thing one needs when flying a biplane halfway across the world. I arranged for it to be shipped at great expense to London, even though I had nowhere to put it. In the early evening, Matt and I took off in a tuk-tuk to do some filming around the town for an hour before I sat down with Ewald and Markus for some serious flight planning.

NOVEMBER 28, AGRA TO VARANASI

On our departure from Agra on Saturday, I was determined to try and get a glimpse of the Taj Mahal from the air and, although aircraft are diverted away from the site, I slipped in a right turn after take-off and managed to catch a glimpse of the pearl-like dome in the mist.

We then tracked the Yamuna River – the most polluted in India – to the east until it joined the Ganges near Allahabad, a confluence marked by another old fort. Flying over miles of burning fields, through a thick pall of smoke made progress tortuous. We passed many towns and villages where several houses were painted a vivid, cobalt blue, which I later learned apparently fends off the malarial mosquitoes that breed in prolific swarms in the nearby paddy fields and waterways.

It was nearly four hours to Varanasi, the old city of Benares, the spiritual capital of India. The Hindu pilgrims come here to bathe in the sacred waters of the Ganges and funeral rites are performed where bodies are burnt on pyres and the ashes spread upon the water. It was a hot and humid place. We found a hotel near the airport and the buffet dinner that evening was a lacklustre affair –

with few other diners around – but I was too tired and hungry to care and, after I finally opted for a lukewarm chicken curry, we all retired early.

NOVEMBER 29, VARANASI TO KOLKATA

I awoke next morning to sharp stomach pains and my mood worsened when we met the worst Indian bureaucracy at the airport. During the three hours it took them to process our paperwork, I stayed with the Stearman on the apron, perspiring from the heat and feeling increasingly unwell. Just as we were about to run out of daylight for the long flight ahead to Kolkata, we finally got away and once we climbed to the cooler air I felt instantly better.

Now clear of the city, we flew over miles of intensively cultivated areas with terraces cut into the hillsides and tree-covered mountains before the terrain flattened into areas of industrialisation with huge coalfields and brick factories with distinctive conical towers. The visibility improved for a while but by the time we got to Kolkata it turned murky again. We were given radar vectors through the control zone and landed at Netaji Subhas Chandra Bose International Airport right at sunset.

We endured a tortuous hour-long drive into the city in horrendous traffic. Our taxi had no air conditioning, so we drove with the windows open, exposed to the burning diesel fumes and car horns which blared every inch of the way. We eventually arrived at the Taj Bengal Hotel and I had to rush to meet the British High Commissioner and his wife for dinner. The stomach pains, which had temporarily eased, came back with a vengeance and I blamed the buffet in Varanasi. Later that night, full-blown food poisoning kicked in. Seldom have I been so ill. I couldn't get up the next day. To my distress, we had to cancel the outreach programme but the crew continued with the media reception without me. I was especially disappointed not to be able to meet with a group of female artists who had brought their paintings to show me.

DECEMBER 1, KOLKATA TO BANGLADESH

Twenty-four hours later, I dragged myself out of bed and felt strong enough to press on to Bangladesh. I couldn't bear to hang around any longer. As always, flying was the best tonic and I felt better the minute I was back in the air and on the move again.

Previously part of British India, Bangladesh was annexed to Pakistan after the partition in 1947 and was known as East Bengal. This later changed to East Pakistan and modern Bangladesh was only established after its own war of independence in 1971.

It was a revelation to fly over countries which had hitherto only been different coloured areas on a map. From the air, I found it profound to see the dramatic changes in terrain which defined individual nations that can appear arbitrary on a map. It wasn't just the geography I found astounding, but also the dimension of history and the scale and reach of what once was the British Empire. The land became more undulating as it rose into the low foothills which marked the border area. Bangladesh appeared even more densely cultivated than India but greener, with more trees, which made it infinitely more appealing.

Once over the hills, the land flattened again and now spread into the vast flood plain that signalled the final stretch of India's sacred River Ganges, lying directly across our route, flowing southwards into the Bay of Bengal. The sprawling delta is the largest in the world and one of the most densely populated places on Earth. Millions depend on the ebb and flow of the river for their livelihoods, yet it brings both bounty and devastation in equal measure. A sweltering monsoon climate prevailed and the sky looked swollen and feverish in the tropical torpor.

Our next stop, Chittagong, was 200 miles to the east of Kolkata around the bay. Described in the seventh century by a Chinese traveller as a 'sleeping beauty rising from the mist and water', Chittagong is one of the world's oldest ports, its harbour a strategic gateway into the Indian subcontinent. It became a major maritime trading hub with Arab sailors and traders dealing in pearls, silk, muslin, rice, bullion, gunpowder and horses. British colonisation began in 1760 when the Nawab of Bengal ceded Chittagong to the British East India Company and the whole Bengal region was controlled by the British for nearly 200 years until the partition.

It was again hot and humid on the ground and, seconds after landing, the mosquitoes arrived in an irritating aerial assault. Despite the air of dereliction and the lack of activity or personnel at the airport, we cracked on sorting the aeroplanes for the night. A stone monument commemorated the presence of the United States Tenth Air Force at Chittagong during the last year of the Second World War. Several American squadrons operated from this runway, including 80th Fighter Group which flew P-38 Lightnings over Burma.

We caught a taxi to the Navy Club on the bank of the Karnaphuli River – an old and distinctly colonial establishment, where I could picture members and memsahibs taking tea and cake on the lawn back in the day. I had seen old 18th century engravings of this river with Dutch merchant ships moored up against a backdrop of tropical jungle, but I didn't linger to take in the contemporary view and, unable to eat dinner, I retired early for the night.

December 2, Bangladesh to Myanmar

As it was Ewald's 50th birthday, we all congratulated him over breakfast and commiserated that he was stuck with us when he could have been back in Europe in the middle of winter. He gave a wry grin and said there was nowhere else he would rather be. Although born and raised in the high Alps of Tyrol in eastern Austria, Ewald had a horror of the cold, didn't like mountains much and so, as a great traveller, it suited him perfectly to be in the tropics, away from the fuss of enforced birthday celebrations.

We took off shortly after and it was back into the humid murk as we headed east towards the border with Myanmar. The ground rose progressively until it became distinctly mountainous and we flew over the first couple of ridges in a light mist. Braced for more bad visibility ahead, we kept climbing and soon found cool, clear air at 5,500 ft. Before us were the incredibly beautiful Arakan Mountains, which lay in gentle parallel ridges in receding shades of deep blue. Jungle covered the slopes and the dense vegetation flowered beneath us in bursts of purple, red and orange, releasing a fragrance which was heaven after the choking smog.

Markus pulled alongside us for some filming in the perfectly smooth air. Ewald and I continued over the eastern side of the mountains and as we cleared the last ridge, several thousand feet below was a big airfield partially obscured by strands of cloud. Ewald asked if he could take control and, knowing what was coming, I handed over the stick. Quickly zipping up the leather pouches where I kept all my maps, I pulled my safety harness tight as Ewald put the Stearman into a steep dive and hitting 140 knots, pulled up vertically into a loop and then rolled off the top. He dived again in a mirror manoeuvre in the opposite direction to make a perfect Cuban Eight, the symbol for infinity – his way of celebrating his birthday.

I took control again as we swept down over the plain towards Bagan. As we descended, red Buddhist temples started to sprout out of the ground, and then hundreds of them appeared as far as the eye could see. Flying low over the top of these stupas in red sandstone, some square with steps like Mayan temples, others with pointed steeples, was simply marvellous, like a scene from *Raiders of the Lost Ark*. The small regional airport, a short distance from Bagan, was surrounded by jungle and high trees. On our landing, the locals ambled out to meet us, very friendly and welcoming.

Although Tim Kelly had booked us a hotel, we decided we needed something a little more comfortable, given we were going to stay for a couple of days, and Matt suggested a place he knew which had traditional Burmese architecture and was set in extensive grounds, blazing with tropical flowers.

That night we celebrated Ewald's birthday properly and I gave him an intricately carved silver dagger I had bought in India. On our second free day we spent the morning cleaning and servicing the aeroplanes, both filthy from the smog. The locals once again came to help, bringing barrels of water on a little cart to help with the clean-up.

DECEMBER 5, MYANMAR TO YANGON

On our departure, we prepared the cameras for air-to-air filming and flew several low passes in formation over the temples, Ewald keeping a good eye ahead for any obstacles while I concentrated on following Markus. It was fantastically exciting and we were all high on adrenaline. Afterwards, the PC-6 diverted to Mandalay to pick up jet fuel, while Ewald and I continued to Yangon, enjoying the most gorgeous flight in hot, clear weather.

We flew low over fishermen in canoes casting their morning nets on the Irrawaddy River and could see straight into the stilt houses which lined the bank and the inhabitants might have had a start seeing us buzz past at eye level.

Fields glowing an almost fluorescent green in the sunshine were bordered by very tall palm trees wafting gently in the breeze. We saw people swathed in dark cloth with pointed straw hats working the fields without machines. Punctuating these fields were grey wooden houses on stilts with rusted red, corrugated metal roofs. Occasionally, we'd see more bright blue painted buildings to ward off mosquitoes.

We landed at Yangon – formerly Rangoon – three and a half hours later, an hour ahead of the PC-6. After we refuelled and tethered the Stearman, we checked into the Oriana Hotel, where we'd be spending two nights while we pursued a special mission.

After an early breakfast, we set off with the cameras in the hope of locating the old Government Technical Institute, which featured so prominently in Amy's story.

On the outskirts of Yangon, flying over the suburb of Insein (pronounced 'insane') in heavy monsoon rain, Amy couldn't find the airfield, which in this case was the local racecourse, and chose instead to land in a small clearing. Too late did she realise it wasn't long enough for landing. She glided in over the trees, hit the ground hard, lurched across the field and ended up nose down in a ditch. There was a sickening crunch as the propeller struck the bank and the undercarriage and wing buckled at the impact. Amy was hysterical, as she knew she'd blown her chance of the record.

What she didn't know was that the sports field on which she'd crashed was the recreation area of a British engineering college and the teachers and students all rushed to her aid and helped with repairs. Three days later she was on the move again and joked how lucky she'd been that the college wasn't a dance school.

After following one false lead, we eventually managed to find the old Victorian institute and the very place she had crashed. As soon as I saw it I knew we were in the right place. The building might have lain disused for years but it still retained its old colonial grandeur.

By a freakish coincidence, some of the college alumni were there preparing to celebrate the 120th anniversary of the institute and were trying to get the building back from the government to restore it to its former glory. Amazingly, they remembered being told about the English woman who crash landed there in 1930. They showed us the playing field with the original grandstand where she had come careening across before hitting the ditch. I found it profoundly moving to be there and took a moment to absorb the significance, picturing Amy there crying in the wreckage of her broken aeroplane. Emotions must have been stirred because that night I woke up in tears.

The closer I got to Australia the more I'd been thinking about my family and feeling trepidation about a looming reunion in New Zealand. It was going to be my mother's 80th birthday in February, with Russell flying in for the party, but I feared it would be wrecked by the conflict between Mum and Julie on one side and Debs on the other. There had only been intermittent contact between them all in the last 10 years, much of this stemming from the continuing fallout over my father. His death might have changed the dynamic but there was still a lot of anger and pain.

My growing fear manifested itself in the nightmare I now suffered. I went back to sleep again but rose before dawn feeling very uneasy. As I sat on a little balcony overlooking the street, a text message arrived on my phone. It was Debs. I hadn't heard from her in weeks, maybe months, yet now suddenly here was a message out of the blue. She reassured me that everything would be all right. She had contacted Mum and Julie and they all agreed to draw a line on the past. I had crossed another Tropic.

December 10, Yangon to Hua Hin

After air traffic control held us up for half an hour on the ground with the engine running before finally clearing us for take-off, we were given a right-hand turn out to the south and routed 25 miles to the west of the city underneath the airline traffic. This was the opposite direction to where we needed to be and flying off course ate into our fuel reserve before we could finally turn east again.

We now flew across the Gulf of Martaban but only when we were over the water did Ewald and I realise we weren't wearing our life jackets. It was a stupid oversight but also an indicator of the pressure trying to get out of some of these places.

Picking up the coast again, we were absorbed by the extraordinary beauty of the terrain – a green, richly fertile land with sugar-loaf mountains covered in dense vegetation. We crossed from the west coast to east coast, crossing the border into Thailand somewhere in between and after five hours finally landed at Hua Hin.

We found a nice little hotel on the beach not far from the airport and, after dumping our kit, went for a long walk in the balmy heat. Later, we sat on the balcony with views of the Gulf of Thailand, eating spring rolls and delicious Tom Kha Gai soup, one of my favourite dishes.

DECEMBER 11, HUA HIN TO SURAT THANI

We continued the next day to Surat Thani, some 230 miles to the south, tracking first inland and then picking up the coast. We did some air-to-air filming around a small cluster of mountains and rock formations and as we flew on I became fixated on a stationary object in the air ahead slightly higher than we were. Only when we got closer could I see that it was a kite. How surreal. Obviously, there must be a string attached, but I couldn't see this or the person holding it several hundred feet below.

As we neared the equator, the landscape and vegetation grew ever more Jurassic. A dense jungle coastline gave way to dark, mysterious islands rising steeply out of the water. Afternoon thunderstorms brewed inland and the sky darkened to purple with streaks of orange. Our next stop, Surat Thani, was not far away and it wasn't long before I touched down behind the PC-6. Light rain started to fall and I prayed there would be no thunderstorms with the Stearman tethered outside for another two-day stopover.

Although our hotel was over an hour away, it was a perfect haven, tucked away in the bush on the side of a hill with a great view of the bay and islands beyond. We spent the next two days relaxing, writing emails, flight planning and filming.

Markus and Matt went off on bikes for an afternoon of exploring on their own and stopping at a roadside cafe, becoming enchanted by a small, tame monkey. When Markus picked it up it climbed onto his head and began humping his left ear. Matt captured the hilarity on film but Markus would soon rue this brief interaction with the randy critter.

December 13, Surat Thani to Penang

From Surat Thani we routed over Phuket and the spectacular Phang Nga Bay, where we flew through the limestone islands and pinnacles of rock which mushroomed out of the pellucid water. Covered in luxuriant foliage with rope-like vines and creepers that dropped straight into the water, these rock formations were made famous in the James Bond film *The Man With The Golden Gun* and it was breathtaking to fly past them at a hundred feet, Matt capturing the epic moment on film. With towering cumulus clouds forming inland, we crossed the border into Malaysia and the terrain immediately flattened out.

We were bound for Penang, a large island off the west coast, and as I approached the runway at George Town, with a 10-knot quartering tailwind, I asked the controller for permission to land on the opposite vector to put the Stearman into the wind. With such a tailwind in a taildragger, there is the possibility of running out of elevator control and the attendant risk of ground looping, so when the controller declined my request I braced myself for the touchdown. I pulled back firmly on the stick for a three-point landing with all three wheels and kept the elevator fully deflected to keep the tail down during the ground roll on the sealed runway. It worked flawlessly.

We were directed to the aero club and secured the aircraft on the lawn next to this small, prefabricated building. We were pleasantly surprised by the inexpensive fuel and, in the absence of any airport personnel, we wandered through to the other side of the security fence without having processed through immigration – a complete contrast to everywhere else we had been.

We took a cab into George Town and had just sat down with cocktails outside our hotel when the heavens opened. As lightning split the sky, we grabbed our drinks and scrambled inside to avoid the downpour.

DECEMBER 14, PENANG TO SINGAPORE

We took off under heavy skies for our trip down the Malay Peninsula. Markus and Matt diverted into Kuala Lumpur to pick up fuel while Ewald and I headed out over the sea before heading due south again with thunderstorms building around us.

We landed at Seletar Airport in Singapore with a monstrous cumulonimbus cloud next to the airfield flashing with lightning. As our wheels touched down the rain started and we were grateful for the waiting ground crew, who pushed us into the big Hawker Pacific hangar before we had even climbed out of our cockpits.

As Singapore was one of our main stops, I had three days of intensive media interviews and outreach events ahead. Singapore Airlines were our hosts and we enjoyed a splendid day at their head office. They invited me to their flight training facility and I had a marvellous time flying one of their simulators.

In the afternoon we visited the Singapore Youth Aviation Club, where I met with the students. Tim Kelly was there in person to help with the whole programme and John Dodd from Artemis also flew in to meet us, which was a great treat. We also met Skip Boyce, who headed up Boeing's South East Asia division, and visited the company's offices and organised for a local girls' school to come to Seletar to see the Stearman.

Later, we paid an obligatory visit to the famous Raffles bar for a round of gin and tonics.

However, just as we relaxed after a productive three days, a potential problem reared its head. We had hoped to fly the Timor Sea from the furthest point east on the island of East Timor. It was the shortest route across the water to Darwin and was what Amy did in 1930. But political tensions between the separatist groups in East Timor and the Indonesian military had flared up once again and we were denied entry permits. As a back-up plan, we had taken the precaution of applying to the Australian authorities – Customs, Immigration and Quarantine (CIQ) – and we now requested permission to enter Australia via a non-official immigration point because we didn't have the range to fly directly to Darwin.

There was another problem. Ever since we arrived in Singapore, Markus had been bothered by an ear infection, no doubt caused by the wretched monkey in Thailand. It hadn't initially impaired him but he now had a livid rash down the side of his head and neck and was evidently in a lot of pain. He took antibiotics but his condition seemed to be getting worse and he remained in his room for four days trying to sleep it off.

DECEMBER 20, SINGAPORE TO BALI

By December 20 we had no option but to press on. Ewald offered to fly with Markus in the PC-6, while Matt came with me in the Stearman, but Markus finally decided that he was okay to fly with Matt for the filming.

Turning clear over the Strait of Malacca, the sea was a gorgeous jade green with hundreds of cargo ships scattered over its smooth surface. We dropped to 1,000 ft and somewhere over the water, crossed the equator. We picked up tropical islands to the south covered in dense vegetation and edged with secret coves and crescents of golden sand. To the west in the distance was the dark coast of Sumatra and somewhere ahead, extending deep into Indonesia, was the monsoon line.

A vast archipelago stretching 3,000 miles from west to east and a thousand miles from north to south, Indonesia is made up of more than 17,000 islands scattered both sides of the equator, including Sumatra, Java, Sulawesi and parts of Borneo and New Guinea. The whole area is geologically unstable with a high degree of seismic and volcanic activity caused by the underlying convergence of three tectonic plates. The explosion of Krakatoa in 1883 was among the most violent volcanic events in recorded history and the earthquake off northern Sumatra, which killed more than 200,000 people in 2004, was the worst natural disaster in the world.

Determined to fly from Singapore to Surabaya on the eastern side of Java, a leg of a thousand miles, Amy tracked down the east coast of Sumatra. When she reached the southern tip of the island of Bangka, she cut across the Java Sea to save time. The weather looked good but miles out to sea, she ran into heavy rain and was forced lower over the water. It was a huge tropical storm and she became engulfed by blackness. What she didn't realise was that a volcano had erupted on Java contributing to the violent atmospherics and the terrifying black clouds. Those looming towers must have seemed like an apocalyptic vision and it was perhaps Amy's darkest moment during her entire flight. She circled round, shrieking in panic and peering down at the shark-infested sea just a few feet below. With the prospect of death now closing in, a shaft of light suddenly penetrated the darkness and refracted into a rainbow against the clouds. Amy darted through the gap in her Gypsy Moth and made a beeline back to the coast. It was another freakishly lucky escape.

Amy's terrifying experience was at the forefront of my mind as we flew at 1,000 ft down the same foreboding, mosquito coast with no beach, just brown, silted water lapping into the mangrove with narrow estuaries snaking off into the jungle. Further south, the rainforest had been cleared and there were miles of waterlogged palm plantations with no roads, just a grid of muddy waterways – not the place to have an engine failure. I gingerly checked the gauges and gave the Stearman an encouraging pat as we purred along.

Markus pulled alongside and for a while we flew in a loose formation, chatting on a discrete frequency. I welcomed the company in such a bleak setting and was encouraged to hear Markus sounding better.

After nearly three and a half hours and 240 miles, we landed at Palembang, which lay inland in the southern part of Sumatra. Although Markus was on the mend, he took himself off for an early night after supper and the rest of us weren't far behind.

We pressed on early the next day, now bound for Semarang on the north coast of Java, around 300 miles away. Again, I started to get a real sense of the vast distances that Amy had been trying to cover. The area around Palembang was flat with a lot of standing flood water and it looked rather squalid as we climbed to 1,000 ft over the city and then kept climbing to find the forecast tailwinds at higher altitude. We picked up the coast again, the same beachless shoreline with silted brown seawater. We crossed the short channel from Sumatra to Java and now, approaching the capital, Jakarta, we headed out over the Java Sea and skirted around the northern side of the control zone at 2,000 ft.

Markus diverted into Jakarta to pick up fuel and that turned into the usual bureaucratic pantomime with eye-watering costs. He was charged $700 for barely an hour of ground handling but managed to negotiate this down to $500. What happened on the ground often took the edge off things, but at least we had enjoyed a brilliant day's flying.

While the crew were off on this fuel diversion, Ewald and I were two hours on the ground at Semarang waiting for them. By the time they finally arrived it was too late to fly on and we were forced to spend the night. We secured the aircraft and drew the covers on as more rain threatened. It was a short drive to our hotel and we worked on the flight planning over an early supper. We were all desperate to get to Bali, where we intended to rest up for a couple of days over Christmas.

The next morning, I woke early, keen to start, and, against a pale sunrise, saw three perfect silhouetted cones of volcanoes. I was determined that we should get some good aerial footage for the film to illustrate the real drama of Amy's story.

By the time we arrived at the airport, the conditions had changed and it was now heavily overcast and all around us were embedded monsoon thunderstorms. Visibility was poor on take-off at Semarang and, just as we got airborne in the Stearman, the air traffic controller advised a route change from our filed flight plan. We were instructed to take a more northerly route, forcing us to navigate our way around the thunderstorms and volcanoes, which in places rose to 15,000 ft. The PC-6 had taken off a few minutes after us but we lost radio contact and didn't see them for the rest of the flight. We had 300 miles to cover and, after a murky first hour, the weather lifted and the cloud broke up.

At one point we found a lower volcano and had a spectacular view of the crater – a big caldera with a brilliant blue mineral lake at the bottom, with open-cast mining and vehicle tracks cut into the crater wall. We circled above trying to get the most dramatic angles on the GoPro cameras and then flew along the solidified lava trail which flowed like a dark river down the valley.

Delighted with our volcano success, we swept down over the richly fertile land beyond. It was all luxuriantly green and intensively cultivated in terraces of neat crops and beyond was the coastal plain which marked the eastern end of Java.

We hopped across the short stretch of water to Bali and picked up the south coast, tracking the beach and marvelling at the opulent houses and swimming pools all the way to the airport at Denpasar.

Although we thought we'd left the worst of the dark clouds behind, we had no idea we were flying into a perfect storm.

After flying nearly 10,000 miles without any problems we now had an utter nightmare on our hands.

Detained

WE landed at Denpasar just a few minutes behind the PC-6 and, as we taxied towards them on the apron outside the ExecuJet facility, a small crowd of people clustered around.

I drew to a halt and before we were even out of the cockpit Markus and Matt came half running towards us. The crowd was not a welcoming party, they warned, but the military and the secret police. We were in some kind of trouble. They didn't know what but it looked serious – and the officers wanted all the cameras.

Quick as a flash, Ewald stood up and leaned across to remove two of the cameras attached to the wing, then jumped down and managed to remove the memory cards from the remaining two cameras before we were surrounded.

One of the officers scanned the Stearman, spotted the two cameras and demanded we hand them over, saying they would make 'a nice Christmas present' for him.

The Indonesian military accused Markus of flying through sensitive airspace and given he possessed cameras, they also accused the crew of spying and filming defence installations.

They herded us into the ExecuJet offices for further interrogation, detaining us for five hours before allowing us to go to our hotel. That was only the start of it, however.

The next day there was another long interrogation by the military and the air traffic controllers but our ExecuJet handler warned me the Indonesians did not like women and it would be better if I remained in the background.

Reluctantly, I left the boys to argue our case, but I couldn't help wondering whether if I'd gone with them I might have been able to make the authorities see sense.

It transpired we had inadvertently hit a friction point between the civilian air traffic controllers and the authoritarian Indonesian military, which was paranoid about security.

Markus had a signed and authorised flight plan for the route from the air traffic controller but had not received the subsequent radio call in-flight with the route change we had received. According to international aviation law, a pilot who loses radio contact should continue with his last instruction, which is precisely what Markus did. Losing radio contact may have been due to the electrical interference from the thunderstorms or the blanketing effect from the volcanoes but, in any event, he flew it according to the flight plan which had been filed and was bemused at the suggestion he had done anything wrong.

We had landed at Bali on December 22 but, due to the hold-up, Christmas came and went. To make matters worse, I had no service on my mobile phone, so communication became difficult. I tried to keep Tim Kelly and Boeing in the loop and I contacted the British Embassy in Jakarta.

On December 28, we had another meeting with the Indonesian authorities and hoped we would be cleared but still no decision was forthcoming and the terrible state of limbo continued. The stress did nothing to help poor Markus, whose condition deteriorated again.

The one breakthrough came from the Australian authorities – Customs, Immigration and Quarantine (CIQ). They were aware of our predicament with the Indonesians and keen to help. They agreed that we could land at Mungalalu Truscott Airbase, the northernmost airfield in Western Australia, to refuel before flying the 400 miles up the coast to Darwin to process through immigration and customs.

We had another consideration. If the Stearman was impounded with no hangarage, it could be outside for weeks in monsoon rains which would cause irreparable damage. It became clear Ewald and I would have to press on if they allowed us. We also had to get through to Sydney and finish the flight. Everybody was waiting for us to arrive – sponsors, media, friends and supporters. We couldn't just not turn up.

Eventually, on the afternoon of December 30, word came through from ExecuJet that the Indonesians had reinstated the permit for the Stearman, meaning Ewald and I were allowed to leave. Markus and Matt were forced to stay and, with a heavy heart, I made the decision to fly on without them.

We didn't really have a choice. There was nothing we could do for them because the military was intent on holding a full investigation and this was going to take yet more time. The boys were in a comfortable hotel and could move around freely so, all things considered, it could have been a lot worse. They weren't happy at being left behind, understandably, and I apologised but the decision was made and it was the right one in the circumstances.

The same officers who had greeted our arrival were there to see us off and the atmosphere was tense. Notwithstanding, I made a point of shaking hands with them all and thanked them extravagantly, and then hugged Markus and Matt. Markus was silent and downcast, but I tried to reassure him we were on the case and would be back as soon as possible to free them.

The Last Leg

December 31, Bali to Kupang

WE were airborne at 8.15am. As the wheels left the ground, I felt weak with relief but, with one last forlorn glance down to where the crew were watching on the apron, we headed east. Conditions were perfect, with brilliant sunshine and a 10-knot tailwind spurring us along, our anxiety soon eased.

We picked our way through the islands, flying along the southern coasts of Lombok and Sumbawa. We could see the occasional golden cove fringed with palms but mostly there were rugged coasts with steep, broken rock fall and jungle rising to hills with volcanoes inland. It felt wild and prehistoric, like flying through Jurassic Park and, indeed, on some of the islands below lurked man-eating lizards – Komodo dragons – which resembled dinosaurs and could grow up to three metres in length. It was another place one wouldn't want to force land an aeroplane.

Thunderstorms threatened to the north and I took a picture of one of these immense cumulonimbus clouds mushrooming into the sky behind us to a phenomenal height, brilliantly illuminated around the edge. Ewald experimented at filming from the front cockpit as we headed out over the Savu Sea to Kupang on the island of Timor.

In total, we spent nearly seven hours in the air, covering just under 600 miles, but just as we were about to call time on a brilliant day's flying, horror struck again.

As soon as we landed at Kupang a swarm of secret service men in civilian clothes came to meet us. One demanded to know where the 'big camera' was, so clearly this had been noted back in Bali and passed on. I showed him the rear locker and just shook my head to his aggressive and repeated demands. He followed me around the Stearman and then attempted to scramble up on the mid part of the wing to look in the cockpit. He had obviously never seen such an aeroplane and had no idea how to get up without damaging it. I screamed at him not to touch the wood and fabric wing and made such a scene that he backed off.

Luckily, the officer was fooled by the Stearman's optical illusion, as looking up at the cockpits from the ground gave no sense of the space within them, particularly the front cockpit which extended to the firewall of the engine. The camera was hidden up there on top of a bag, which Ewald had tied to the inside of the fuselage frame. As the man walked a short distance away, he was straight on to his mobile phone, no doubt reporting to his superiors back in Bali.

We were seriously rattled by all of this but tried to appear perfectly relaxed and friendly as people hovered around us. We had pre-arranged fuel and a bowser appeared within a few minutes, so I climbed up the side of the engine and onto the top wing to take the hose.

Our concern now was how to get the camera from the front cockpit to the rear locker undetected. Ewald and I formulated a plan under our breath and then waited for a suitable moment.

While Ewald continued talking with the rest of the secret service men a few yards away, a commotion began when a small airliner taxied up and the passengers and crew disembarked. They milled around the apron for a few minutes but when the pilots walked over to look at the Stearman I saw an opportunity. With all the activity around the plane, I quickly dragged the fuselage cover over the cockpits and discreetly managed to move the camera underneath like a conjuring trick, lifting it first into the rear cockpit and then into the back locker. I then locked it shut and pulled the cover into place.

All this was highly stressful and we were quite shaken by the menacing attitude. It didn't bode well for the crew back in Bali.

After two hours we finally got away to a hotel and only then realised it was New Year's Eve. In just a few hours it would be 2016 but, as with Christmas, we were not in the mood to celebrate and all our thoughts were with Markus and Matt.

JANUARY 1, KUPANG TO DARWIN

I spent a dreadful night, beside myself with worry about the camera and the fear that the secret service men would be back in the morning to terrorise us again and prevent us from leaving.

We were up and out before dawn and arrived at the airport just after sunrise at 6am to find it deserted. We quickly pulled the covers off and stowed the camera up front again. The rest of our preparations were done at high speed as we kept looking nervously around. By 6.30am we were strapped in with our life jackets on and 15 minutes later we were in the air.

Hardly able to believe our luck, we took off towards the south and headed out over low hills, dodging a few strands of morning stratocumulus. Then, suddenly there was the sea, and freedom. I yahooed with relief as we crossed the coast and Ewald raised a thumbs-up from the front cockpit.

We headed straight out over the water in brilliant sunshine, cruising along at 1,500 ft with a light tailwind, and I cracked into a packet of Oreo biscuits for a celebratory breakfast.

For pioneering aviators, water crossings were always the most perilous, as the chance of being rescued if something went wrong was almost non-existent. Amy had been very anxious about the last treacherous part of her journey over the Timor Sea, the final leg into Darwin. The Royal Navy had positioned a ship halfway across the sea for Amy to take her bearings and when she located this, she flew low over the ship's deck and threw a bread roll over the side at the sailors as she swept past. She was now so excited at the prospect of arriving in Darwin that tears of relief poured down her face. With the coast of Australia in sight, she also whooped wildly with joy and slapped *Jason's* side like a horse, urging him on to the finish line and a moment of unimaginable triumph.

On New Year's Day 2016 we didn't see a single ship. For three and a half hours across a wide, empty sea we saw nothing but waves and the patterns of the wind on the shifting surface. It didn't matter. I loved every moment. The isolation just seemed to add to the thrilling beauty and the Stearman roared on, breasting the air waves like a marvellous wind horse.

Suddenly, through the haze was the outline of land – Terra Australis. Every sailor since time began who set out to some new world must have had that same feeling of wonder.

A map revealed the complex and convoluted coastline of what is the Kimberley region of Western Australia. Mungalalu-Truscott Airbase lay a few miles inland on the Anjo Peninsula and, built in 1944, it was a staging post for flying boats and Allied bombers making attacks on Japanese targets in the Dutch East Indies. The site was chosen because it was the point on the Australian mainland closest to Java, where the Japanese forces were concentrated. The Japanese were never able to find the airbase on that remote peninsula fringed with mangrove, although they had looked for it and a search party had once landed just a few miles down the coast.

As we approached the long runway in scrub bush, I cursed under my breath. We were coming into a hot, gusting crosswind. I came in quite fast with full left aileron deflected to counter this and wheeled the Stearman on, managing to keep it straight as we bowled down the runway. Ewald complimented me on the handling but it was nothing compared to the relief of finally landing in Australia. The handful of Aussies on the base gave us a fantastic reception. Although we were technically in quarantine, we had lunch in the little canteen and the base manager took us on a tour of the airfield. A Liberator bomber had crashed just after take-off on May 20, 1945, near the north-west end of the runway, killing 11 men in the process. There was nothing left of the bomber's fuselage, but sundry parts and pieces of metal were still in remarkably good condition, uncorroded and glinting in the sun, 70 years after the accident. The big radial engines with blackened pistons were still largely intact – a poignant reminder of the lives that were lost all those years ago.

Grateful for the hospitality from our Australian friends and suitably refreshed, we said goodbye and set off again mid-afternoon for the 400-mile flight to Darwin, in the Northern Territory.

We now flew a dramatic red coastline with countless miles of sand, effectively a desert with a beach, virtually devoid of human habitation. We discussed landing on the sand to go for a swim but it was merely a fantasy to keep ourselves amused. We needed to get to Darwin before nightfall. As we flew over the southern reaches of the city, the sun was setting and we landed at 6.23pm after more than four hours in the air. Over the course of another very long day, we had flown for seven and a half hours and covered close to 700 miles.

Surrounded by tropical bush with palm trees running down one side of the runway, this was where Amy had landed and the moment was charged with historical significance.

A couple of journalists and film crew from a local TV channel were waiting so I did an interview in front of the Stearman. Our handler, David Fleming from Darwin FBO – a very pleasant chap and endlessly helpful – strolled out to meet us on the apron. Once we'd gone through immigration he drove us along Amy Johnson Drive, out of the airport, to our hotel on the seafront and joined us for a drink. As we sat on the terrace in the clear darkness, we finally toasted the New Year and our relief at being away from Indonesia.

Given we lost more than a week of our schedule in Bali, our plan now was to get to Sydney as fast as possible. A small tropical cyclone had been hovering to the east of Darwin and Tim Kelly, now in Sydney, used this as the excuse for our delayed crossing of the Timor Sea in his media updates. We thought it best to keep the situation in Indonesia under wraps so as not to inflame things further.

JANUARY 3, DARWIN TO TENNANT CREEK

With 3,000 miles of predominantly desert between us and Sydney, we planned on flying two legs a day, which meant eight hours in the air with a fuel stop.

We took off early into a peerless morning, heading due south. Once clear of the city, the landscape morphed into low mountains with escarpments and then miles of black swamp with thin, white tree trunks sticking out of the ooze like bones. This was all Aboriginal land and it was four hours before we came to Kalkarindji, a remote indigenous settlement with a dirt airstrip. In true 1930s barnstorming style, we buzzed the town and, thinking that we might have to revert once again to motor fuel, noted a petrol station in the high street. Then we circled to land.

I shut down the engine and it was like an oven door had opened. It must have been nearly 50°C on the ground. Flies swarmed around, landing on our faces and lips and crawling behind our sunglasses. I'd never experienced anything like it. We climbed out and, moments later, a flatbed truck pulled up and the driver, a tall Aboriginal called Michael, wearing a classic Australian bush hat with corks hanging around the rim to ward off the flies, came to greet us. His wife Lorraine also stepped out to say hello and we all shook hands.

'We saw you on the news this morning, love, and figured you might be looking for fuel,' he said.

I couldn't help laughing. There we were, seemingly in the middle of nowhere, but here a local knew all about us.

Michael offered to whip round 'the family' to find some jerry cans and promptly drove off again, returning 15 minutes later with three of them but we still needed to fill them with fuel. It transpired the garage we had spotted from the air was closed with a broken pump, so motor fuel wasn't an option. Ever helpful, Michael now suggested he take us to one of the local cattle ranches to see if they might be able to give us some Avgas. We all drove off in his truck to the dusty yard of a big farm. The farmer's wife appeared and took us to her husband's helicopter barn to see what fuel he had and was kind enough to fill our cans. She also phoned ahead to Hooker Creek airport further south in Lajamanu to confirm if they had Avgas. With that, we scrambled back to the strip with an hour and a half's fuel to get us to the next stop.

It was an hour's flight to Lajamanu, where there was a sealed runway with several hangars and a functioning fuel pump. The heat was almost unbearable and as we refuelled another couple of locals, Mick and Louisa, came to say hello and kindly invited us to their home for a cold drink and a quick lunch. We gratefully accepted, but by the time we got airborne again it was nearly 4pm. There were still 230 miles to cover to get to our next stop at Tennant Creek and we would be pushing it to get there before dark. We flew low over the flat, arid terrain counting off the miles.

January 4, Tennant Creek to Uluru

We were up at dawn again with two legs to fly 430 miles. The first leg was to Alice Springs – as in Nevil Shute's famous book, *A Town Like Alice* – gateway to the red desert of central Australia.

We stopped to refuel and flew on again an hour later to the west of the town to film the low ridge of mountains and beyond. Out in the dry scrubland, several miles away, was a big satellite and radar communications centre with huge, white 'golf ball' like structures. It was a restricted area so we kept well clear.

We now tracked south-west deep into the desert, and it became a landscape of endless red sand. There was little in the way of vegetation but as we flew on I grew intrigued by the sight of single and sparse tree trunks, which resembled the etiolated shapes of human beings, like strange Giacometti figures, and turned out to be juvenile desert oak. Instead of leaves they have silver green needles, which become flame resistant and shed during the dry season, forming a circle around the base of the tree which acts as a protective fire guard. Another native shrub, a mulga – a type of Acacia – also made distinctive dots, which made me suddenly understand the pattern and rhythm of Aboriginal art. It occurred to me that the early Aboriginals must have been able to picture the desert from the air.

The red sand gave way to salt, and the desert now became bleached by vast stretches of whiteness. Saline lakes formed in the middle of these salt pans, like pale yolks and beyond this mineral plain, the land once again resumed its red hue.

Then, in the distance, the red rock, that unmistakable island mountain which rises from the desert to a height of nearly 1,200 ft. This was Uluru, or Ayers Rock, as it was previously known. The site is sacred to the Pitjantjatjara people and it was not difficult to see why. It exudes a numinous power and as we got closer I was beside myself with excitement at the sheer, jaw-dropping spectacle of it. The colour must be seen to be believed. The rock glows red in the dawn, like a burning heart, and again during the sunset.

We landed just after 3pm, and it was another sporting landing with a stiff crosswind. Once again, the locals were fantastically friendly and the team from Professional Helicopter Services Ltd (PHS) helped us push the Stearman into a big hangar, which was otherwise used to house helicopters, for the many tourist flights around the rock.

The next day we had a lie-in until 10am and then made our way back to the airport to work on the aeroplane. Ewald wanted to do a full maintenance check and oil change while I cracked on with cleaning it. A couple of PHS boys, Tom and Clint, came to help and we all toiled away for nearly six hours in sweltering heat, but at least we were under cover from the sun. We arranged to do an early flight around Uluru the next morning and it took nearly an hour and a half to process the access permit with the local Aboriginal authority.

Later that afternoon we caught up once again with Caroline O'Donnell from Artemis. She had been waiting for us to arrive in Sydney but with our delay, had flown to meet us en route. We had a relaxing couple of hours chatting by the pool at the hotel and then I tidied myself up for yet another media appointment. I had to do a live interview with ITV at 7pm that evening, so we set that up at one of the viewing points with Uluru in the background. Afterwards, we met up again with Clint, the helicopter pilot, for a drink and while we were sitting in the bar, a girl who had been sitting reading nearby, came over to talk to us. She had heard me mention Amy Johnson and quite by chance she had been reading an article on Amy which she showed me. It seemed an extraordinary coincidence. I suddenly realised that this very day – January 5 – was the anniversary of Amy's death in 1941.

JANUARY 5, ULURU

We were all up at 5am the next morning for the air-to-air filming flight around the rock. Clint was piloting the Bell Ranger helicopter with Caroline sitting in the front seat and Ewald in the back with the camera and the door open.

I took off in the Stearman in cool, still air and the helicopter closed in alongside. It was one of the great flights of the expedition. Uluru was an almost unbelievable sight, crouching on a shadowed earth but itself lit up like a glowing coal. We were only allowed to fly on the illuminated side, the other part of the mountain is out of bounds for cultural reasons, nor is it permitted to fly over the top. I flew several passes in formation with the helicopter and then peeled away to do my own sight-seeing. I couldn't resist flying a few exuberant wingovers and one loop. Caroline managed to snap a picture with her phone and put it out on social media after we landed. The picture of the *Spirit of Artemis* against the backdrop of Uluru, the most iconic sight in Australia, became the most popular hit that day on the BBC website.

After we landed we had breakfast with Clint's girlfriend, Reena, also joining us. Later that morning I did two more press interviews and although we planned a star-gazing tour in the desert that evening we had to cancel as I was too busy.

An email arrived from the British Embassy in Jakarta about the crew. The High Consul in Bali had visited Markus and Matt but otherwise there was no progress with their release. Everything had shut down over the New Year and a date had been set for the investigation hearing, but it was mired in military officialdom.

Coupled with that frustrating news, was an update from Markus, who was still struggling with his health. Something had to be done to rectify this terrible situation.

JANUARY 6, ULURU TO OODNADATTA

I was awake at 4am after a restless night. I wrote to Markus and to various people at Boeing who were doing their best to help us in Indonesia. The American Ambassador was being very proactive and even the Royal Navy First Sea Lord, the wonderful George Zambellas, had written on our behalf to his counterpart in the Indonesian navy. It seemed everybody was doing their best to help and I was encouraged to believe that this diplomatic pressure would somehow break the impasse. In the meantime, we had to press on.

We were away at 6.30am for what was going to be another two-leg 500-mile day. Reluctantly, we left Uluru behind, glowing in the early sun, and headed south-east into a 15-knot headwind. Ahead of us was the Simpson Desert and for nearly 300 miles the outback stretched below us. We spotted the occasional kangaroo bounding around – even these were red – and the odd bigger group. Somewhere down there were half a million camels, an introduced species, but we didn't spot one.

After flying nearly 300 miles, we landed at Oodnadatta, derived from the indigenous word 'utnadata' which means 'mulga blossom'. For tens of thousands of years, it was a stop on the old trade route for Aboriginal people, and today there are still fewer than 300 residents. We landed on a long dirt strip used by the Flying Doctors. We had arranged for fuel here and after 10 minutes a truck pulled up with a barrel on the back. The driver was a white Australian with a grey ponytail and pink cowboy hat, who was also the eccentric owner of the famous Pink Roadhouse in this remote desert town. He invited us back for a cold drink, so we loaded into the truck with him and drove into town. As the name suggested, everything at his low, single-storey establishment was bright flamingo pink – including the petrol pumps and two kayaks out front, which were clearly a joke in a waterless desert.

He cheerfully told us: 'Never mind the airport, love, you could have landed here on the main street and pulled straight up to the pump.'

Looking at that dust blown, empty road, which looked like something out of a Hollywood western, I could well believe it.

January 7, Oodnadatta to Griffith

From Oodnadatta, we flew to Woomera Royal Australian Air Force Base, 230 miles to the south-east and had a splendid night in the mess with the officers. The families on the base along with some of the local air cadets came to see us and hear me give a talk about the expedition in the bar.

Next morning, we were airborne by 7am. It was 245 miles to Broken Hill over Lake Torrens and the ranges to the east. There were more kangaroos and the surreal sight of two emus strolling along in the desert, side by side, as if they were taking a walk in the park.

After another quick fuelling stop, we pressed on for another 260 miles to Griffith. Now that we were within striking distance of Sydney we talked long into the night about what we'd achieved. We had covered around 4,000 miles in eight days in gruelling temperatures of nearly 50°C, but it was some of the best flying I had ever had. After all the bureaucracy and officialdom of Asia, Australia was like being back in the 1930s, with little in the way of restrictions and limits, meaning we could fly exactly as we wanted. And it was just the three of us – Ewald, me and our love affair with the Stearman. I didn't want to break the spell. With his incredible kindness and devotion, Ewald had never faltered for a second. Looking at his long, feathery blond hair, lean, weathered cheeks, and eyes that were pale blue like the sky, it struck me he was just like an eagle. Such an unusual man, he could move perfectly in three dimensions and was entirely devoid of ego.

JANUARY 8, GRIFFITH TO SYDNEY

The next morning, we flew another 240 miles into another Royal Australian Air force base at Richmond. It was a lovely flight over the blue mountains, with a few lingering strands of morning cloud and we swept down the eastern side over what was now subtropical forest.

On landing, we were met by several officers and a group of female air cadets for the usual round of photos before I gave another little talk about our flight.

We then freshened up for the last hop into Sydney, now just 30 miles away.

I'd always imagined the Sydney Opera House would be an amazing sight from the air. Strangely, though, it wasn't. From 1,500 ft above it looked like a miniature and the structure resembled upended clam shells stuck on the edge of the harbour.

We buzzed overhead before tracking along the harbour and out to sea for the long approach into Sydney Kingsford Smith Airport.

We touched down at 1.40pm in front of a tremendous crowd that had gathered at the ExecuJet FBO – not quite the tens of thousands that had greeted Amy but a few hundred nonetheless and, among them, some familiar faces. Tim and Caroline were there, along with a fantastic gathering of women from the Australian Women Pilots' Association and several famous veterans of the air. It was a lovely touch.

We cracked into the champagne and posed for photos before I conducted several obligatory press interviews. It was all great but, honestly, I would have given anything just to fuel up and keep going. I wanted to fly on up the east coast to Cook Peninsula and Ewald wholeheartedly agreed.

The Stearman would not be airborne again for quite some time, however. We had just three days to dismantle the aeroplane and get it packed into a container for shipping to America for its next big adventure. Working under pressure with the ExecuJet team, we got it done with not a moment to spare. At the very minute the container truck left a huge thunderstorm broke over the airport – a fittingly atmospheric denouement to the Australian flight.

Two days later, I was on a commercial flight back to Jakarta.

I had a crew to rescue.

Fate is the Hunter

WHILE in Sydney, I received an interesting email from a female government minister in Indonesia.

Susi Pudjiastuti, the Minister for Fisheries, had seen the publicity surrounding our flight in a Jakarta newspaper and was writing to congratulate us.

She had made a name for herself with a no-nonsense approach to illegal fishing and piracy in Indonesian waters – by blowing up the trespassing boats to deter foreign interlopers. Susie had a special interest in aviation and had set up her own eponymous airline 15 years earlier. Susi Air Charter now operated throughout Indonesia with services extending to Singapore, Hong Kong and Japan. When the earthquake hit Sumatra in 2004, Susi's airline was one of the first responders with food and medical relief.

When Susi wrote to me, she had no notion of our difficulties. She invited me to come and see her if I was ever in the country again.

I wrote back immediately, saying, as it happened, I was on my way back to Jakarta with a little problem she might be able to help with.

I arrived in Jakarta on Saturday, January 16 and next morning met the British Consul Mike Hancock, who had been to Bali to check up on Markus and Matt but had no progress to report with their investigation. On Monday morning I phoned Susi's office and spoke with her personal assistant, Fika Fawzia. Before I could explain our situation, Fika stopped me with the news that Susi had suffered a terrible tragedy. Her eldest son, who was training to be a pilot in Florida, had died suddenly in the night of heart failure at just 31. It spoke volumes for the kind of woman Susi was that, even in her grief, she still wanted to help. Through Fika, she arranged for me to meet that afternoon with Luhut Pandjaitan who, as Minister for Security and chief of staff to President Joko Widodo, was one of the most senior ministers in the Indonesian government.

At the ministry that afternoon I met Luhut, who was incredibly handsome and charming, like a movie star. He expressed surprise that I was on my own. I refrained from replying that was because my crew was under detention by his military.

Luhut listened attentively to the whole story and vowed that the situation would be sorted before I left the country the following day. Mightily relieved and grateful that someone was finally listening to us, I left with renewed hope.

By the next night, however, nothing had been sorted and I flew back to Australia with a feeling of unease once again. Ewald met me in Melbourne, where we had a busy day ahead of presentations and meetings. We flew back to Sydney that evening, from where I went on to New Zealand for my family reunion, while he returned to Bali to see Markus and Matt.

It was now January 22 and Ewald found that, far from being released, the boys had been subjected to a 12-hour interrogation by the military with no interpreters present. They had been made to sign documents in Indonesian without being sure of what it was they signed. Matt had made some statement to the effect that he had 'filmed for himself because he was interested' and I was deeply concerned he had said something incriminating.

I had no idea what the boys had filmed – apart from volcanoes – but their captors were claiming to have 'evidence'.

Matt, clearly scared out of his brain, sent me a link about capital punishment in Indonesia and one clause referred to crimes committed in aircraft and the filming of military instal-lations. Such a crime was punishable with death by firing squad.

In fact, two Australian drug smugglers had been tried and shot a few months before, which had caused a major diplomatic row between the two countries.

I couldn't believe it. The situation was getting worse. I tried to reassure Matt by saying I wouldn't let the Indonesians shoot him and made hurried plans to return to Jakarta. It was easier said than done, however. There were no direct flights and the best option routed via China and took 24 hours.

When I finally arrived in Jakarta, Ewald came to meet me and together we saw Skip Boyce from Boeing, who had hosted us in Singapore, to discuss how to proceed. We agreed we needed to speak to Luhut again. I got in touch with his aide-de-camp, Agus Barnas, while Skip, through his Asian network, contacted the minister's office directly and managed to speak with Luhut. Despite Luhut's earlier assurances, the case was more complicated than he had first thought. The military were concerned about anomalies with the flight – apparently the PC-6, captured on radar, had descended to 4,000 ft over a military airfield. The question was what Matt had caught on film. Had he inadvertently filmed the military airfield? Even he wasn't sure.

The following morning, I met again with Mike Hancock, the British Consul, but as far as the Foreign Office was concerned, 'their hands were tied'. I told Mike that Boeing and the American ambassador, Robert Blake, were being very proactive and he was slightly defensive, saying that he thought the Americans were being 'rather forward'.

I said we needed a bit of 'forward' at this stage in the proceedings when everything else seemed to be failing.

Markus was, by now, in a bad way. In addition to his infection, which had been diagnosed as shingles, he had also caught dengue fever and was admitted to hospital suffering hallucinations. Our fear was that he might start haemorrhaging internally, which in extreme cases with this mosquito-borne disease can be fatal. Matt was doing his best to support him but it was a terrifying ordeal. We arranged a flight for Markus's girlfriend to fly out from Switzerland to look after him.

With everything in a terrible limbo, I arranged to meet Susi Pudjiastuti in her office on Friday, January 29. Also joining us was Agus Barnas, who brought the so-called 'evidence' – an oblique photograph of the 'military airport' from nearly three miles away, shot at a height of 4,000 ft. If this was their only evidence of espionage, it was a very thin case. We all agreed that better pictures were available on Google Earth and the airport was not used exclusively for military purposes. Civil airliners operated there on a scheduled service and passengers could easily take photographs out the window on their mobile phones.

Ewald brought Markus's original flight plan, which Agus had never seen. It had been signed by the air traffic controller and proved the authorisation of the routing over the seemingly sensitive airfield. In the many exchanges between the air traffic controllers and the military, a copy of this flight plan had conveniently disappeared. Agus took a copy and left soon after.

Susi picked up the phone to the Indonesian president and said how ludicrous the situation was and how badly it reflected on Indonesia. I listened with amazement. When she hung up she gave me a dazzling smile and reassured me the crew would be released, it would just take a bit more time. That was how things worked in Indonesia. Susi then poured me a large gin and tonic and proffered a box of cigars, before lighting up one for herself. As we sat talking, I noticed she had a tattoo from her ankle, up the side of her calf, before disappearing under her skirt. She truly was 'the girl with the dragon tattoo', a most extraordinary person.

While Ewald flew home to Austria, I stayed on and waited to see what would happen next. For three days, I waited at the hotel in complete radio silence.

On February 4, I was summoned to the ministry. It was like a court martial. There were 30 uniformed men in the room for the hearing conducted in Indonesian.

My heart was pounding. Fika Fawzia, who translated, and Agus joined me.

After several officers addressed the meeting, I was finally invited to speak. I had been briefed on Indonesian protocol and their 'face-saving' culture but couldn't resist a bit of British candour. I said I was dismayed at the chain of events, triggered by an innocent situation and that the personnel and resources that had been deployed to investigate our case had been disproportionate. I assured the assembled company that I hadn't flown my vintage biplane halfway around the world to spy on Indonesia. By detaining our support crew, they had nearly ruined the expedition and caused great stress to all of us, especially Markus and Matt. I ended my speech on a conciliatory note, however, expressing the hope that the situation could now be quickly resolved. Finally, I thanked Susi, Luhut and Agus for their interventions.

I'm not sure whether any of this made the slightest impression on those inscrutable military men. Their expressions remained impassive throughout but, as the meeting ended and we filed out of the room, many of them came forward to shake hands and several wanted photographs with me in front of the Indonesian flag and coat of arms. I smilingly obliged but considered all of it bonkers.

Not long afterwards, the crew was finally released.

I got back to Auckland just in time for my mother's 80th birthday – and our family reunion. It felt very significant, not just for Mum's birthday, but for everything. It was a time for healing and for moving on into a new era for my family.

After the stress of the last few weeks, I returned to the UK refreshed and rejuvenated and ready for my next challenge.

And I would need all the strength I could muster.

The Suicide Club

RETURNING to the UK in February 2016, I went into full planning mode for the next expedition – a US transcontinental flight along the historic airmail route.

Embarking to North America was, in many ways, a homecoming. I was bringing the Stearman home, 74 years after it was built at the Boeing factory in Wichita, Kansas. Our starting point for the journey – scheduled for May – was Seattle, where William Boeing started business in 1911. Barely 120 miles to the north was McConnell Creek, where I spent my early childhood. I had come full circle, around the globe.

Boeing had played a significant part in my personal journey, and not just because of the Stearman. William Boeing sold the first aeroplane he built – a float plane in 1911 – to the New Zealand government to carry airmail. I had seen archive photographs of this aeroplane – Boeing had supplied two of them – moored at Mission Bay in Auckland, where I got married in 1989 and why I chose the venue. On that date, March 3, back in 1919, Bill Boeing and Eddie Hubbard made the first experimental international airmail flight from the US to Vancouver, also in British Columbia.

From 1918 to 1926 the American government established the first scheduled airmail service in the world, the US Transcontinental, between New York and San Francisco, using surplus Curtiss 'Jenny' biplanes from the First World War. The service was then contracted to civilian operators to encourage commercial aviation. Boeing secured the route between San Francisco and Chicago and built a flourishing airmail operation.

The aviation companies who controlled the airmail routes grew into airlines, and those routes became the civil routes for the mass air travel of today. US anti-monopoly laws eventually forced Bill Boeing to break up his company into three separate entities – United Aircraft Corporation, the Boeing Airplane Company and United Airlines.

The mortality rate among those first airmail pilots was shocking, worse than flying in combat in the First World War. Of the first 40 pilots, 31 died, such was the extreme risk of flying in all weathers at all hours of the day and night. Due to the pressure of getting the mail through, coast to coast, the pilots jokingly called it the 'Suicide Club'.

Now, after flying 14,600 miles from England to Australia, I was about to fly my 1942 Boeing Stearman the 3,000-mile US Trans-continental route from west coast to east coast along that same historic airmail route. The Stearman had crossed the Pacific Ocean on a cargo ship and at the end of February arrived at the Historic Flight Foundation at Paine Field, Seattle, where John Sessions and his team of engineers were waiting to unload the container.

I made my way to the west coast in March to meet it, stopping off in Nashville for the International Association of Women in Aviation (IAWA) conference, where I was a keynote speaker. I then flew to Chicago to spend a day at Boeing headquarters before flying on to Seattle. Ewald had arrived a few hours earlier and we drove up to Everett together. We were reunited with the Stearman the next morning and it was something to see it there, wingless in the hangar, waiting to be transformed once more into a bird of flight. John's team all pitched in to help with the reassembly and four days later the *Spirit of Artemis* was back in the air, albeit with a few minor glitches. The manifold pressure gauge was not working in the rear cockpit and I noticed that when the Stearman was in a turn, a fine spray of fuel dispersed off the top wing. The seal on one of the fuel tank screw lids had disintegrated during the shipping.

As preparations for the US flight continued, I returned to London at the end of March to fulfil a packed programme of events. Among several unexpected awards and recognitions that came my way because of my expeditions was being made Honorary Lieutenant Commander RNR by the Royal Navy and, in early April, I visited the Britannia Naval College at Dartmouth for an induction course. A few days later, I flew to Geneva to give a presentation to the United Nations. Then, the night before I flew back to Seattle, I gave the Cobham Lecture for The Honourable Company of Air Pilots (HCAP) at the Royal Aeronautical Society in London. Their Royal Highnesses Prince and Princess Michael of Kent attended and, in a terrific gesture of support, the princess came dressed in a flying jacket and scarf, like an old-fashioned aviator.

The Honourable Company had awarded me their Master's Medal earlier in the year for 'raising awareness of science and technology in general, and aviation in particular, amongst young women across the world'. It was a tremendous honour and something I was grateful to receive. However, not everyone agreed. I was informed that the then Master of HCAP had received a personal call from Rutherford complaining about the award. The Master had described this call to colleagues subsequently as 'highly abusive'.

I met with two HCAP officials, accompanied by my Boeing project manager Tim Wheeler, who was able to verify that Boeing understood my flights were supported and were happy for me to fly with crew and passengers as I saw fit. There had been no sleight of hand or fraud. The expeditions had generated a lot of publicity for the greater cause of women in aviation and Boeing were happy to endorse them. HCAP seemed satisfied and I left for the US hoping I could focus solely on what would be another challenging expedition.

Little did I know my world was about to come crashing down – in more ways than one.

Bird Down

I FLEW back to Seattle on April 27, still on course to depart in five days' time and with my support team now in place. With me was Ewald and my old friend Rebecca Thompson. She was going to help drive our support vehicle. Meeting us in Seattle was Tim Kelly, who would once again handle my PR, and Simon Fanthorpe, a British cameraman who lived in Los Angeles. Rather than take him with us the whole way, our plan was to hire a camera-ship at various places so he could film the key bits.

We arrived in time for the Clipper Round the World Race, which I was due to fly over, and then I flew from Paine Field to historic Boeing Field for the official departure.

On May 1, I had the most fantastic flight along the Seattle water-front, past the Space Needle and then inland towards Mount Rainier, a huge volcano cloaked in snow and another part of the Pacific Ring of Fire. Ewald and Simon were in a Cessna flying alongside, filming this fantastic spectacle.

MAY 2, SEATTLE TO FLORENCE

For the official start to our US transcontinental flight, I took off late morning from Boeing Field after a terrific send-off, elated to be in the air. I roared off, heading west over the sounds, an intricate web of inland waterways surrounded by forest. I was on my own but accompanying me in the Cessna were Simon and Ewald.

It was nearly a hundred miles to the coast but suddenly, there it was, the Pacific Ocean – a vast expanse of hazy blue with waves rolling in from a distance, forming long white parallel lines, which advanced and dissipated into the wide, flat beach. The locals landed on that beach – but I just flew a few feet above without letting the wheels touch, before roaring on through the miasma of sea haze.

Down the coast I went until, three hours later, I reached Astoria, Oregon. After a quick refuel and a bite of lunch we pressed on to Florence. From here, the Cessna took Simon back to Seattle and it was Ewald and me once again, caught up in the romantic adventure of the flight. Two hours later we landed in Florence and, after we'd tethered the Stearman, some local flying club members arranged a taxi to take us into town, where we found a little hotel and a restaurant for dinner.

MAY 3, FLORENCE TO SANTA MONICA

After an early start, we flew along the coast over towering redwood trees – some nearly 200 ft tall – looking straight down the trunks to the forest floor, hoping to see bears lurking below.

We stayed on the coast, flying a parallel course to the inland mail route of Portland, Albany and Eugene. From Oregon, we passed into northern California and stopped at Arcata, routinely one of the foggiest places on Earth, but which today was simply overcast.

From here, we headed to San Francisco, winging right over the top of the Golden Gate Bridge. I felt a rush of vertigo as I always do when looking straight down at manmade structures. The Pacific was dark blue green, churning with white caps, and in the distance I could see the skyline of the city and the infamous Alcatraz Island and its former prison.

Our next stop was Santa Rosa, where we reunited with the crew. I arranged for us all to stay with an old friend, Ed Wallis, who had a big house and a vineyard at Diamond Mountain near Calistoga. I had met Ed 30 years before in London when he was looking to buy an airship from my Greek friends, George and Alexander Spryou, who had a company called Airship Industries. We ended up staying for four blissful nights due to bad weather, but Ed cooked up a storm with barbecues and lavish breakfasts.

We continued to Sonoma and picked up the coast again for a lovely flight down to Monterey, where offshore we saw the occasional whale sending plumes of spray into the air.

We refuelled and flew on to Santa Monica, the coastal city west of Los Angeles, where we received another tremendous reception from the flying community at the historic airport where McDonnell Douglas was based and was the home of the iconic DC-3. Sadly, the airport was now threatened with closure despite the best efforts of the locals. Here, we benefited from the kindness of local pilot and Stearman owner Randy Sherman, who we hadn't met yet but let us use his hangar and paid for dinner that night. We finally met our mysterious benefactor when he arrived at the airport two days later with Clay Lacy, a famous pilot who had been the youngest pilot to join United Airlines and made his name flying Learjets in the 1950s and 60s with a host of celebrities. He had even flown with Charles Lindbergh as his passenger. Clay had learnt to fly Stearmans when he was just 13 years old and now 84, he had nearly 50,000 flying hours, more than anyone else on the planet.

May 10, Santa Monica to Grand Canyon

We were 10 days and nearly 2,000 miles into the US transcontinental flight and ahead of us was going to be the most spectacular part of the flight – the Grand Canyon. Leaving Los Angeles, we flew on to Boulder in the Mojave Desert before heading on to the Grand Canyon Airport. That night I could scarcely contain my excitement for what lay ahead the following day.

MAY 11, GRAND CANYON TO WINSLOW

The day began with a morning scenic flight along the rim of the canyon with our cameraman Simon in the front cockpit and then we landed back at Grand Canyon Airport to get ready for a full day of air-to-air filming. Our camera ship was a Cessna 172, which had just arrived from Phoenix, flown by Patrick McGarry, who knew the terrain well and briefed a route taking us past all the most dramatic parts.

While Simon and Patrick loaded up the camera equipment into the Cessna, Ewald and I prepared the Stearman with GoPro cameras, four in all, mounted on various parts of the wings and tail.

We got airborne again by mid-morning and tracked east from the Grand Canyon to the Vermilion Cliffs, the steep and winding escarpment of rock glowing red in the morning sun. From there we headed to Lake Powell, that dramatic reservoir on the Colorado River that could have been the surface of Mars. Then we flew into Monument Valley, the vast tableland interspersed with the iconic red buttes as far as the eye could see.

We landed at Winslow in the late afternoon to refuel for the last leg of the day – a flight to Phoenix, a hundred nautical miles to the south. While we were on the ground we opted for a short diversion to a famous crater of a meteor strike from the Pleistocene age, reckoned to be the best of its kind in the world and only 15 miles to the west.

It was on taking off for that last detour – after what had been one of the most amazing days I had ever experienced – that disaster struck.

As I recounted in the opening prologue, I had only climbed to 80 ft when the Stearman suddenly suffered a loss of engine power and we came crashing back down to earth.

It took a while for the dust to settle. We were only about a mile from the airfield and for nearly 40 minutes nobody came. We discovered later the emergency services had gone directly to the airport and didn't know where we were.

While Ewald tried to determine how the aircraft lost nearly 300 rpm of power, I was on the phone to Simon Howell, my long-suffering insurance broker back in London, where it was 2am. Despite the ungodly hour, he answered.

I drew a deep breath and said, 'Simon, you're not going to believe this ...'

I also phoned Randy Sherman and was immeasurably relieved to hear his deep, calm tones. Immediately, he offered me his own Stearman to finish the flight – an immensely gracious offer but one I couldn't accept. It seemed terribly disloyal to my own aeroplane. We had come a long way together – literally – since its restoration in 2013, flying over 30,000 miles.

A woman who witnessed the crash from a road a few hundred yards away, picked her way through the scrub, calling out to check we were okay.

It was kind of her to be concerned but, in a typically British response, even though we'd just had a narrow brush with death and our aeroplane was a crumpled heap, I said we were perfectly fine.

In truth, however, I was anything but fine.

I was in a state beyond tears. It felt like everything was over – that my beloved Stearman was no more.

For some people, however, knowing I had come crashing down to earth wasn't enough. They wanted me ground into the dirt, my life annihilated.

Men Behaving Badly

BETWEEN 2016 and 2018 a sequence of events shook me to the core. It's tempting to pretend they never happened, but they are part of my story. Perhaps I was naïve, and what follows shouldn't have been a tale of the unexpected. But I was grieved and astonished by the depths of bitterness some men evidently felt towards me and the lengths to which they would go in pursuit of my public humiliation.

Three days after the Winslow crash, the worst seemed to be over. I released a short statement to the British media, along with pictures of the badly damaged Stearman. The crash briefly featured on ITV and BBC news and in various British papers.

Then came a report in Canada's *National Post*, claiming that the crash had 'reignited a debate that has been going on in the general aviation community for years. Can the self-described 'Bird in a Biplane', famous for her solo flights across continents, continue to enjoy lucrative sponsorship and media attention when the journeys are flown with an experienced pilot in the front seat?'

The principal source for the story was Sam Rutherford.

Inaccurately stating that he'd been with me for the 'entire journey from Cape Town to the UK in 2013' (we dispensed with his services when we reached Crete), he claimed to be speaking out for the greater good of 'the film crew, sponsors, the press, everyone', by exposing the falsity of my alleged claims to have flown entirely solo. 'If someone climbs Mount Everest alone, it's a bigger deal than if they do it with a team.' No shit, Sherlock.

He was right that at the outset I'd told him the Africa flight would be solo. But, as he well knew, the plan had evolved as it became apparent that I was going to have to carry sponsors and others who might be relevant to the film. His assertion that an Artemis director had flown to Kenya to tell me to stop describing the flight as 'solo' was untrue.

Rutherford also took issue with Annette's film *The Aviatrix* depicting the journey as '10,000 miles, with no modern technology — just a joystick and pedals'. It was basic stick and rudder VFR flying but of course I had a simple nav/comm Garmin 540 in the Stearman and my iPad with the route. I wasn't involved with post-production and editing so had no control over the film publicity. *The Aviatrix* included several sequences of me flying with other people and couldn't have been shot at all without them. If I was trying to deceive anybody, it wasn't a very convincing way to do it.

Another Rutherford charge was that I spoke at the Seattle Museum of Flight in April 2016 before a backdrop stating that I had flown 'alone' across Africa. *The National Post* report carried a photo of me and the slide, which showed a map of Lady Heath's route through Libya and Tunisia captioned 'six weeks alone in an open cockpit'.

That image had come from Nylon Films' early promotional material. I hadn't seen any of the slides before I did the talk, and the route shown was Mary Heath's, not mine. We had flown from Egypt straight across the Mediterranean to Crete. It would indeed have been less than honest had I pretended this meant me – nor did I.

Years later I was embarrassed to discover that two press releases, from Artemis in 2013 and Boeing in 2015, had referred to my 'solo' flights. Had I known at the time I would have corrected them, but I can understand how the marketing departments would run with a simplified message about a solo flight and the media would latch onto the theme of a lone female flyer.

The National Post acknowledged there were those in the 'aviation community' prepared to argue that my critics were 'trying to attack a woman in aviation, an industry dominated by men', but the thrust of the report was that my expeditions were a confidence trick perpetrated on the world.

The other source quoted was another familiar name – Mike Flynn, described as a 'pilot and former journalist who is active in the general aviation community'. I later discovered he was a former BBC Radio Wales broadcaster and hobby pilot, who had relocated to Thailand. While denying that he was 'trying to hack down a tall poppy', Flynn fantasised that I was so 'well-connected with British royalty' that I was 'up' for the award of OBE.

As I later learned, Flynn was also active on the Professional Pilot Rumour Network (PPRuNe), an online aviation gossip forum, both under his own name and as 'Jay Sata'. Numerous posts in the wake of the crash reprised the theme that I was a fraud, incapable of flying or navigating without men beside me, an uneducated adventuress, shamelessly deploying feminine wiles to achieve undeserved honours.

One 'Cazalet 33' opined that I was 'a mediocre private pilot and rather poor navigator' but 'manipulative' and 'brilliant at the bullshit', pushing my 'gender agenda' and playing 'the Amelia Earhart card'. Amelia too had been 'a piss-poor navigator' who 'plied her personal charms' and 'found the funds to rebuild an aeroplane which she cracked up through being a bit of a crap pilot.'

Tough on the boys, but at least I was in distinguished company.

Then there was 'Canopener' of New Zealand, who announced that 'a little detective work down under would unveil the truth from all the smoke and mirrors' and reveal the 'blatant dishonesty exhibited by TCT and her groupies … the charlatan needs to be stripped of all her dubiously obtained awards and this forum is a valuable tool in ensuring that the subject is kept in front of the aviation community'.

When Terry Holloway, a lifetime vice president of the Air

League, spoke up in my defence on PPRuNE, he received an email from Flynn advising him to distance himself from me.

No detail of my dishonesty seemed too small. I was denounced for trying to pass myself off as an RAF pilot by wearing service wings on my flying suit. Actually, the wings in question were 1944 issue, bearing the crown of George VI, a treasured gift from my old friend, Christopher Blount. Was I trying to pass myself off as a Second World War veteran?

In July 2016 it became clear that this abuse couldn't just be dismissed as boys' changing room gossip. The Honourable Company of Air Pilots warned that their formal letter sent to me a few months previously to notify me of their Master's Medal award had been published in full online, complete with my home address. The poster on PPRuNe was 'Jay Sata', who two years later would boast that he had been fed information by a past Master of HCAP, himself a prominent pseudonymous poster on PPRuNe.

In August, returning to my London flat after several months away in America and then Hungary, I was alarmed to see a man hanging around the entrance to the building with a clipboard. He introduced himself as a freelance journalist, wanting to talk to me about the controversy surrounding my flights. He declined to say whether Rutherford had put him on my case. Much later, Mike Flynn admitted he had been in contact with the journalist.

In September the Marketing Director of the Royal Navy Royal Marines Charity, at whose upcoming fundraising gala dinner in Plymouth I was to be guest speaker, contacted me. I was informed Rutherford and Flynn had made telephone calls – recorded by Naval intelligence – complaining that I was a charlatan who should not have been booked to speak. Emails had been received from them and others in the same vein, some foretelling my imminent disgrace at the upcoming annual general meeting of the Light Aircraft Association in October. I was to be exposed and humiliated by the passing of a motion to rescind the Bill Woodhams Trophy for navigation made to me in 2014.

I had been an LAA member for many years, but only gradually did I find out what had been going on. Rutherford had joined the association in April 2016 and immediately started emailing its officers with demands for my public disgrace. Simultaneously, on the LAA chat forum, which was similar to PPRuNE, a thread was initiated devoted to denunciations of my fraudulence and calls for my humiliation.

Several LAA members joined in the witch hunt and, by September, two had been recruited to present a motion at the AGM demanding the LAA strip me of the Woodhams Trophy on the grounds that I had 'brought the Association into disrepute'.

The motion presented to the LAA directors wasn't even accurate. It stated the 2014 award had been made 'in respect of flights from South Africa and to Australia', even though the latter hadn't then happened. But while acknowledging that it was 'factually incorrect', the board accepted it, said the chief executive, 'in the spirit of democracy'. The motion was sent to LAA members as part of the AGM agenda and, in the absence of any accompanying explanation, they could reasonably conclude that, in common with the rest of the list of resolutions, it was endorsed by the board.

By this time, I was on a tour of South Korea and China, speaking at Dulwich College International Schools. I had flown out two days after the RNRMC gala dinner to a series of exhilarating, uplifting occasions that temporarily took my thoughts away from what lay ahead.

However, feeling I needed to do something before I left, I briefed a barrister and served legal papers on Rutherford, Flynn and the PPRuNE forum citing harassment and breach of my private information and asking them to stop. With hindsight, not a good idea: Flynn displayed them online as a badge of honour. Nothing came further of the letters and I never received a response.

An instance of my deceitfulness much quoted online was the claim Rutherford had made in the *National Post* that when I had spoken at the Seattle Museum of Flight in April 2016 I had pretended to have flown alone across Africa.

To clear up any doubt about this one slide, I contacted Barry Latter, a docent at the Museum of Flight and board member of the Historic Flight Museum. In a message of October 13, 2016, he wrote to the LAA saying: 'Ms Curtis-Taylor never once claimed to have accomplished her epic flight, either African or transcontinental to Australia as a totally solo pilot. In fact, she was emphatic in praising the contributions of her support team, including the times members of that team flew with her.'

Unsurprisingly, his words were not circulated to LAA members ahead of the presentation of the motion.

On October 22, 2016, the morning after my return from Asia, I drove from London to Turweston Aerodrome in Northampton-shire for the Light Aircraft Association AGM. As I entered the hall, the chairman intercepted me and told me that I was wasting my time and might as well go home, since the motion was certain to pass.

When the debate began, the proposer, whom I barely knew, majored on my having uttered the word 'solo' at Herne Bay in 2014, thereby demonstrating that I was a liar. How my alleged offence had brought the LAA into disrepute he did not explain.

Several members spoke against the motion. One, who had done several long-distance flights, asked who else in the room had flown any aeroplane the length of Africa, never mind an open cockpit one. Nobody had. I said I was dismayed that the LAA had not thought fit to advise me beforehand of a motion that was the cul-mination of a malicious online campaign.

When the vote was taken, just 17 hands in the room were raised in support. There were 53 against. By more than three to one the meeting exonerated me of bringing the LAA into disrepute.

And yet I lost by a landslide.

It was then announced that of 114 postal votes submitted, 106 were for the motion, eight against. 36 more had been entrusted to the chairman as proxy. He cast them for the motion, enthusiastically supported by a former president of the Association, who sat on the front row, waving his stick to signify his affirmation. It was my erstwhile foe from Shuttleworth Sir John Allison. I always knew aviation was a small world, but it seemed to be shrinking and contorting before my eyes as I watched this play out.

With the announcement of the result, I got up and walked out in protest. Most of those present people came with me. There were cries of 'foul' and 'shame'. It was unusual at an AGM for more than a handful of votes to be cast by or for members not present. On this occasion an unprecedented motion attacking an individual member had been carried almost entirely by the votes of people who had not heard a word spoken for or against.

Within weeks the LAA secretary resigned and subsequently joined me in my fight for justice. The lifetime Vice President decried the actions of the board and came out in public support of me. The chairman of the Awards Committee that had given me the trophy in the first place also resigned.

The instinct of any institution that has been accused of behaving badly is to close ranks and dig in. In January 2017, the Governance, Strategy and Process Committee a sub-group of the LAA board concluded that the disparity in voting 'could be explained by the detailed factual information available to the proxy voters via the internet after having discounted the non-factual debate carried out on various social media sites'. If this meant anything it was that those who came to the AGM must be incapable of accessing the internet and therefore less knowledgeable than non-attenders!

The immediate aftermath for me was the mortification of the BBC headline, 'Biplane adventurer Tracey Curtis-Taylor stripped of award'. Most of the national newspapers ran the story on similar lines. Almost identical accounts in the *Mirror* and *Daily Mail* added to the 'revelations' about the duplicity of the 'former waitress' the opinion of the 'veteran member' who proposed the motion. 'She made these claims about flying solo, or at least that is what we were lead (*sic*) to believe, and now it has come out that they were not that at all ... I am delighted that her name will be removed from the annals of the Light Aircraft Association ... I think she is a boastful lady who needs bringing down a peg or two'. He had, of course, 'the greatest of respect for women pilots'.

And there perhaps I should have left it. But I felt a burning sense of injustice. I was horrified that senior governing members of the LAA, which I had come to view as family after eleven years of happy membership, facilitated the process with evident relish.

The successful completion of the American flight in the spring of 2017 provided a welcome distraction, but I could not let it be. I spent eye-watering sums on legal correspondence with the LAA, whose chairman eventually suggested I could have proposed my own motion to reinstate my award if I could persuade a majority of members to support me.

I had just undergone surgery for a painful kidney condition, but could not resist the challenge. Evoking Freedom of Information, I requested redacted copies of the postal votes cast by LAA members in 2016, from which it was apparent that some voted solely for the motion against me and ignored the rest. I also recruited a proposer for the restoration of the award in the venerable figure of Stewart Jackson, Vice-President of the Association, a man of conscience who had been horrified by what it had done in his name. In the face of this, the board decided it would talk to me after all. In mid-2018 we met at the RAF Club in Mayfair. The meeting was polite but less than comfortable. They hinted at a possible 'compromise', but wouldn't elaborate.

In August 2018 Stewart submitted his motion to the LAA: 'The Annual General Meeting acknowledges that its resolution of

October 2016 to rescind the award of the Woodhams Trophy to Tracey Curtis-Taylor was unjustified, unjust, and inappropriate to the values of the Light Aircraft Association.' The board then let it be known that they would put forward one of their own, proposing, without comment, the reinstatement of the Woodhams Award to Tracey Curtis-Taylor. At the time I thought this was a spoiler; I now believe it was an attempt by the LAA to extricate itself from an embarrassing situation of its own making, but without any admission of error.

The aviation social media networks pulsated with rage. On PPRuNE, LAA Hangar Chat and Ops-Normal anonymous, angry men denounced my temerity. Along with my 'entourage' I was obviously bent on revolution. The passing of the motion would be followed by 'all manner of other undesirable actions being brought to bear'.

Paradoxically, I was also in league with 'the establishment', trying to overthrow the democratic will. The trolls were 'the proles', defending their freedom: 'If every contributor to this thread can galvanise five LAA members and ensure those votes are posted it's job done'.

'Canopener' rejoined the keyboard warriors. 'TCT's wiki page is a gross imbelishment (*sic*) … her website is smoke and mirrors. Trust me … I know'. Then he suggested: 'For those of you that haven't worked it out I'm Tracey's ex-husband Steve Taylor.' He said he had contacted both 'Jay Sata' and Sam Rutherford to give them a 'bit of support', but added, 'I have no desire to fuel the spontaneous self-combustion of Tracey, nor do I hold any grudge or harbour bitterness towards Tracey.'

Wasn't that magnanimous of him?

The date 21 October, 2018 was to be, according to the *Express*, 'D-day for 'Bird in a biplane' versus 'sexist' men who brought her down'. It proved to be an anti-climax.

Stewart, who sadly died a few months later, was too ill to attend.

His speech, urging the Association to put right the injustice it had done and not 'look like an out-of-date club of misogynists', was read out by the acting chairman and heard in silence. I was allowed three minutes to speak in support, my words punctuated by injunctions from the chair that members should close their ears to quotations from 'confidential' documents.

It hardly mattered. The LAA had moved into the world of advance voting by email – 87 per cent of the votes had already been cast. The motion was thrown out by 389 votes to 82. The board's motion was then presented by the acting chairman. The gist of his speech was that the Association had been dragged into a distasteful private dispute. Chairman and board were blameless, but perhaps members might be so good as hold their noses and restore the trophy to a temperamental troublemaker? It was rejected by 277 to 202.

The Times reported on 22 October: 'Voters in the association, which is 95 per cent male and has an average age of 61, were untroubled by the risk to their image.' My instant reaction was quoted. 'It's discrimination. This is how women have been closed out of aviation … This was two years of trying to right a wrong but the bigger struggle goes on.' The report included Sam Rutherford's admission that he had been 'very active' in an online campaign to secure votes against me. Yet he was 'all for more women coming into aviation – my wife and daughter fly'.

If in October 2016 I could have accepted the vote that I had brought the LAA into disrepute and was accordingly stripped of my navigation award, shrugged my shoulders and moved on, I might have saved myself a lot of heartache and money too. Although I had expended a lot of effort into heaving up a flat stone far enough to discover much unpleasant activity going on underneath, try as I might, I didn't shift it.

I subsequently resigned from the Association and removed my 1941 Ryan aeroplane from the British register to avoid ever having to deal with these people again. A greater loss to the LAA was the resignation, in protest at its conduct, of its patron Prince Michael of Kent.

In a further twist to the tale, I was contacted in November 2018 by an LAA member, who had been so troubled by events at the 2016 AGM that he had written to request the terms, conditions and regulations regarding the awarding of the Woodhams Trophy. On 5 December, 2016 he got a two-page response from the chief executive officer, attached to which were the rules of the Awards Working Group, the final clause of which was, 'The working group decisions are independent of the board and are not subject to challenge.'

If the only body that could rescind the award was the body that made it, the motion presented in 2016 AGM should never have been entertained. I immediately wrote to the CEO, who replied on 1 December, 2018 that the document I had referred to was not brought into effect until November 2016, after the AGM.

In other words, within days of facilitating the public stripping of the award from me, the LAA board legislated to ensure this could never happen again. Needless to say, there was no mention of the rule change at the 2018 AGM. The board's motion was presumably intended to right the wrong without admitting it.

If I had to choose between malignant misogyny or fatuous self-importance to explain the conduct of the Light Aircraft Association I'd probably incline to the latter. But the anguish that it caused and the sheer amount of time – not just mine – that it wasted is hard to forgive.

Spirit of Victory

WHILE this circus played out at home, I had the wreck of the Stearman airlifted from America and transported back to Ewald's workshop in Hungary. I was not there when the Stearman was delivered but our cameraman, Johnny Irish, captured the moment. The Hungarians stood around in a half circle and there was an audible intake of breath and then a stunned silence when they first set eyes on the shattered fuselage, stripped of wings and landing gear, looking like a dismembered torso. Ewald appeared momentarily overwhelmed and brushed a tear away before patting the engine as if it were an old friend.

The whole team now set about rebuilding the Stearman for a second time. A new set of wings were already prepared and another Lycoming R-680 engine was on the testbed.

Seven weeks later, when I arrived, I dumped my bags in the office and walked straight through to the workshop. The Stearman was shrouded in pale sheets of polythene which hung off the top wing and fell like a shining veil over the whole aircraft. It was top lit from the high windows of the hangar and the effect was electrifying. Only dimly visible in outline, it looked like a fully formed moth with wings spread in its chrysalis. I stood in a state of almost religious awe staring at this vision.

Working round the clock for seven weeks, Ewald and his team wrought a miracle. I had come to realise that he was that rarest of beings – a true artist, who had brought all his skill, genius and dedication to bear on the thing both of us loved the most.

We flew the Stearman back to England together in time for the

2016 Farnborough International Air Show. As it was Boeing's centenary year, the air show was a celebration of the company's hundred years of aeronautical achievement and it was a tremendous honour to be a small part of that history with the Stearman. I could never have imagined that I would be so happy, just two months after the crash.

Over the summer, I had a busy programme of events lined up. I took part in the Amy Johnson Festival, held in her hometown of Hull, attended the graduation ceremony for engineering students at the University of Portsmouth and participated in several events with the Royal Navy.

In the autumn, I attended the unveiling of the bronze statue of Amy Johnson in Herne Bay with Prince Michael of Kent – the successful culmination of two years of fundraising by the local community, spearheaded by the redoubtable Jane Priston. It was a stirring occasion to see the figure of Amy, clad in flying jacket and breeches with her hair tucked into a flying helmet and her arm raised to shield her eyes, as she looked out across the water where she had lost her life.

On the face of it, I tried to get on with things but I was still having to deal with relentless attacks online, raising doubts about the cause of my crash in America. It must have been disappointing for them that the accident report detailed the cause of the crash as contaminated fuel which had formed a grey sludge in the carburettor of the Stearman. When the FAA accident inspector had cleared this, he got the engine running normally again on the testbed.

Deeply agitated by all of this and having difficulty sleeping, I started seeing a psychotherapist a friend had recommended called Dr Le Fevre. Using a piano keyboard, the doctor sat opposite and struck two alternating notes at either end of the scale while I followed the two keys with my eyes going backwards and forwards like an old typewriter while we talked through the issues. The combination of the sound and the rapid eye movement apparently engages both sides of the brain, which has the effect of rebalancing the cognitive part with the emotional and irrational part. I was somewhat sceptical of this and thought it was some kind of hypnosis, but after several sessions the result was dramatic and I calmed down.

After a deeply restorative Christmas holiday to Myanmar with my old travel buddy, Diana Rigg, I decided, in spring 2017, to go back and re-fly America. My fantastic sponsorship with Artemis Investments had come to an end, almost certainly damaged by the awful publicity with the LAA, so I needed a new name for my aeroplane.

Suddenly, it was obvious what that should be. Someone had once commented that the Stearman was really my long-lost horse, Victor, and I was struck by the prescience of that remark. After all that had happened, this felt like a transformative moment. And so, the Stearman became the *Spirit of Victory* and emblazoned on the fuselage and on the tail fin was our new emblem – the winged horse. Victor would be with me forever in the sky which was my heaven on earth.

Triumph Over Adversity

WE shipped the Stearman to Los Angeles to our great friends in Santa Monica, Randy Sherman and his son Max, who had helped us so brilliantly before.

Ewald and I flew into Los Angeles two weeks later to join the Stearman, once again berthed in Randy's hangar. It took us three days to put it back together and now I didn't hang around. After all the allegations about fraudulent solo flying, I told Ewald that, sadly, he couldn't come with me this time. He was upset and felt I was pandering to the trolls. I was indeed weary of the criticism and relentless insinuation that I couldn't fly my own aeroplane, but it was more than that. Now we were in America, on what felt like home turf, I wanted to be on my own with the Stearman as much as I could, having on several legs promised to take friends from Boeing. Ewald understood, hired a vehicle and prepared to drive across America with tooling for the Stearman and the rest of our kit to meet me at the various stops. Max Sherman, a writer and seasoned traveller who had driven across America on his own and written a book about his journey, offered to come with us to help with the ground support and the filming. We jumped at his kind offer and he became part of our little crew.

June 23, Santa Monica to Mesa

I wanted to fly across America in just over two weeks, and we got away from Santa Monica as soon as the morning mist cleared. I flew in formation with a helicopter, piloted by Steve Stafford, who had huge experience flying in movies. With him was Simon

324

Fanthorpe, our cameraman from the first American expedition, all set up for the filming with the side door of the helicopter open to the elements.

We took off towards the Pacific Ocean and I turned to the right up Venice Beach and then doubled back along the line of hills to the north and along the edge of the city. We wanted to film the iconic 'Hollywood' sign and I did several passes, circling steeply around each time, to get the footage.

The helicopter stayed with me for a few more miles as we flew over the city and then I headed on alone into the blinding sunshine. I flew over San Bernardino and Palm Springs and then the Joshua Tree National Park.

Ahead was the Sonoran Desert, which covered great swathes of California, Arizona and north-western Mexico. Two hours later I landed at Blythe on the border with Arizona in burning heat. The temperatures reached 124°F (51°C) that month and I quickly filled up the tanks with the help of the man driving the fuel truck, before dragging a cover over to protect the cockpit from the searing heat and running across the melting tarmac to the shade of the office. My iPad was so hot I put it on a shelf in the fridge in place of an ice cream which I ate before sitting for half an hour by a fan trying to cool down.

It was another 175 miles or so to Phoenix which took another two hours of flying. I buzzed along at 2,000 ft, cool in the cockpit, and thoroughly enjoyed the flight through that arid, rock-strewn landscape. The Stearman didn't miss a beat in the heat. In Phoenix it was even hotter. They were closing the airports there because of the high temperatures, but I landed at Falcon Field, in Mesa, without a problem.

JUNE 24, MESA TO SANTA FE

As this was the leg into Winslow-Lindbergh Airport, I took Ewald with me to lay old ghosts to rest. When the airport came into view with its triangle of runways and distinctive old airmail hangar, I flew a wide circuit around the field and passed over where we had crashed. Looking down, I felt a sense of detachment from the events of a year ago. We landed and, after taxiing onto the apron, saw the familiar figure of Josh, the man who had raised the alarm and helped so much in the aftermath of the crash. He was amazed to see us again. I couldn't resist hugging him. We stayed there for an hour talking with the team at the Wiseman FBO and refuelled before flying on to New Mexico.

Our next stop was the state capital Santa Fe. We stayed for two nights to see the sights and lodged with one of Randy and Max's friends.

JUNE 26, SANTA FE TO AMARILLO

Located high in the mountains of the Sangre de Cristo range, Santa Fe is over 7,000 ft above sea level and I wanted to get away early before the air lost even more density with the heat.

The Stearman and I happily roared on to Amarillo, with me reliving my childhood belting out the Tony Christie hit song for the two and a half hours it took to get there.

The boys arrived an hour later and Ewald took Max on a local flight in the Stearman, while I worked on my flight plan for the next leg in the comfort of the pilot's briefing room. We found a motel near the airport and dined in a local mall on the inevitable Texan steak.

JUNE 27, AMARILLO TO WICHITA

We headed to Wichita and Lloyd Stearman Field. This was big Stearman country and around the airfield aircraft owners had their own hangars and houses. Dwayne Clemens, the airport manager and owner, let us use one of the private hangars during our two night stay. There was a wonderful restaurant full of Stearman memorabilia with overhead fans like propellers and Stearman Burgers on the menu. Simon joined us once again for filming and we visited the old disused Boeing factory at Wichita Municipal Airport, where my aeroplane was built in 1942. I stood for several minutes in the empty building, absorbing the mood and trying to visualise the huge assembly line which in the 1930s and 40s produced more than 10,000 Stearmans.

JUNE 29, WICHITA TO CREVE COEUR

The next leg crossed the notorious 'Tornado Alley', that extends from north Texas to the west of the Great Lakes. It was heavily overcast and threatening rain with reported tornado activity around Kansas City, so we waited for a couple of hours until conditions improved. Max came with me, sick bag at the ready. I warned him that if he threw up in my plane it would be the end of a beautiful friendship. But conditions turned out to be smoother than expected and we had a lovely flight across the prairies, even spotting a few free-roaming mustangs grazing below.

After an hour and a half, we landed at Miami County Airport on the outskirts of Kansas City, where Geraldine Wilmot from Boeing was waiting to greet us. I had first met Irish, fun-loving Geraldine in Seattle and we instantly became friends. Her joy at the prospect of flying the next leg in the Stearman was touching. We flew to the lovely airport of Creve Coeur in Missouri over miles of forest and the Missouri River glowing in the afternoon sun.

There is nothing more conducive to cocktails than landing in a biplane on home paddocks in the sunset. As Geraldine and I climbed down from our cockpits, Tim Wheeler, my wonderful project manager from Boeing, handed us each a brimming glass and we toasted the Stearman in proper 1930s style.

JULY 2, CREVE COEUR TO GALESBURG

After two days at Creve Coeur and St Louis, I took off again, this time with Tim Wheeler on board. On either side of my wings were Pete and Marie Spear and Tye Hammerle, who had flown in from Kenosha to meet us in their Stearmans. We lined up together for a formation take-off before I led our three-ship in a wide circuit around the airfield and then came in for one low pass together down the runway. We then climbed away towards Galesburg, the home of the National Stearman Fly-In where I had been guest speaker the year before. We flew over beautiful rolling corn fields, forests and river, the two Stearmans following me in a loose formation.

On landing at Galesburg, we were greeted by the rest of the Stearman team, lovely people all. Becky Patterson put us up for two days, enabling Ewald to work on the plane and take part in some joyrides. It was hugely enjoyable to have some precious downtime with our friends, without the relentless pressures of the earlier expeditions.

JULY 5, GALESBURG TO CLEVELAND

I flew on alone to Stark County, Ohio, where I met another friend from Boeing, Chris Bohl. She flew with me into Cleveland, along the shores of Lake Michigan. We landed two hours ahead of Ewald and Max in the car, and enjoyed a very civilised champagne lunch.

We stayed with Randy's kind and accommodating friends Kenny Roller, his partner Jennifer. The following day Ewald took Kenny flying while I went to explore the Cleveland Museum. In the 1920s and 30s Cleveland Airport was famous for air racing. It was here in 1929 that Lady Heath had her devastating crash, after which her life spiralled downwards.

JULY 7, CLEVELAND TO WILLIAMSPORT

Randy flew in to meet us and joined me on the next leg into Williamsport, Pennsylvania, all rolling, dark forested ridges under a cool sky. Here appearances can be deceptive. The Appalachians are prone to fog and low cloud during the winter and were once a notorious death trap for airmail pilots. Unable to see what was ahead and with compasses overreading in areas of lower temperatures and pressures, several flew into the sides of mountains.

July 8, Williamsport to Long Island

16 days after leaving Santa Monica, the end of the trip was looming. I flew one more short leg to MacArthur Airport, in Ronkonkoma, where we stayed one night before the final run into Republic Airport, also on Long Island.

At the American Airpower Museum, I had a marvellous welcome. Stearmans formed a guard of honour on the apron and a pipe band from a local school struck up as I taxied in. I was greeted by the president and manager of the museum, and after being shown around, was presented with a beautiful leather flying jacket. Once again, it was a privilege to meet so many kind people driven by the same passion that drove me. And, when the time came, the whole team of museum volunteers would pitch in to help us dismantle and pack up the Stearman.

July 9, New York City

For the last day of our transcontinental journey, we prepared to film my final American flight, fittingly into New York City. Again we commissioned a helicopter to carry our cameraman Simon, the plan being to take off from Republic Airfield in the sunset, fly along the south coast of Long Island and into New York Harbour. I was both nervous and excited as I strapped myself in. *The Spirit of Victory* gleamed in the late afternoon sun as I cast my eyes over the wings and wires. The helicopter was going to position off my right wing and the last words of the pilot at the briefing were, 'Just ignore me and fly normally.'

I was conscious of breathing fast as I went through the start-up checks, primed the engine, glanced behind to make sure we were clear, then flicked the ignition to 'both' magnetos and hit start.

The nine-cylinder radial engine roared into life and I could feel my heart roaring with it. I checked the gauges and waited for the oil temperature to rise as I dialled up the radio frequency. A light wind blew across the runway as I taxied out. The helicopter was already airborne and hovering on the runway threshold waiting to film my take off. Lining up on the centreline, I pushed the throttle forward and felt that familiar, thrilling surge of power as the Stearman accelerated down the runway. I eased forward on the stick to raise the tail, kicked in a bit of the right rudder to counter the gyroscopic swing, and seconds later we were in the air.

As I climbed, the helicopter closed in on my starboard side and we settled into a smooth level flight as we headed south-west to the coast. For several miles, we tracked the southern shoreline of Long Island until we turned north around Brighton Beach. Ahead was the Verrazzano-Narrows Bridge, which connects Brooklyn with Staten Island – the gateway into New York Harbour.

I often think man-made features are a disappointment from the air, but New York is the great exception. The skyscrapers of Manhattan were a dreamscape, mirroring a thousand suns in that radiant sunset.

I gripped the joystick as if my life depended on it. On one side was the beating proximity of the helicopter. On the other was the awesome, overwhelming beauty of that vertiginous skyline. I was in a time and place that stood outside normal existence. Only the Stearman felt real. Ahead was the slender green column of the Statue of Liberty, reaching up into the sky with her burning torch. I flew towards her like a moth to a flame and circled overhead.

I knew then that I had reached some great height in my life, beyond the measure of an altimeter. The greatest of all human dreams was so close, I could almost reach out and touch it.

Epilogue

AT the Royal International Air Tattoo at Fairford in 2012 – for the public launch of my aeroplane – the base commander's wife told me that, despite always wanting to be a pilot and spending her life around aviation, she had never managed to fly. Life had somehow got in the way of her dream. She was genuinely excited to hear about my forthcoming Africa flight and begged me to show her the Stearman.

When she clapped eyes on it – with its double cream white wings and gleaming British racing green fuselage she gasped and, gripping my arm, exclaimed through tear-filled eyes: 'Oh, I wish it was me, I so wish it was me!'

It was so moving to hear that I started crying with her. I knew only too well from my own experience how often the burdens of life conspire to keep you tethered to the ground.

I wanted to take her with me, but of course that was impossible.

The question people most ask me is, what does it feel like to fly such an aeroplane?

That takes me right back to a particular moment at Ardmore Airfield, in Auckland, New Zealand in 1989, where parked up in the Warbirds hangar, was an SE5a, a replica of the single-seat fighter from the First World War. When I saw it, I thought it beyond possible to fly that aeroplane.

However, I ended up buying a share in the SE5a syndicate and it was to provide one of my first experiences of open cockpit flying.

Piloting my own Boeing Stearman many years later took things to another level. As I described earlier, when recounting that first time, it is an intensely visceral experience – pulling the propellor through by hand, then climbing up the wing into the rear cockpit, strapping in, pulling on the leather helmet and goggles and starting up. That first crackle of pistons with the accompanying burst of smoke; then lining up on the grass runway, pushing the throttle to the wall and feeling the surge of power; the blur of things flashing past; that first sense of uplift and the realisation that you've left the ground is, as I've described, truly like a whole orchestra striking up in your chest.

It makes you want to sing at the top of your lungs but the wind takes your breath away. The feeling is of exquisite happiness. You feel as if you're exactly where you should be, in some higher element of space, freedom and beauty.

My expeditions were not just for the joy of it, although that was a big part of course.

I was also on a mission.

In flying an old aeroplane, it was a journey back in space and time, to the golden age of aviation between the wars when solo pilots were setting long distance records and pushing themselves and their aircraft to the limits of endurance.

A handful of female pilots played a pivotal role during these years. They prevailed despite an obstructive male establishment which banned women from flying commercially and prevented them from earning a living as pilots. These women wanted to prove that they could fly as well as men and they wanted the same opportunities. They were pioneers and pathfinders and their historic contribution to aviation has been under-rated and over-looked in an industry which remains resolutely male. In 2022 just five per cent of commercial pilots are women.

The parallels between those pioneer women and myself weren't exact, of course. I was not trying to set or break records, as these women were, still less to out-perform them in some way. Rather, I wanted to pay my own tribute to them and to remind the world of what they achieved, invoking their journeys as far as possible, although separated in time and technology by nearly 90 years. They flew alone, without navigation aids, radios or airspace restrictions in what was predominantly British Empire territory. I was flying with a support and film crew in the highly bureaucratic and restricted post-9/11 world. And whereas they were flying the modern sports planes of their day, with fuel and oil and engineering support readily available, I was flying a vintage aeroplane and we had to be largely self-sufficient.

Most of all I wanted to fly in a way that captured on camera something of what it's like to take an old aeroplane such distances and low level over some of the most spectacular terrain in the world. To buzz along in an open cockpit biplane at 85mph for over 30,000 miles across five continents over fields and forests, across mountain ranges, through valleys and canyons, over deserts and tropical jungles, tracking miles of surging coastline and some of the great rivers of the world, island-hopping across vast archipelagos, remote coral reefs and shark-infested seas, was an epic odyssey.

With world-class sponsorship and the pioneers as brave and inspirational role models, our team was able to create a global programme reaching out to girls and young women wherever we went: on the flight to Australia alone we made 62 stops in 23 countries. Wherever we stopped I spoke at schools, colleges, academies and conferences and conducted dozens of media interviews. I met with thousands of schoolgirls and spread the message about the fantastic opportunities in aviation and aerospace. A male preserve for most of the 20th century, the aviation industry was crying out for pilots and engineers and at last actively recruiting women. We became a kind of flagship for female aspiration.

If that was the mission, there proved also to be a subplot which threatened to turn the dream into a nightmare. Perhaps it was inevitable, perhaps my own fault, that someone with a personal grievance would try to bring me down. That his endeavours achieved traction with angry men in the rarefied world of the aviation community, many of them with limited flying experience themselves, is a commentary on the misogyny and cynicism which still prevails in the industry today. Women are soft targets, not equal partners. Rather, they are curiosities who may be praised and patronised, but then firmly put back in their places. I was no exception. What I experienced perhaps also bespeaks the tenacious survival of an old boy network, suspicious and resentful of the intrusion into its world of someone outside the establishment, who didn't go to the right sort of school, wear the right sort of uniform or have the right sort of relatives. Out of all this came a greater realisation about the destructive nature and unfairness of imbalanced power.

And yet I feel that these flights were transformational, not only for me personally but for women in aviation. If, at times, I felt terrible disappointment at the injustice of some of the things that happened, that did not stop me. I never lost sight of the real journey. My story has elements of both triumph and failure, but it is fundamentally about the redemptive and ultimately transcending power of flight.

Acknowledgements

MY thanks to Andrew Lownie, my agent, who suggested that I write a book in the first place and to Douglas Wight, my ghost-writer, who helped sculpt the story with inimitable skill.

Also to my dear friend, Andy Connell, my history and Latin teacher at Appleby Grammar School, for his intellectual heft and unflagging support over so many years.

Without the brilliant and generous help of Ewald Gritsch and his team of Hungarian engineers at Rare Bird Aviation none of this would have been possible.

I am inestimably grateful to my expedition sponsors: *The Boeing Company; Artemis Investment Management LLP; GIC Re of India; ExecuJet Aviation Group; The Taj Group (India); The Koc Group (Turkey); Singapore Airlines; The Britain is Great Campaign (the UK Government); The Royal Navy; The Goodwood Road Racing Company; Tag Aviation Farnborough; Belstaff UK.*

And additional support from: *The Royal Air Force; The Historic Flight Foundation, Paine Field, Seattle; The American Airpower Museum, Republic Airport, New York*

And in addition, the engineers, pilots and volunteers of the Shuttleworth Collection for their invaluable technical assistance and support.

I can never adequately thank the people who have helped me in the course of the past 12 years. They have shared their hearths, great reserves of wisdom and humour, and kept my courage up. I hope they will understand if I simply list their names in alphabetical order, and express my deepest gratitude.

Nick Adams; Mark Austin; Christopher and Susan Blount; Christine Bohl; Jonty Brame; Miriam and Mike Brooks; Melissa and Damian Brousse; Philip Cayford; Chantal and Greg Chamandy;

Tom Chandler; Brian Collier; Christopher Cully; Lynne Custance; Anthea and Ian Davidson; Miles De Lange; Gene De Marco; Christopher Devereaux; Pieter De Zeeuw; Monika Drzewicz; Simon Fanthorpe; David and Camilla Freeman; Bronwynn Glass; Jonathan & Diana Green; Derick Gunning; Barbara Harris; Dr Mike Hayes; Belinda Hill; Matthew Hill; Jacques Holender; Mark Jones; Terry Holloway; Simon Howell; Chris and Gill Huckstep; Tim Kelly; Mike and Deb Kurth; Clay Lacy; Martine Le Coultre; Mark Lewis; Peter Livanos; Emma Lorejo; Michael Loveridge; Sarah Macaulay; David Mamet; Chad and Stacey Mankse; Mark Martyrossian; Robert Marshall; Tim Mather; Geoffrey Matthews; Richard Melman; Frances and Andrew Morton-Jenkins; Sue and John Milne-Bennett; Paul Murphy; Carol and Adam Mynott; Caroline O'Donnell; Michael O'Leary; Steve Parkinson; Kimberly Pearson; Lorena Philp, Annette Porter; Christine and Christopher Potter; Kelly Pratt; Jane Priston; Ian Rawlinson; the late great Diana Rigg; Jill Rippchen; John Rose; Susie Schroder; Andy and Jackie Sephton; Dr Randy Sherman; Max Sherman; James Slade; Marie and Peter Spear; Alexander Spyrou; Julian Stephens; Ingrid Strahammer; Rebecca Thompson; Nick Timms; Greta Warden; John Wellington; Tim Wheeler; Graham Williamson; Geraldine Wilmot.

Of special memory are my father's three older sisters, now sadly departed: Mary Spry, Elizabeth Brame and Muriel Macbean, who provided a lifelong example of loving kindness and a particularly female kind of strength and stoicism.

Finally, my love and gratitude to my own three siblings, Julie, Debbie and Russell, who have enhanced my life beyond measure.

Tracey Curtis-Taylor
October 2022

US TRANSCONTINENTAL FLIGHT 2016-17

SEATTLE

PORTLAND

MEDFORD

SAN FRANCISCO

FRESNO

LAS VEGAS

WINSLOW

ALBUQUERQUE

AMARILLO

LOS ANGELES

PHOENIX

KA